MW01121535

The Impact of YouTube on U.S. Politics

The Impact of YouTube on U.S. Politics

LaChrystal D. Ricke

LEXINGTON BOOKS
Lanham • Boulder • New York • London

Published by Lexington Books
An imprint of The Rowman & Littlefield Publishing Group, Inc.
4501 Forbes Boulevard, Suite 200, Lanham, Maryland 20706
www.rowman.com

16 Carlisle Street, London W1D 3BT, United Kingdom

British Library Cataloguing in Publication Information Available

Library of Congress Cataloging-in-Publication Data

Ricke, LaChrystal D.
The impact of Youtube on U.S. politics / LaChrystal D. Ricke.
pages cm
Includes bibliographical references and index.
ISBN 978-0-7391-8349-6 (cloth : alk. paper) -- ISBN 978-0-7391-8350-2 (electronic)
1. Communication in politics--Technological innovations--United States. 2. Political campaigns--
Technological innovations--United States. 3. YouTube (Electronic resource)--Political aspects--Unit-
ed States. 4. Social media--Political aspects--United States. 5. Internet--Political aspects--United
States. I. Title. II. Title: Impact of Youtube on United States politics.
JA85.2.U6R54 2014
320.973--dc23
2014020471

Printed in the United States of America

To Michael, my perpetual champion.
And Joann, my interminable mentor.

Contents

ONE

The Participatory Web and YouTube

The potential communicative impact of the Internet has been a topic of discussion since the early 1990s. Nobody was really sure how or when the Internet would begin to make its impact, but many in the telecommunications industry knew that it would. While the future direction of Internet-based technologies was uncertain, Dan Schulman, then an executive at AT&T and the future CEO of Virgin Mobile USA, remarked that the changing communication structure of the Net was creating a "tsunami of change, unseen and unfelt now, but sure to wipe away the world as we know it when it arrives."[1]

Although primarily situated as a commercial enterprise, YouTube has become a pervasive and vital political communication tool. Its structure, including ease of use, person-to-person connectivity, and asynchronous interactivity, have ushered in a wave of political communication, campaigning, and engagement that connects people to politics, and politically to one another, in ways that far outreach previous communication technologies. It is arguable that perhaps no other communication medium in the history of politics has expanded so substantially and had such an impact on the political communication spectrum in such a short period of time. In just a few election cycles, the proliferation and expanse of YouTube has had a measurable impact on politics in the United States. Now that the platform has been utilized as a political tool across multiple election cycles, there is enough information to begin discussing its broad political impact with an eye toward the platform's political impact in future elections.

The purpose of this volume is to discuss the broad and evolving political impact of YouTube. This text is positioned to provide a historical, descriptive, and conceptual discussion of the important ways in which YouTube has been implemented into the areas of political campaigning, communication, and engagement. To provide a synthesized illustration of the ways in which YouTube has become a requisite political tool, the text provides a discussion of political YouTube videos and strategies spanning across the 2006, 2008, 2010, and 2012 election cycles. The text discusses the importance of YouTube as a vehicle for political communication and provides examples of successful integration of YouTube into political communication strategies, as well as some failures on the part politicians and campaigns to adequately engage the populous via the medium. Finally, the volume will aim to address the overarching question of where the relationship between politics and YouTube may lead in the future.

POLITICS AND TECHNOLOGY

In order to understand the contemporary impact of YouTube, it is important to first discuss the evolution of political technologies and the ways in which the political Internet has provided a venue through which political and citizen voices have been allowed to advance. Developing communication technologies have always provided interesting alterations to the political spectrum and have often fundamentally transformed the ways in which campaigns and politicians communicate with constituents. The advancement of mass media technologies have consistently necessitated the melding of campaign communication platforms and strategies. With the emergence of each new communication technology, former, dominant communication methods tend to become less salient with regard to reaching certain portions of the constituency. Now, this is not to say that any one new communication technology will render previous forms of communication ineffectual, but to assert that as new communication platforms evolve, they may, over time, emerge as dominant methods of message dissemination. For politicians to remain viable and effective in emerging media environments, they have always had to implement innovative methods of leveraging communication technologies to consistently reach and engage as many potential voters as possible. The most successful political campaigns understand this and work to create comprehensive campaign platforms that embrace new communication technologies and pair them appropriately with the tried-and-true methods of campaigns' past.

   YouTube provides an interesting exemplar as to how online communication technologies have been and are being used to enhance the reach and salience of established traditional mass media. In the 1930s, radio surpassed precinct leafleting as the primary method of campaign communication. However, contemporary candidates still spend a great deal of time and money dispersing large armies of staff and volunteers to amplify in-person voter turnout initiatives and have used YouTube as a means of increasing volunteer participation in such on-the-ground activities. In the 1960s, television supplanted radio as the dominant platform for the distribution of campaign messages and became the media on which a majority of campaign expenditures were allocated. Yet, candidates in nearly every contemporary federal election still use radio to reach particular voter demographics. During the 2008, 2010, and 2012 elections traditional radio advertisements from many candidates were also distributed via YouTube. Since radio ads are often geographically bound, redistributing the ads through YouTube amplifies the population base that may hear it and greatly extends the reach of traditional media strategies. For example, one radio spot for presidential candidate Ron Paul in 2008 was listened to over 58,000 times on YouTube.

In the late 1990s, Internet technologies began to play a significant role in political campaign communication. As the Internet, and its users, began to evolve technologically, Internet use became an integrative behavior for many individuals. Much like reading the newspaper, listening to the radio, or watching television had historically provided a staple avenue through which to access political news and information, the Internet quickly became a vehicle individuals turned to for politics. By the 2008 election, the Internet had become a significant source for political news with 24 percent of Americans noting they regularly found campaign information online, an increase of 11 percent from the 2004 election, and 42 percent of people ages 18–29 reported regularly using the Internet to access political information.[2] As Internet-based technologies evolved, they began playing an increasingly dominant role in message dissemination and consumed larger portions of campaign media expenditures. While contemporary campaigns are still largely dependent on both radio and television, quite often there is substantial overlap between the types of political messages that generate traction across radio, television, and Internet platforms.

THE POLITICAL INTERNET

Widespread use of candidate websites began during the 1996[3] presidential election and the rise of online mobilization and fundraising efforts during the 1998 midterms.[4] As revolutionary as these tactics were at the time, they still maintained a systematic method of campaign-down communication and were not structured as methods for constituent engagement, rather just as new methods for information distribution. Political media of this era tended to be monological, continuing to produce one-way, non-interactive political discourse despite distribution methods divergent of past media forms.[5] However, the quickly evolving interactive functionalities of the Internet rapidly altered the traditional information structures of political communication. Unlike preceding mediated tech-

nologies, the Internet allowed voters to evolve beyond being passive receptors of political information and allowed them to become active seekers, producers, and interpreters of it.

As the U.S. political system was forced to move past the broadcast
entertainment architecture which had dominated political communication for decades, it was also forced to relinquish the centralized control
over content production and distribution that it was used to. The Internet
ushered in a generation of political audience members that consumed
less television, desired to control their own media, knew how to use the
Internet to find information about candidates and campaigns, and understood the decentralized and user-generated structure of the Net. As the
number of Internet-savvy members of the electorate increased, the expectations of political transparency and the number of online opinion leaders
and trendsetters, or "influentials," grew as well. These changes, both in
structure and audience, brought new voices to the United States' political
system and fundamentally altered the political landscape.

NEW POLITICAL VOICES

The rise of the political Internet lessened individuals' reliance on mainstream media outlets, many of which were well known for their agenda-
setting and gatekeeping behaviors, and allowed users to seek out alternative political viewpoints. While some argued that the Internet was simply
frontier-style journalism, where opinions were most often disguised as
fact, the Net created opportunities for peer-to-peer sharing and social
networking that altered the flow of information and, ultimately, the overarching power of mainstream media. Political media mavens that knew
how to leverage the power of broadcast media to influence politics and
public opinion were now under attack from a medium that many of them
did not understand.[6] Media giants, such as Rupert Murdoch, CEO of
News Corporation, began to realize the power of the Internet versus
broadcast media when he noted that the *Fox News Channel* was unable to
influence popular public opinion regarding the war in Iraq due to alternative information being available online.[7]

The political Internet also enabled the rise of the Netroots, a community of people who became politically active through online interaction[8],
and provided an environment where the Millennial generation became
increasingly politically active.[9] Internet usage is integrated into the normal behaviors of these two user populations and they consistently, and
actively, share their opinions and ideas with others. They use official and
unofficial political websites, candidate websites, social media, and You-
Tube more frequently than other demographics and are relatively easy
for politicians to find online because they have organized themselves into
overlapping social media circles. When Netroots and Millennials con-

verge or collaborate online, they are disproportionately more influential than the general population with roughly 69 percent of them being considered "influentials" in contrast to only about 10 percent of the general population being considered as such.[10]

CHANGING POLITICAL LANDSCAPE

The political Internet not only changed the political atmosphere by allowing new voices to enter the conversation, but there were also measurable economic advantages associated with politicking online. The cost of creating, producing, and distributing campaign content and advertisements fell quickly, allowing lesser-funded campaigns, especially those with savvy media advisors, to more effectively and often successfully compete against incumbents or candidates with more substantial war chests. For example, in 1965, a sixty-second commercial, which would air just three times on national television, would enable a candidate or party to reach 80 percent of the country's prime 18- to 49 year-old demographic. However, by the early 2000s, demographics' shifts in media consumption and the growing median age of evening news viewers necessitated a change in political strategy to reach younger demographics. In 2002, because the 18–49 year-old demographic had begun to move online for news and information and to consume more targeted television, reaching this same level of demographic saturation would have required 117 prime commercials.[11] By the 2010 election, YouTube's video targeting tools made it easy for campaigns to strategically place in-stream advertisements by targeting location, demographic, and audience interests for a fraction of the cost of broadcast television commercials.[12]

Campaigns that began to embrace an open-source approach, where control was not centrally located within campaign headquarters, but rather distributed throughout multiple contributors, became successful in recruiting volunteers, targeting financial donors, and bringing new voters into the electorate. In order to successfully capture the audience's attention, politicians had to quickly determine how to create political content that people surfing the Internet would actually want to stop and watch. In an environment where audience members had an exponential number of things to look at, politicians discovered that more authentic messages, delivered by credible messengers, provided a competitive advantage over the campaigning techniques that had dominated politics throughout the previous decades.

Perhaps the first politician to fully grasp and embrace the political Internet was Howard Dean. While he gained a great deal of attention during his unsuccessful 2004 presidential bid for the "Dean Scream," his work as the Chair of the Democratic National Committee is most indicative of his understanding of the evolving political Internet. After taking over as DNC Chair in 2005, Dean promised to take the Democratic Party's message to all fifty states, regardless of states' partisan voting proclivities. Pulling on volunteers from his presidential campaign, Dean placed 183 organizers into party operations around the country. These organizers were knowledgeable of how to encourage political involvement through online interaction and how to leverage the Internet for grassroots organizing. After a year, the average Democratic vote in the Congressional districts where organizers had been placed increased 9.8 percent, which was more than double the increases that Democrats saw in all contested congressional campaigns in 2006.[13]

Howard Dean appeared to understand early on that those who devoted their energies and finances to the political Internet would gain the upper hand during future election cycles. This is a lesson that holds true as the political Internet continues to evolve via websites such as YouTube. Contemporary political Internet users rely heavily on online video, Web 2.0 technologies, and social media in such a manner that new voices are continually added to national political discourse and campaigns generate new methods to disseminate campaign information, advertise, generate funds, and engage potential voters.

POLITICS AND ONLINE VIDEO

The percentage of Internet users in the United States who have incorporated video viewing into their habitual online behaviors is consistently increasing. By May 2011, roughly 71 percent of online adults reported having used an online video sharing website, representing a 33 percent increase in this behavior from 2006. Further, 28 percent of Internet users reported participating in some type of video sharing each day.[14] Contemporarily, an estimated 97 percent of marketers use online video for content marketing, making it the most utilized and fastest growing content format with an annual growth rate of 55 percent.[15] Web pages featuring video have a 41 percent higher click-through rate than similar sites with plain text[16] and users on social media are highly likely to engage with and share videos.[17] Facebook posts with videos are shared twelve times more frequently than text-only posts and estimates predict that by 2017 mobile video will represent over 65 percent of global mobile data.[18] With the rise of video-on-demand services and the decline of traditional television viewership, online video is predicted to account for 90 percent of all web traffic by 2015.[19] Voters now expect to retrieve on-demand political and campaign information through online video and social networking and the growing dominance of online video will provide an environment ripe with potential political audience members.

Just as online video has also become an important political tool, YouTube has become an important political pulpit. In recent elections, campaigns have created, uploaded, and shared thousands of videos to You-Tube that have launched candidacies, implored public participation, distributed campaign information, recruited volunteers, and solicited donations. These videos have generated audience views in the hundreds of millions and have saved campaigns millions of dollars in communication distribution expenses. Utilization of online videos offer politicians a level of image and message control that is outside the purview of the mainstream media. Campaigns are now better able to specifically target messages, rebut opponent attacks, and speak directly to their constituencies through affordably produce, highly targeted, and accessible messages that are easily shared across the political Internet. Digital videos allow politicians to situate campaign-engagement tools within the Internet environments that potential supporters are familiar with and that have become a bedrock through which to digitally reach both supporters and undecided voters. Appropriately conceptualized and strategically placed online videos can quickly and affordably reach a vast audience and boost campaigns' momentum through the generation of thousands, or sometimes hundreds of thousands, of views and shares.[20]

The public is increasingly turning to online video as a source of political news and information, as a way to connect to campaigns, and cided voters. gn. el ch a means of sharing political content with others.[21] During the 2004 presidential election, only 13 percent of online users reported watching campaign-related videos online. By the 2008 presidential election, 35 percent of online Americans reported watching online political videos to view unfiltered campaign materials, candidacy announcements, candidate debates, and political speeches.[22] During the election, Democratic voters were more likely to watch online videos than Republican supporters (51 percent to 42 percent) and supporters of then-candidate Barack Obama were more likely to engage in all manner of online political video engagement than supporters of any other candidate.[23]

During the 2010 midterm elections, 31 percent of online Americans reported watching campaign-related videos. This represented an increase of 12 percent from the 2006 midterm election and a 63 percent increase in the cumulative number of adult Internet users consuming online campaign-related videos.[24] The increase made online video consumption the Internet-based political activity with the most substantial growth between 2006 and 2010.[25] Additionally, during the 2010 election, 8 percent of political social media users, Internet users whose primary political engagement occurs via social media platforms, reported sharing online photo, video, or audio content related to the campaign.[26] Both Democratic and Republican supporters consumed more online video in 2010 than in 2006, with the number of Republican voters engaging with online political video roughly doubling between the two election cycles. Both Democratic and Republican voters were more likely to watch online political video than non-voters.[27]

During the 2012 campaign, 66 percent of registered voters who used the Internet reported watching previously recorded candidate speeches, press conferences, debates, and political advertisements, as well as live candidate speeches, press conferences, and debates online.[28] During this election, political social media users did not just view online video, they also reported using videos to engage with others with 23 percent of on-line voters recommending online political videos and 62 percent having had an online political video recommended to them.[29] Among voters who reported following the election closely, 73 percent recounted watching online political video versus 45 percent of those whom reported following the election less closely. In terms of party affiliation, both Republican and Democratic voters were equally likely to consume online political videos during this election.[30] Demographically, and potentially politically important, non-White users, populations which have historically had lower levels of political engagement, are using video sharing sites at higher frequencies than Whites, with 79 percent of non-Whites reporting using online video sharing sites regularly.[31] For political campaigns that continually work to increase citizen engagement and voter turnout amongst traditionally politically disenfranchised voter blocs, heightened participation in video sharing by non-White users may become an integral factor in future political campaign strategies.

THE PARTICIPATORY WEB

Web 2.0, also referred to as the participatory web, references a conceptualization of the Internet as a platform through which individuals, many with no specialized training or education, are the primary developers of web content.[32] These individuals participate in rapidly expanding Internet platforms, such as social media, wikis, blogs, podcasts, and RSS (really simple syndication) feeds, to write and develop content, videos, applications, and websites.[33] Web 2.0 is a social web.[34] It is characterized by masses of users participating asynchronously in the creation of content. These platforms capitalize on attributes such as collaboration, tagging (the assignment of a non-hierarchical keyword to a piece of information), hyperlinking, and viral marketing and have both fundamentally and dynamically expanded the ways that individuals both communicate through and participate with the Internet.

The characteristics of Web 2.0 have created an interactive, content-rich Internet architecture which has substantially impacted political campaigning, political communication, and public engagement. Through participation in these platforms, the traditional hierarchies of political communication have shifted; politicians, political parties, and campaigns are no longer the sole, or in some cases even the primary, creators and disseminators of political messages. Through Web 2.0 platforms, political

Internet users are no longer simply passive viewers of Internet content, they have become prosumers of political information and active participants in the development of political material.

In the Web 2.0 environment, it is requisite for politicians and political parties to maintain profiles on multiple platforms in order to effectively facilitate public communication and engage potential voters. Through the creation of communication structures that are horizontal and focused on engagement and relationship building, campaigns are able to connect with the constituency in ways not possible through less interactive mass media platforms. Properly leveraging Web 2.0 capabilities allows politicians to successfully pursue new avenues for information dissemination, fundraising, and mobilization. This Internet environment benefits from viralability, the conceptualization and development of a video or message with specific orientations intended to make it attract viral Internet attention. Additionally, it provides a space for the fast distribution of inexpensively produced, micro-targeted political content. Via Web 2.0, campaigns can quickly distribute agenda-driven political messages and monitor, practically in real-time, the success of this content. Messages or advertisements that do not achieve the desired level of viralability can be inexpensively and quickly altered and redistributed. This significantly increases the circulation of campaign messages and can substantially impact campaigns' ability to reach targeted audiences through which they can encourage sharing and cross-posting of political content.

YOUTUBE

While multiple video sharing websites exist, YouTube is the most trafficked video sharing site in the world and is a Web 2.0 platform with a substantial impact on the political Internet. Preceded into the online video sharing frontier by other pioneering websites, such as Metacafe, launched in 2003, and Vimeo, launched in 2004, YouTube was fundamentally different in that it was the first video sharing site where the site owners were not the primary content developers. YouTube was originally based on the "Hot or Not" principle, where anyone with website access had the ability to upload content that anyone else could view; if the video was "hot" it would receive views and online traction, if it was "not" it would fade out of existence.

YouTube began as a venture-funded technology startup supported by an 11.5 million dollar investment by the venture capital firm Sequoia Capital.[35] While there are many narratives surrounding the impetus of YouTube's launch, the most basic is that the site's developers had found it difficult to easily share the videos they were making with their friends. In the beginning, and even somewhat to the present date, there has been uncertainty and contradiction as to what YouTube is actually for. In its early days, YouTube marketed itself with the byline "Your Digital Repository," functioning primarily as a personal storage facility for video content. As the site began to evolve and embrace its new moniker "Broadcast Yourself," it attracted more users and began to fundamentally alter the online video experience.

By combining the functionalities of social networking with easy-to-use flash video player applications, YouTube enabled simple and fast video uploads, shortened video download times, reduced the cost of creating and sharing video, and created a new online sharing experience. Through YouTube, all one had to do was click an onscreen image of a video and they could instantaneously share it with anyone. Initially, YouTube did not have high adoption rates; however, it did offer many attractive features, such as a free and integrated interface, a minimal required level of technical knowledge, and basic community functions that made it easy to link to other users as friends. These features helped to quickly propel the site to its current position of dominance in the digital video domain.

Just a year after its launch, the site boasted over thirty million unique users and roughly 649 million videos had been streamed or downloaded from the site.[36] This growth represented a staggering 1,922 percent increase in the site's viewership traffic from 2005. In September 2006 alone, over six million videos were uploaded to YouTube, one million more than were uploaded the previous month.[37] In October 2006, YouTube was acquired by its current parent company, Google, and by early 2008 was consistently rated by various web metric services as one of the top ten most viewed websites globally. In December 2006, *Time* magazine featured "You," the user (reflected in a mirror on the magazine's cover) who uploads videos representing creative and social expression onto YouTube, as its "Person of the Year." The accompanying article noted that, "YouTube is to video browsing what a Wal-Mart Supercenter is to shopping: everything is there, and all you have to do is walk in the door."[38]

YouTube has continued to show exponential growth and has become the flagship online video sharing website. Through consistently evolving features, YouTube has emerged into multiple roles in the digital video environment, functioning simultaneously as a high-volume website, a broadcast platform, a media archive, and a social network. However, this substantial and consistent growth makes keeping up with usage statistics challenging. YouTube reins as the world's third most viewed website, behind Google and Facebook,[39] it functions as the second largest search engine platform in the world behind Google, and is the world's largest video sharing platform. In early 2011, YouTube emerged as the premier site through which Internet users watch video by surpassing a staggering benchmark of one trillion views, equating to roughly 140 views for every person on Earth.[40] Unique visitors to the site surpass over 800 million each month who spend an estimated four billion cumulative hours watching videos. Each day, average YouTube users spend between fifteen and twenty-five minutes watching content and it is estimated that for each minute of each day, there are 2.8 million views, equating to over two billion YouTube views every single day.[41] On an average day, the viewing audience on YouTube nearly doubles the number of prime-time audience members of all three major U.S. broadcast networks combined.

There is an exceptional amount of content uploaded to YouTube. It is estimated that over seventy-two hours of video are uploaded every minute of every day, with more video content being uploaded to YouTube in a sixty-day period than has been broadcast on the three major United States television networks in the past sixty years.[42] YouTube also has a substantial social media reach, with estimates indicating that roughly 500 years' worth of video is watched via Facebook every day. YouTube is accessible on over 350 million mobile devices and over 10 percent of its global views come from mobile technology. Between 2010 and 2011, there was a 200 percent increase in the number of videos watched on mobile devices per day, with an average of three million YouTube videos being viewed on mobile devices every day.[43] On average, over 700 YouTube videos are shared via Twitter each minute of each day, representing a 200 percent increase in this activity between 2011 and 2012, and more than 3 hours of video is uploaded to the site through mobile devices every minute. [44]

YouTube is localized in forty-three countries and operates in sixty languages globally, with an estimated 70 percent of the site's worldwide traffic coming from outside of the United States. Domestically, YouTube users are predominately male (however, only by a very slight margin), tend to be of a younger demographic, with 63 percent of users being under thirty-four years old, and come from households with higher than 50,000 dollars in annual income.[45] They tend to have no college education and have children living in the household. While individuals of Caucasian ethnicity represent the largest demographic of YouTube users, when comparing individuals of a specific ethnicity with the overall Internet usage of that ethnicity, individuals who identify as Hispanic, African American, and Asian proportionally have higher usage patterns than Caucasians.[46]

YouTube has been able to achieve incredible growth by lowering the cost of video creation, providing an inexpensive and easy method for sharing videos, and embracing both Web 2.0 and social media functionalities. Although users are not required to maintain a YouTube profile, the desire to do so and become a member of this fast-growing online community is evident. YouTube's features, such as video recommendations, one-click video sharing, embeddable video players, and comment functionalities, consistently allow it to engage with new and expanding audiences. These elements, combined with YouTube's shift in concept from a video repository to a platform for social expression, help to position YouTube

within the user-led revolution that is indicative of emerging and expanding Web 2.0 platforms and one that is particularly attractive to political
Internet users.

POLITICALTUBE

In 2006, YouTube somewhat inadvertently emerged as a significant force
upon the United States' political landscape. During an informal campaign gathering, remarks made by a senator seeking reelection were
caught on video, uploaded to YouTube, and marked one minute and
three seconds that dramatically altered how politics, politicians, and campaigns function in a digital media environment. Attempting to emphasize his campaign's theme of "positive and constructive ideas," Senator
George Allen from Virginia, went off script and personally addressed a
young staffer filming the event for the opposition's campaign. In his
remarks, Allen welcomed S. R. Sidarth, a young man of Indian descent, to
America and "the real world of Virginia," and referred to the young man
as "macaca," a term that many consider a racial slur. Sidarth took the
video back to the Jim Webb campaign and having no other means of
distribution, the campaign posted it to YouTube. On video, the remarks
made by Allen gave the perception of a sitting U.S. Senator belittling a
young immigrant and perhaps even questioning his immigration status
by welcoming him to America.[47] The video was riveting for its viewers
and quickly gained momentum, with both online and mainstream media
outlets picking up the story and broadcasting the video widely.

In previous, pre-YouTube era political campaigns, this exchange
would have most likely not even been a blip on the political radar. It
occurred at a small, informal gathering, and may have only resulted in a
short story that could have been easily denied by the campaign or craftily
politically spun. The ability for this seemingly trivial political misstep to
reach hundreds of thousands of viewers and attract the attention of the
mainstream media nationwide was an early indicator of the potential
political power of YouTube. Following the "macaca moment" going viral,
Allen attempted to reframe the situation and regain his footing in the
campaign, outspending Webb three-to-one, but attempts to mitigate the
impact of his remarks were unsuccessful.[48] This and subsequent You-
Tube videos of Allen opened channels of criticism for Webb and increased voters' knowledge of and attention to the race. That year, voter
turnout reached the highest level for a midterm election in Virginia's
history, with an increase, centered predominately on college campus and
in inner-city neighborhoods, of 14.6 percent compared to the previous
election.[49]

The power of this specific viral video and resulting political buzz was
not only evident in Allen's loss to Webb in 2006, but again in 2012 when

Allen was defeated by Tim Kaine for a seat in the Virginia State Senate. Comment threads on mainstream news websites discussing Allen's 2012 campaign were filled with comments about the "macaca moment," with site users posting comments such as ". . . the macaca moment will haunt Allen forever," "it's hard to understand how this racist Republican Allen can have any kind of shot in this race," and ". . . this guy is trying to run for office again? Priceless!" The original YouTube video has generated over 700,000 views and thousands of comments, with users posting comments about the video as recently as February 2014, over seven years after the original video was posted.

While the campaign of 2006 birthed the video-stalker, staffers who attend opponents' events and hope to catch a viral-video-worthy moment on camera, YouTube quickly evolved from a distribution network for "gotcha" videos into a site where serious politicking could take place. By mid-2006, many of YouTube's unique monthly visitors were heavily engaged with political videos, with "politics" being the second most popular general type of channel or topic cluster behind "humor." Political campaigns also began to leverage the platform to strategically reach audiences, engage and mobilize potential voters, and raise funds. YouTube also proved to be a valuable platform through which campaigns could affordably and easily disseminate political advertisements. The YouTube platform increasingly became not only a valuable campaign tool, but also, in some cases, a campaign battleground with candidates using the site to post videos of speeches, clarify policy initiatives, distribute attack advertisements, rebut opponent's or mainstream media attacks, and engage in political debate.

In March 2007, YouTube launched You Choose '08, a voter education initiative aimed at effectively bringing candidates and voters together. The site expanded election content for easy public consumption by grouping the YouTube channels for all seventeen presidential candidates under one banner page. The platform, described by YouTube as "The World's Largest Town Hall" for political discussion, enabled political candidates to easily inform potential voters about their campaigns via video.[50] You Choose '08 was the election's centralized hub for candidate-controlled YouTube channels, where viewers could access campaign videos, speeches, informal chats, and behind-the-scenes footage. You Choose '08 also included updates from campaign staff, 'insider' information, candidate endorsements, issue-related commentary, satirical and humorous sketches, and a great deal of user-generated content. The platform also encompassed video content from partner news organizations, such as the *Associated Press*, *CBS News*, and *The New York Times*, as well as content from local news stations and bloggers. Local and national media, the League of Women Voters, *PBS*, *MTV*'s Rock the Vote and multiple state and university voter guides listed You Choose '08 as an important, nonpartisan resource for the 2008 U.S. election.[51]

YouTube also instituted a variety of initiatives aimed at establishing dialogue and engagement between the candidates and voters. Citizens could connect with candidates by subscribing to, commenting on, sharing, favoriting, and rating candidates' videos. Individuals had the opportunity to create and share their own political videos, post text or video responses to videos and clips posted by the campaigns, and create video web logs (or vlogs). In addition to these community features, the platform instituted a candidate Spotlight that gave each candidate a week in the "Spotlight" on the News and Politics homepage. During their time in the spotlight, candidates would post a video question to the YouTube community and viewers would have the opportunity to upload video responses. According to YouTube, candidates would monitor users' responses throughout the week and post a video at week's end reflecting upon and discussing what they had noticed. The goal of the Spotlight was to let the candidates know what the public was thinking about important political issues facing the country and to provide a space where the public could engage with the candidates across the level platform that YouTube had created for politics.[52]

You Choose '08 highlighted candidates' views on important topics via a frequently updated playlist function and provided viewers with links to five timely political videos each day, which culminated with a "Best of the Week" post to allow the audience to catch up with any important political moments they may have missed during the week. The platform initiated YouTube's political functionality by inviting public participation, highlighting public opinion, and archiving America's political moments. Following the 2008 election, the platform expanded to focus on upcoming Congressional, state, and local elections and connected users with similar YouTube platforms in the United Kingdom and Spain. The platform was named by *Time* magazine as one of the fifty best websites in 2007[53] and eventually evolved into CitizenTube, YouTube's news and politics blog featuring breaking news from citizens, organizations, activists, and politicians.

By the 2008 election the public had begun embracing YouTube as a source of serious political information. With over 39 percent of voters reporting watching at least one political video online during the election,[54] campaigns began implementing YouTube as a viable platform for serious political messaging. Campaigns began heavily utilizing the platform as it provided them with an embedded audience that was easy and cost-effective to reach. During this election, seven presidential candidates announced their campaigns via online video through various online channels and 110 candidates for elections across the country registered official YouTube channels.[55] Campaigns posted videos of speeches, rallies, and advertisements and sought to leverage this new medium to engage with a specific demographic of potential voters—the political social media user. The 2008 election cycle saw the generation of thousands of YouTube videos, posted by the campaigns, mainstream media, and the public, with candidates' official videos receiving over 200 million views and videos generated by either individuals or groups not associated with the campaigns being viewed over one billion times.[56]

During this campaign, both major party candidates, John McCain and Barack Obama, used YouTube to reach potential voters. However, the Obama campaign provided the first glimpse into the future political power of YouTube by unleashing an army of videographers who posted roughly 2,000 videos of speeches, rallies, door-to-door organization initiatives, and of average Americans sharing their personal stories.[57] This movement invigorated the campaigns' grassroots supporters and generated a substantial number of page and video views.[58] Between July 2008 and the November election, the Obama campaign posted nearly 800 videos, in sharp contrast to the 100 posted by the McCain campaign.[59] By November 2008, over 50 million unique viewers had spent roughly 14 million hours watching Barack Obama's campaign-related videos on YouTube.[60] The successful integration of YouTube into overarching campaign strategies and prolific use of the platform by potential voters led many to dub the 2008 presidential election "The YouTube Election."[61] Understanding the increasingly crucial role of YouTube in contemporary politics, in January 2009 both Congress and the White House launched dedicated YouTube channels.

By 2010, YouTube had become a fixture in United States' politics. In February 2010, President Obama used YouTube as a platform to honor his promise of increasing transparency in government and of his administration by participating in an exclusive interview with YouTube users. Following the 2010 State of the Union address, the public was invited to submit follow-up questions for the president and vote for which questions he should answer via CitizenTube. In sum, over 11,600 questions were submitted and there were 660,000 votes on which questions Obama should answer. Steve Grove, YouTube's News and Politics director, hosted the interview at the White House by showing President Obama a citizen-generated YouTube video and then allowing Obama to respond to questions related to foreign policy, health care reform, small business development, job creation, and college tuition costs. President Obama answered the questions with a mixture of narrative and policy discussion. The full interview was uploaded to both the White House website and YouTube where it generated over 1.1 million views and over 13,000 comments.

In 2011, YouTube launched the YouTube Politics Channel (YTPC), a dedicated channel within the platform that would serve as the hub for locating and accessing political videos, campaign messages, political debates, news broadcasts, and political parodies during the 2012 presidential race. The creation of the YTPC was a response by Google to the public's increasing appetite for gathering political information online and campaigns' increased use of the Internet as a platform for framing and distributing messages. It served an important role as a mechanism in Google's attempt to solidify its position as a dominant provider of digital political content and as a go-to source for political news and information.[62]

The YTPC sought to provide a holistic view of what politics looked like in a YouTube environment and to centralize political videos in such a manner that it directed YouTube traffic specifically to the YTPC. The YTPC emphasized the horse-race nature of political campaigns by accumulating analytical data, such as graphs and charts comparing candidates' YouTube reach, and constructing candidate profiles that condensed their core YouTube statistics. The various features of the YTPC also provided ways for assessing the popularity of candidates' online videos and methods for tracking the latest political videos, which gave users a reason to frequently return to the hub for more information.

The YTPC served as a clearinghouse for political video during the election, with videos being cultivated from a variety of sources including the candidates' official YouTube channels and websites, various media outlets, and everyday citizens. The site also employed a third-party outlet that searched and monitored user-generated content across a variety of social media platforms and allowed YouTube to bring attention to trending videos that were captured or produced by ordinary people.[63] The YTPC served as a fully-functioning social video tracker and made it easy for its more than 35,000 subscribers to easily keep connected to political videos during the 2012 campaign.

During the 2012 presidential election, campaigns seemingly acknowledged the need to produce videos with social media sharing in mind and incorporated viral messaging strategies into many additional and novel forms of campaign communications. By April of 2011, when Mitt Romney officially entered the presidential race, nearly 600,000 videos, generating nearly two billion views, mentioning Obama or Romney had been uploaded to YouTube.[64] The Obama campaign made YouTube the central video hub of the campaign by directly linking its official YouTube channel to its official campaign website.

Throughout the election, the Obama campaign consistently uploaded new and dynamic videos, averaging four new videos every day, on a wide range of topics including advertisements, policy announcements, and rebuttals. By the election's conclusion, the Obama campaign had uploaded over 3,000 videos to its official YouTube channel. The channel generated roughly 9.2 times as many video views and 9.6 times as many followers as the Romney channel[65] and in July of 2012 the channel had reached a staggering 200 million views.[66] While the Romney campaign did not generate as many subscribers or channel views as Obama, Romney's channel had 35,000 subscribers and the channel's 300 videos were viewed over thirty-three million times, reaching a substantial constituent population.[67]

YouTube's steadily increasing coverage of politics has also forced mainstream news organizations to re-evaluate their strategies in attempts to regain splintering audiences caused by reliance on online media. News networks have begun to understand YouTube as an increasingly popular supplement to mainstream news and have made moves to distribute their content through YouTube rather than expecting audience members to come to them for information.[68] Similar to political campaigns, news organizations have been forced to remake their political landscape, develop new methods for creating and distributing information, and cultivate new partnerships to better engage with an online audience.

CONCLUSION

YouTube has become a fixture in campaigns and political communication. It is anticipated that as the medium continues to grow and expand, so too will the ways that the platform impacts campaigns, political communication, and democratic engagement. Recent election cycles have demonstrated the political power of YouTube and are indicative that future politicking will need to embody methods that are divergent from traditional politics of the past and build on the lessons and momentum drawn from the 2006, 2008, 2010, and 2012 elections. As video production becomes even more accessible and affordable, and distribution through traditional websites and Web 2.0 environments becomes even more prominent, online video and YouTube will play an ever-increasing and important role in the political landscape. The number of Americans using online video sharing sites is increasing and evidence indicates that members of often highly sought-after voting blocs are using online video sharing somewhat extensively.[69] These, and other factors, require political campaigns to increase their level of knowledge and understanding of how to most effectively leverage YouTube to reach the broadest constituency base possible. Politicians, the media, and the public alike have recognized the important role that YouTube now plays in the political landscape of United States' politics.

ORGANIZATION OF THIS VOLUME

Part I of the volume will focus primarily on the multiple ways that YouTube has impacted political campaigning. This section explores how the strategic integration of YouTube functionalities into political elections has helped campaigns more effectively distribute targeted messages, provided more control over candidates' political and personal images, increased the potency of advertising dollars, produced new methods for raising funds, and modernized political debates. Part II of the volume discusses how elected officials utilize YouTube as a method of communicating with constituents while in office. A survey of the YouTube channels of sitting U.S. Senators and Congresspersons offers a glimpse into how elected officials use YouTube as a method to keep their constituency up-to-date on their work while in office. An in-depth look at the official White House YouTube Channel provides a case study illuminating how the Obama White House has used YouTube as a means of consistent communication with the American constituency. Finally, Part III of the volume examines how Americans have begun to increasingly use YouTube as a means of engaging with political campaigns by discovering new ways to connect with candidates and new avenues through which to engage in public deliberation. The final chapter in the volume will discuss the potential future relationship between YouTube and politics and provide some discussion as to how the platform may be used in future elections.

NOTES

1. Morley Winograd and Michael Hais, *Millennial Makeover: MySpace, YouTube & the Future of American Politics* (New Brunswick, NJ: Rutgers University Press, 2008).
2. Andrew Kohut, *Internet's Broader Role in Campaign 2008: Social Networking and Online Videos Take off* (Washington, DC: Pew Research Center for The People & The Press, January 11, 2008), http://www.people-press.org/2008/01/11/Internets-broader-role-in-campaign-2008/.
3. David Farrell and Paul Webb, "Political Parties as Campaign Organizations," in *Parties without Parisians: Political Change in Advanced Industrial Democracies,* ed. Russell Dalton and Martin Wattenberg (London: Oxford University Press, 2000), 102–28.
4. Daniel Shea, Joanne Green, and Christopher Smith, *Living Democracy* (New York, NY: Prentice Hall, 2011).
5. Stephen Coleman, "Connecting Parliament to the Public via the Internet: Two Case Studies of Online Consultations," *Information, Communication and Society* 7 (2004): 1–22.
6. Morley Winograd and Michael Hais, *Millennial Makeover: MySpace, YouTube & the Future of American Politics* (New Brunswick, NJ: Rutgers University Press, 2008).
7. Ibid.
8. Jerome Armstrong and Markos Zuniga, *Crashing the Gate: Netroots, Grassroots, and the Rise of People-Powered Politics* (White River Junction, VT: Chelsea Green Publishing Company, 2006).
9. Marcela Garcia-Castanon, Alison Rank, and Matt Barreto, "Plugged in or Tuned out? Youth, Race, and Internet Usage in the 2008 Election," *Journal of Political Marketing* 10 (2011): 115–38.
10. Joseph Graf and Carol Darr, *Political Influentials Online in the 2004 Presidential Election* (Institute for Politics, Democracy, and the Internet, February 5, 2005), http://www.ipdi.org/UploadedFiles/influentials_in_2004.pdf.
11. Martin Peers, "Buddy, Can You Spare Some Time?," *The Wall Street Journal,* January 26, 2004, http://online.wsj.com/article/0,,SB107508223269211274,00.html.
12. Ryan Lawler, "Political Ads Find Their Way onto YouTube," *Gigaom,* November 1, 2010, http://gigaom.com/2010/11/01/political-ads-find-their-way-onto-youtube/.
13. Elaine Kamarck, "Assessing Howard Dean's Fifty State Strategy and the 2006 Midterm Elections," *Forum* 4, no. 3 (2006).

14. Kathleen Moore, *71 percent of Online Adults Now Use Video-Sharing Sites* (Pew Internet & American Life Project, July 26, 2011), http://pewInternet.org/~/media//Files/Reports/2011/Video percent20sharing percent202011.pdf.

15. Nicole Perrin, "US Digital Ad Spending: Online, Mobile, Social," *Emarketer.com*, April 2011, http://www.emarketer.com/Reports/All/Emarketer_2000794.aspx.

16. Jennifer Dunphy, "How Video Marketing Powers SEO," *Econsultancy.com*, April 12, 2012, https://econsultancy.com/blog/9583-how-video-marketing-powers-seo.

17. Jay Samit, "All Politics Is Social: Social Media Engagement Will Decide Election 2012," *SocialVibe*, June 2011, http://advertising.socialvibe.com/political_solutions.

18. Cisco, *Cisco Visual Networking Index: Global Mobile Data Traffic Forecast Update, 2013-2018*, White Paper, February 5, 2014, http://www.cisco.com/c/en/us/solutions/collateral/service-provider/visual-networking-index-vni/white_paper_c11-520862.html.

19. Emily Reeves, *Leveraging Online Video*, Digital Whitepaper (Stoneward, October 2012), http://www.stoneward.com/wp-content/uploads/2012/10/October-Digital-Whitepaper.pdf.

20. Karen Jagoda et al., *Social Networks Supercharge Politics: Turning Action into Votes in 2010* (Washington, DC: E-Voter Institute, 2010).

21. Kristen Purcell, *The State of Online Video: 69 percent of Internet Users Watch or Download Video Online; 14 percent Have Posted Videos* (Washington, DC: Pew Internet & American Life Project, June 3, 2010), http://uploadi.www.ris.org/editor/1276126693PIP-The-State-of-Online-Video.pdf.

22. Aaron Smith and Lee Rainie, *The Internet and the 2008 Election* (Pew Internet & American Life Project, June 15, 2008), http://www.pewInternet.org/Reports/2008/The-Internet-and-the-2008-Election.aspx.

23. Ibid.

24. Aaron Smith, *The Internet and Campaign 2010* (Washington, DC: Pew Internet & American Life Project, May 17, 2011), http://www.pewInternet.org/~/media//Files/Reports/2011/Internet percent20and percent20Campaign percent202010.pdf.

25. Ibid.

26. Ibid.

27. Smith, *The Internet and Campaign 2010*.

28. Aaron Smith and Maeve Duggan, *Online Political Videos and Campaign 2012* (Washington, DC: Pew Internet & American Life Project, November 2, 2012), http://www.pewInternet.org/~/media//Files/Reports/2012/PIP_State_of_the_2012_race_online_video_final.pdf.

29. Ibid.

30. Ibid.

31. Moore, *71 percent of Online Adults Now Use Video-Sharing Sites*.

32. Tim O'Reilly, "What Is Web 2.0: Design Patterns and Business Models for the next Generation of Software.," *O'Reilly*, September 30, 2005, http://oreilly.com/web2/archive/what-is-web-20.html.

33. Mark Warschauer and Douglas Grimes, "Audience, Authorship and Artifact: The Emergent Semiotics of Web 2.0," *Annual Review of Applied Linguistics* 27 (2007): 1–23.

34. Jennifer Dooley, Sandra Jones, and Don Iverson, "Web 2.0 Adoption and User Characteristics," *Web Journal of Mass Communication Research* 42 (June 2012), http://wjmcr.org/vol42.

35. Miguel Helft and Matt Richtel, "Venture Firm Shares a YouTube Jackpot," *The New York Times*, October 10, 2006.

36. Andrew Lipsman, *Worldwide Internet Audience Has Grown 10 Percent in Last Year, according to Comscore Networks London* (London, UK: Comscore, March 6, 2007), http://www.comscore.com/Insights/Press_Releases/2007/03/Worldwide_Internet_Growth.

37. Ibid.

38. John Cloud, "The YouTube Gurus," *Time Magazine*, December 25, 2006.

39. Laura Fitzpatrick, "Brief History YouTube," *Time Magazine*, May 31, 2010, http://content.time.com/time/magazine/article/0,9171,1990787,00.html.

40. YouTube, *YouTube Statistics*, 2013, http://www.youtube.com/t/press_statistics.

41. Fitzpatrick, "Brief History YouTube."

42. YouTube, *YouTube Statistics*.

43. Ibid.

44. Ibid.

45. Quantcast, *YouTube.com Traffic and Demographic Statstistics*, May 10, 2013, https://www.quantcast.com/youtube.com#!demo&anchor=panel-GENDER.

46. Ibid.

47. David Karpf, "Macaca Moments reconsidered...Electoral Panopticon or Netroots Mobilization?," *Journal of Information Technology & Politics* 7 (2010): 143–62.

48. Winograd and Hais, *Millennial Makeover: MySpace, YouTube & the Future of American Politics*.

49. Carl Cannon, "Generation 'We' — the Awakened Giant," *National Journal Group* 39, no. 10 (2007): 20.

50. Karen Breslau, "Steve Grove: How to Run for President, YouTube Style," *Newsweek Magazine*, December 22, 2007, http://www.thedailybeast.com/newsweek/2007/12/22/steve-grove-how-to-run-for-president-youtube-style.html.

51. Terri Towner and David Dulio, "An Experiment of Campaign Effects during the YouTube Election," *New Media and Society* 13, no. 4 (2011): 626–44.

52. YouTube, *You Choose '08 Spotlight*, April 11, 2007, http://youtube-global.blogspot.com/2007/04/you-choose-spotlight-mitt-romney.html.

53. Maryanne Murray Buechner, "50 Best Websites 2007: YouTube's You Choose '08," *Time Magazine*, July 8, 2007, http://content.time.com/time/specials/2007/article/0,28804,1633488_1633507_1633520,00.html.

54. Andrew Kohut, *More than a Quarter of Voters Read Political Blogs* (Washington, DC: Pew Research Center for The People & The Press, October 23, 2008), http://www.people-press.org/2008/10/23/section-1-the-Internet-and-campaign-2008/.

55. Albert May, "Who Tube? How YouTube's News and Politics Space Is Going Mainstream," *International Journal of Press/Politics* 15, no. 4 (2010): 499–511.

56. Nikki Schwab, "In Obama-McCain Race, YouTube Became a Serious Battleground for Presidential Politics," *U.S. News and World Report*, November 7, 2008, http://www.usnews.com/news/campaign-2008/articles/2008/11/07/in-obama-mccain-race-youtube-became-a-serious-battleground-for-presidential-politics?page=2.

57. John Hendricks and Lynda Lee Kaid, *Communicator-in-Chief: How Barack Obama Used New Media Technology to Win the White House* (Lanham, MD: Lexington Books, 2010).

58. Amanda Michel and Ed Pilkington, "Obama Passes YouTube Milestone as Online Videos Remake Campaigning," *The Guardian*, July 24, 2012, http://www.theguardian.com/world/2012/jul/24/obama-youtube-milestone-online-videos.

59. Bob Boynton, "Going Viral — the Dynamics of Attention," in *YouTube and the 2008 Election Cycle in the United States* (presented at the Journal of Information Technology and Politics Annual Conference, University of Massachusetts — Amherst, 2009), 1138.

60. Brian Kelly, "How Presidential Candidates Can Use Online Video to Run an Effective Campaign," *Huffington Post Tech*, September 19, 2012, http://www.huffingtonpost.com/briankelly/how-presidential-candidat_b_1892222.html.

61. Terri Towner and David Dulio, "An Experiment of Campaign Effects during the YouTube Election," *New Media and Society* 13, no. 4 (2011): 626–44.

62. Jennifer Martinez, "Google to Launch YouTube Politics," *Politico*, October 6, 2011, http://www.politico.com/news/stories/1011/65296.html.

63. Jennifer Preston, "New Politics Channel on YouTube," *The New York Times*, October 6, 2011, sec. The Caucus, http://thecaucus.blogs.nytimes.com/2011/10/06/youtube-launches-new-politics-channel/.

64. Olivia Waxman, "YouTube Videos Mentioning Obama and Romney Reach 2 Billion Views," *Time Magazine*, August 29, 2012, http://techland.time.com/2012/08/29/youtube-videos-mentioning-obama-and-romney-reach-2-billion-views/.

65. Jim Folliard, *2012 Presidential Candidates Use Online YouTube Videos in Campaign* (Fairfax Video Studio, November 20, 2012), http://www.fairfaxvideostudio.com/news/2012-presidential-candidates-use-online-youtube-videos-in-campaign-20121120.cfm.

66. Michel and Pilkington, "Obama Passes YouTube Milestone as Online Videos Remake Campaigning."

67. LaChrystal Ricke, "YouTube and the 2012 Presidential Election: An Examination of How Obama and Romney's Official YouTube Channels Were Used in Campaign Communication.," in *Presidential Campaigning and Social Media: An Analysis of the 2012 Election.* (New York, NY: Oxford University Press, 2014), 246–58.

68. PBS NewsHour, *Pew Study: More Viewers Choose YouTube for Breaking News* (PBS, July 16, 2012), http://www.pbs.org/newshour/bb/media/july-dec12/pewyoutube_07-16.html.

69. Kathleen Moore, *71 percent of Online Adults Now Use Video-Sharing Sites* (Pew Internet & American Life Project, July 26, 2011), http://pewInternet.org/~/media//Files/Reports/2011/Video percent20sharing percent202011.pdf.

Part I

YouTube and Political Campaign Communication

In 1998, Lynda Lee Kaid stated that "when political communication is assessed in the next millennium, maybe only ten years from now, the entire process by which we now define political campaigning will be completely different."[1] As the following chapters discuss the ways that YouTube has altered the political communication landscape, it is clear that Kaid's prediction resonates with the evolving political campaign landscape that YouTube has helped to foster.

Political campaign communication has been greatly transformed by YouTube. Candidates no longer reach audiences solely via static, campaign-down communication tactics; rather, they must now engage in multiple, varied, and dynamic means of campaign communication. As contemporary voters increasingly expect to use the Internet for campaign outreach, politicians have begun to capitalize on technological advancements to better inform and target them.

Political YouTube channels have begun to function as campaign microsites—small websites that are separate from campaign's official websites—that allow for the production and distribution of targeted-content that can be effectively indexed by search engines. The increasing sophistication of online campaign messages allows for them to be more effectively categorized for online searching and more narrow campaign messages help campaigns more successfully target specific online demographics.

Analysis of the content and features across an array of political YouTube videos and channels offers a glimpse into how YouTube has been used during recent political campaigns. Candidates have used the platform to more effectively control campaign agendas and for heightened political and personal image management. Campaigns have figured out how to reach more substantial and more responsive audiences through considering viralability and microtargeting in campaign advertisement and fundraising videos. The mainstream media have used YouTube as a platform for political debating, helping to bring about an increased level of authenticity, transparency, and access to voters.

The information and examples contained within this section exemplify the multitude of ways that YouTube has impacted political campaigning in the United States. Each chapter discusses the benefits and challenges that campaigning in the YouTube environment may bring and offers suggestions regarding where research on the relationships between YouTube, candidate messaging, advertising, fundraising, and political debates my lead during future election cycles.

NOTES

1. Lynda Lee Kaid, "Research Trends in Political Campaign Communication," in *Communication: Views from the Helm for the 21st Century* (Boston, MA: Allyn and Bacon, 1998), 123–26.

TWO

Political Message Development and Image Control

In 1994, California Senator Dianne Feinstein became the first political candidate to construct and use an official campaign website. Although very basic by contemporary standards, this website initiated the use of the Internet as a developing political communication channel. Campaign websites gave politicians a higher level of control over political message development and dissemination and permanently changed how politicians communicated with potential voters. Websites as digital campaign tools created a central location where voters could locate detailed information about candidates and connect with other like-minded voters through rudimentary discussion boards. These early websites paved the way for platforms such as YouTube in contemporary political campaigns to provide campaigns with new channels of message delivery that allow them to more effectively target and engage potential voters. This chapter provides examples of how campaigns have used YouTube for campaign announcements, for information and image control, and discusses how YouTube has given rise to the multi-voicedness of the Internet.

ONLINE CAMPAIGNING

Political campaigns quickly learned that Internet technologies allowed them to more effectively manage public perception of their candidate, distribute information directly to the public and the mainstream media, and raise questions or generate press regarding the positions of opposing candidates. As Internet usage among the public expanded, campaigns realized they had to follow these voters online.[1] These early digital communication strategies began to upset conventional wisdom regarding the role of money and media in political campaigns. The boundless online communication options increased lateral communication structures and helped to minimize the public's hierarchical relationship with traditional media.[2]

As the political Internet continued to evolve and play a larger role in campaign communication, the traditional four M's of political campaigning—money, media, message, and messenger—needed reconsideration.[3] The Internet enabled candidates who had minimal financial support from the major parties, or those who were outspent in traditional media by their opponents, the ability to leverage Netroots supporters and translate online support into offline action, money, and votes. Proper utilization of online technologies began to create a snowball-effect amongst supporters; one that increased campaign momentum and excitement and made incumbency no longer a hurdle that could not be overcome by lesser known candidates.[4] By effectively using extensive online networks, campaigns could ensure that campaign messages were heard and that the ideal potential audience was reached.

It is estimated that 88 percent of social media users are registered voters and that six out of ten social media users expect political candidates to maintain a social media presence.[5] While generally true of a younger audience, with roughly 70 percent of 18- to 34-year-olds maintaining this expectation, older members of the electorate also now expect politicians to have a social media presence.[6] Fifty-seven percent of 45- to 54-year-olds, and 52 percent of those over age 55, expect to be able to gather political information specifically through social media sites.[7] However, 63 percent of those aged 18 to 34 compared to 40 percent of those 55 and up will specifically use social media to make decisions about the candidates.[8] Additionally, 38 percent of social media users believe that the political information they glean from social media is as impactful in their political decision making as information from traditional media outlets.[9]

Contemporary political candidates have had to become increasingly aware of both their ability to craft and manage their political personas and their need to adhere to the ever-changing expectations of their audiences. Campaigns now leverage the public's widespread use of YouTube for both its online video and social networking capacities to build their political brand and cultivate political followings. The next sections will discuss how campaigns use YouTube to broadcast candidacy announcements, for information and image management, and to combat mainstream media interpretations. The impact that third party outlets and viral videos can have on campaigns' ability to manage their candidates' messages and platforms will also be addressed.

CANDIDACY ANNOUNCEMENTS

In the time between the 2006 mid-term election and the 2008 presidential campaign, there was question among the political establishment regarding what impact a platform like YouTube may have on political campaigns. While some campaigns were resistant to move political communication online because of a diminished locus of control, others quickly understood that in order to effectively court a wide berth of voters, they needed to move many traditional campaign functions online and onto social media platforms.

In 2008 some major party candidates began using YouTube to announce candidacies and follow up on announcements made via more traditional media outlets. By the 2012 election, YouTube had become a go-to channel for campaigns, with nearly 600 candidates for political office around the United States hosting official YouTube channels.[10] YouTube's unlimited platform space allows politicians to create digital yard signs for their campaigns. Politicians can substantially develop and market the theme and feeling of a campaign and offer supporters many options to become engaged with the campaigns early on. For example, some campaigns have asked the public to vote on campaign theme songs and others encourage early participation in the election process through volunteering.

Campaign announcements are vital to the success of the overall campaign because every candidate, regardless of incumbency, needs to persuade the public that they are the appropriate choice to serve in office.[11] Strategically announcing one's candidacy for office has long-reaching repercussions. Research indicates that liking or disliking a candidate, often measured by an assumption regarding the candidate's appearance of trustworthiness, precedes adoption of the candidate's issue orientation.[12] Meaning, that if voters do not like a candidate, or find them trustworthy, during their candidacy announcement, the candidate may have no future option to persuade voters on their platforms or policies.

Although YouTube has proven to be a viable and valuable campaign communication tool, collectively, very few major party candidates have elected to use it as the primary vehicle through which they announce their candidacies. Most major party candidates have elected to continue to use more traditional forums for candidacy announcements, such as stump speeches, rallies, and television interviews. Often, however, videos of these announcements are then posted to YouTube and official campaign websites. While not heavily utilized by campaigns, YouTube announcements can offer candidates the ability to promote themselves and their platforms through strategically crafted and distributed online videos. Candidacy video announcements can allow voters to connect with candidates' personal qualities, like perceptions of sincerity and honesty, which research indicates most voters evaluate prior to assessing candidates' competence and potential effectiveness.[13] While a limited number of candidates have announced their candidacies specifically through YouTube, those who have elected to use YouTube for campaign announcements have done so in a variety of ways.

In 2008, Democratic nominees John Edwards and Hillary Clinton both announced their presidential candidacies through YouTube videos. Edwards announced his candidacy in a short video filmed in front of a house damaged during Hurricane Katrina in New Orleans. Edwards stood in the foreground of a group of young volunteers working on the house and asked the public for their help in his efforts to better America. He encouraged the audience to get involved with the campaign immediately and directed them to his official campaign website. Edward's announcement reached over 176,000 viewers on YouTube, a day prior to his "official" announcement in front of the press. His video gave the impression of humbleness, showing that he, along with the kids in his video, was physically working to make America better. This strategy was meant to craft a positive image of Edwards for the voters, an important function of political messaging.[14] Further, Edwards empowered viewers by asking them to be agents of his campaign through sharing his videos with their networks and helping bring about the change his campaign was advocating for. While Edward's strategy of reaching out to a population of potential supporters who could easily and quickly distribute his announcement throughout their social networks was novel at the time, it has become a prominent and potent online political tactic.

Hillary Clinton marked the official start of her campaign with a YouTube video titled "I'm In," where she encouraged viewers regardless of geographic location or political ideology to join the national election conversation. She then carried this theme through three additional YouTube videos posted on three subsequent days called "Let the Conversation Begin." In these live webcasts, Clinton answered questions cultivated from submissions to her presidential campaign website. She also talked about her favorite movies and joked about her football-fanatic brothers. While the announcement video generated just over 76,000 views on Clinton's official YouTube channel, it amassed over 313,000 unique visitors on the official campaign website. The conversation videos, which were an attempt to make Clinton seem like an "openhearted neighbor, eager to bond over coffee,"[15] did not generate huge viewership numbers on YouTube, averaging only around 5,400 views across the three videos.

The disparity between viewership on YouTube and on the campaign website was likely caused by the fact that this was the Clinton campaign's first real use of YouTube as a platform for message disbursement. Because the campaign had cultivated an embedded audience on the campaign's website, it had difficulty getting this population to migrate to YouTube. YouTube, however, provided higher engagement functionalities for the audience as Clinton's website offered no options for interaction between the candidate and the public. The choice to post the announcement to YouTube first was likely an attempt to mitigate public complaints that attempts to interact with the campaign through the official campaign website were being screened by staff prior to being posted to the website. Strategically, it was important for Clinton to open the channels of communication between the campaign and the voters and to earn users' trust that their thoughts and opinions were being received and were valid. If campaigns can earn voters' trust first, they can then persuade them to vote.[16]

The Obama and McCain campaigns both used YouTube to expand upon campaign announcements following official announcements made in more politically traditional environments. Shortly after announcing his candidacy at a rally in Springfield, Illinois, the Obama campaign posted a twenty-two-minute video of the rally on the official campaign website and to YouTube; the YouTube video amassed over 192,000 views. While the official announcement was not made via YouTube, the campaign used the platform to distribute the video and to energize constituents about his campaign. Although John McCain announced his own candidacy during a public forum in New Hampshire, the campaign's posting of the video "America: Meet Sarah Palin," shortly after she was announced as McCain's running mate to its official YouTube channel set YouTube ablaze. During the last leg of the campaign, from August to November 2008, over 54,000 different YouTube videos of interviews, parodies, and impersonations of Palin, which generated over a half billion views, were uploaded to YouTube.

In 2012, Republican candidates Newt Gingrich and Tim Pawlenty used social media and YouTube as part of their campaign announcement strategies. Gingrich became the first politician to officially announce a presidential run via Twitter.[17] The video, which featured Gingrich in a studio setting alone speaking directly to the camera, discussed the candidate's previous political successes and his desire to focus on various initiatives. It generated over 179,000 views on YouTube. Strategically, the video allowed Gingrich to link ideological, value, appearance, and job dimension characteristics together to heighten his level of public persuasion regarding his fitness for office.[18] Pawlenty announced his candidacy in a YouTube video posted one day before his first official campaign stop in Iowa. The video, a mash-up (a video that is edited from more than one source to appear as one) of video clips and direct-to-camera moments by the candidate, focused on how Pawlenty's past and upbringing provided him the courage to deal with issues facing the country. Strategically, the video, which amassed over 167,000 views on YouTube, allowed the audience to develop an impression of Pawlenty through the messages and images that the campaign collected and mashed-up for the audience. While YouTube had become a more prominent platform for the distribution of campaign communication, Gingrich and Pawlenty were the only mainstream Republican candidates to use the platform for candidacy announcements.

Obama's 2012 campaign also used YouTube as part of its reelection launch by simultaneously posting an announcement video to YouTube and emailing it to supporters. The video, which generated over 1.3 million views on YouTube, was posted the night before the official beginning of the reelection campaign. The video was a compilation of video interviews featuring individuals from around the country discussing why they believed Obama should be reelected. There were marked differences between these candidacy announcements. While the Gingrich and Pawlenty videos highlighted themselves and their accomplishments, the Obama video contained a hallmark characteristic of his 2008 campaign, the use of average citizens to tell the story of the movement. Another marked difference between the announcement videos was the direct embedment of a one-click fundraising widget into Obama's video that allowed supporters to easily donate to the campaign without navigating away from YouTube.

While only a few mainstream campaigns have used YouTube to explicitly announce candidacies, most have used the platform to subsequently post videos of announcements that took place via other venues and to link these videos across social networking sites.

The campaigns that have used YouTube as a primary platform for candidacy announcements engaged in many important strategies that helped mold early images of the candidates for the audience. Candidates' self-presentations in these videos are fundamental in early campaign communication as they allow candidates' to construe and negotiate their identities through the public[19] and allow voters to evaluate candidates' homophily.[20] Both of these factors have been found to be important in the public's future voting decisions. It is anticipated that as online video becomes a more consistent tool of political campaigning, YouTube as a distribution point for candidacy announcements will become more commonplace.

POLITICAL INFORMATION AND IMAGE CONTROL

The Internet has transformed how individuals, political institutions, and organizations communicate and negotiate evolving political information and roles.[21] The Internet is one of the most powerful tools in campaign communication and the shaping of candidate images because it gives politicians the ability to speak directly to their audience.[22] The expanse of the Internet provides campaigns unlimited space through which to thoroughly articulate policy positions, biographical details, and other important information.[23] Campaigns and candidates must simultaneously negotiate two different sets of images: political images and personal images. Political images involve candidates' party identification, ideological commitments, issue positions, and relationships with other political figures and interest groups.[24] Personal images include candidates' traits and characteristics, such as age, intellectual ability, and speaking style.[25] YouTube can be a powerful force in the creation and maintenance of both candidates' political and personal images.

As media channels are increasingly moving toward a system of consumer-driven platforms and away from the producer-driven agendas of the past, the channels through which campaigns disseminate information are becoming more important.[26] YouTube helps transform traditional political communication by giving campaigns limitless space through which to spread messages to potential voters. This makes it easy for the public to obtain important information and allows the public to exchange opinions and share content directly with one another. Unlike traditional mediated platforms that are finite in terms of space and costs, YouTube allows campaigns to provide potential voters a multiplicity of videos covering a wide range of topics. This provides viewers with opportunities to better understand candidates, both as politicians and as people, and heightens the persuasive nature of campaign communication. YouTube provides an ideal venue for campaigns to discuss issues and policy stances, provide rebuttals to statements made by opponents or media outlets, and manage the image of their candidates.

POLICY DISCUSSIONS AND REBUTTALS

Mainstream news media diminishes lengthy political statements or speeches down to the most appealing sound bite, drastically limiting the proportion of candidates' speeches or press conferences that are heard by the public. Through YouTube, campaigns can provide the public with access to entire speeches, full-length press conferences, discussions from the House or Senate floors, and other public presentations via a forum immune to the intermediary influences and interpretations of the mainstream media.

While it may assumed that the public would not be exceptionally interested in watching entire political speeches on YouTube, videos of political speeches and other presentations frequently draw substantial viewership numbers. For example, President Obama's acceptance speech following his 2012 reelection drew in a YouTube audience of over nine million, former U.S. Representative Ron Paul's "What If" floor speech in 2009 garnered nearly 350,000 views, Mitt Romney's 2012 nomination acceptance speech at the Republican National Convention amassed over 600,000 views, and former President Bill Clinton's address at the 2012 Democratic National Convention drew over 2.1 million views. These large viewership numbers can likely be attributed to a variety of reasons including YouTube being an attractive platform for information distribution for first-time and younger voters.[27] The increased levels of interactivity on YouTube can also influence the public's perception of candidates and increase their understanding of candidates' policy stances.[28] Contemporary voters expect to have access to on-demand information about candidates and their agendas and tend to engage more fully with political messages in digital environments.[29] Voting-age social media users have indicated that when seeking out political information online, 94 percent will watch the entire message and nearly 40 percent will share that message with an average of 130 online friends and family.[30]

Hillary Clinton's 2008 presidential campaign is a good illustration of a campaign using YouTube to effectively manage both the candidate's political and personal images. Historically, female political candidates have faced challenging rhetorical choices when using mainstream media outlets for the distribution of campaign messages.[31] YouTube allowed Clinton's campaign to experiment with rhetorical messages, readjust when the messages were not entirely well received by the audience, and reconceive the campaign's voice as it moved forward in the election. The use of online videos allowed the Clinton campaign to distribute political messages exactly where she wanted, to the voters, rather than having her campaign messages broken down into talking points by mainstream media outlets.[32] In a video titled "Ask Hillary," Clinton is seen on her campaign bus, meeting with college students and answering questions from Facebook postings. The video is interspersed with clips of Clinton and her daughter, Chelsea, at various stops on the campaign trail, and snippets of college students sharing their opinions of Clinton as a future president. The video helped to change the voice of the campaign by shifting political dialogue in a way that both helped to socialize the candidate in the minds of potential voters (i.e., her personal image) and influence their perceptions her as a candidate (i.e., her political image). During the election the Clinton campaign posted 353 videos to YouTube, many directed to strategically targeted voter segments, such as college students, nurses, beauticians, and several other groups. Although these videos did not generate substantial viewership numbers, they provide a good illustration of the campaign's use of YouTube to respond directly to the needs of specific demographics.[33]

President-elect Barack Obama used YouTube as the distribution method for his first address to the American public following his election in 2008. His first video to the American public was viewed over one million times, perpetuated many of his campaign's prevalent themes, and capitalized on the social media infrastructure he constructed during the election. The Obama administration would go on to use YouTube as a primary vehicle for the distribution of his weekly presidential address, forgoing radio as the primary medium for the first time since the weekly address had been re-popularized by Ronald Reagan in the early 1980s.

YouTube essentially allows campaigns to run their own media networks.[34] Campaigns have used YouTube's multimedia and interactivity functions to circumvent the traditional structures of media information dissemination and often use campaign-produced videos to create and strategically direct media attention. With a growing population turning to online outlets for political information, campaigns can use YouTube to create an alternative network of information outside of the gatekeeping functionalities of traditional media. Campaigns can place specific information directly into the platforms where their constituencies are gathering news and information. YouTube allows campaigns to offer viewers a wide range of information, including different types of videos and links to related content. When necessary, campaigns can also strategically use mainstream news clips to help increase their credibility or as part of rebuttal strategies. The ability to use YouTube for this type of political image control is invaluable when attempting to connect with voters who retain a higher level of trust in traditional media organizations than in online political communication.

YouTube also provides campaigns with measurement techniques that help ensure the success of political messages. Campaigns are now able to instantaneously track what messages resonate with voters and adjust messages as necessary to more effectively engage their audience. Because of this, voters now play an increasingly important role in the construction and dissemination of campaign messages, which has lessened the authoritative role of the traditional news media.[35] However, because users now have more options for accessing political information and actively seek out specific political content, campaigns must be certain they are actually discussing what potential voters are interested in. For example, during the 2012 election, polls indicated that while both Obama's and Romney's campaign rhetoric was heavily focused on the economy, the online public was more responsive to Obama's discussions about immigration and women's issues and to Romney's messages about health care and veterans' issues.[36]

POLITICAL REBUTTALS

YouTube has also given campaigns new ways to quickly respond to attacks made by opponents and mainstream media outlets. In a pre-YouTube media landscape, campaigns may have been forced to wait until the next day's news cycle to provide a rebuttal statement to an attack or to clarify something a candidate may have said during a speech, debate, or public appearance. Alternatively, YouTube gives campaigns a platform through which to disseminate an almost instantaneous public response. This ability is very important to political campaigns because once voters feel angry, uneasy, fearful, or disgusted by a candidate, it is likely they will vote against them.[37] YouTube gives campaigns a well-populated platform to question, challenge, redistribute, and modify messages[38] and the ability to rely on the interactive and shareable nature of YouTube to quickly distribute rebuttal messages.

One of the most illustrative examples of a candidate capitalizing on YouTube to rebut a message plaguing their campaign in the mainstream media comes from Obama's 2008 presidential campaign. Amidst media reports connecting Obama to inflammatory and controversial remarks made by his former pastor, Reverend Jeremiah Wright, Obama gave a speech in front of an audience at the National Constitution Center in Philadelphia, Pennsylvania. The speech, titled "A More Perfect Union," addressed racial tensions and inequality in the United States and implored the public to move beyond race in order to collectively address shared social problems. Prior to YouTube, a speech such as this, given in front of a local audience would have likely been reduced to a short sound bite on national news, if it were covered at all. However, instead of simply just giving this speech and hoping that a sound bite or two were picked up by the mainstream media, the campaign uploaded the full thirty-seven-minute speech to YouTube. The speech quickly became one of the most-viewed videos of the campaign, with over 85 percent of Americans reporting having at least heard about the speech.[39] The speech generated over seven million views on YouTube and was remarked to be "arguably the biggest political event of the campaign" to that point.[40] It was opined to be the speech that helped elect Obama to the presidency.[41] Rather than letting the controversy linger and allowing the media to continue to interpret the situation for the voting public, the Obama campaign advantageously capitalized on YouTube to quickly and definitively counter attacks from the mainstream media.

In 2012, the Democratic National Committee used YouTube to circulate a video mash-up rebutting statements made by Mitt Romney in an attack advertisement against Obama. The DNC seized the opportunity to use clips of Romney's own statements to reframe claims made in his ad "Too Many Americans," which touted the elevated number of Americans living in poverty following Obama's first term. The DNC countered with its own advertisement, titled "You're Fired," which featured clips of Romney musing about firing people and an infamous 10,000 dollar bet that Romney made during a 2011 primary debate with Texas Governor Rick Perry[42] to prove that Romney was out of touch with the American people and only believed in "half of America."[43] In mashing-up and distributing this rebuttal advertisement, which generated over 80,000 YouTube views, the DNC appropriately leveraged YouTube as a platform through which the viralability of this message would resonate with the online population and be shared quickly across social media platforms. This video also provides a clear example of how campaigns can use YouTube to simultaneously elevate their own candidate while shaping a negative image of its opposition.[44]

IMAGE MANAGEMENT

In a digital environment, effectively managing a candidate's image and presence is vital. Voters will inevitably evaluate candidates' personal qualities, beliefs, and attitudes to determine how closely these characteristics' mirror their own when making voting decisions.[45] YouTube allows campaigns to effectively manage a candidate's image and work to strengthen the relationship between voters and the campaign. Because of this, campaigns have become increasingly savvier in their use of YouTube to manage the political and personal images of candidates. Strategic use of YouTube videos can help facilitate a feeling of interpersonal engagement between campaigns and voters. This may help individuals feel more personally connected to and invested in candidates and is a prominent reason viewers report watching political videos.[46] Properly leveraged YouTube videos can help candidates build their political brand, generate political buzz, reach potential voters, and translate online enthusiasm into engagement, fundraising, and votes.

The Obama campaigns and administration have always heavily utilized YouTube for both policy and image management. During the 2012 campaign, around 17 percent of the videos on the *Obama for America* YouTube channel served to connect supporters with Obama, the person, and not necessarily Obama, the candidate.[47] These videos worked to establish Obama as an average person having dinner with teachers, army veterans, and firefighters, and as a family man, through video montages of the Obama family during special events and one commemorating the Obama's twentieth wedding anniversary (this video alone generated 1.1 million views). There were also funny videos, including Obama singing at press conferences, fist-bumping Michelle, and dancing with television show host Ellen Degeneres, which at over 3.5 million views is one of the most popular Obama videos to date on YouTube. These videos serve to better connect the public with the candidates' personal image and make significant strides towards making the candidate seem widely relatable.

After facing wide-spread criticism for not being as relatable as his opponent, Mitt Romney's 2012 campaign posted two specific videos to the campaign's *Believe in America* YouTube channel aimed at helping to modify the image of the candidate and the campaign. The first was a ten-minute video introducing Romney to the public via testimonials from Romney himself, his wife Ann, some of his children, and others whom Romney had impacted through his professional and political service. The video discussed Romney's upbringing and family life, his role in the 2002 Salt Lake City Olympics, and his record of achievements as a businessman. The video sought to better connect the candidate to undecided voters who may have thought negatively about his personality because of media portrayals and opposition attacks. The video also worked to generate a perception of the everydayness of Romney by discussing topics like his father's rise through poverty and his wife's battle with Multiple Sclerosis. Just before the election, the campaign distributed a video depicting a rally of over 10,000 supporters that Mitt Romney and running-mate, Paul Ryan, hosted in Red Rocks, Colorado. The video aimed to demonstrate the support and momentum that the campaign had generated as well as to spread the campaign's message of job creation. YouTube allows campaigns to construct and manage the specific personal image they want to portray directly to the voting public in a manner that would be difficult and extremely expensive to manage solely through mainstream media outlets.

Videos featuring personal narratives, either from candidates or the public, create identification and agency for voters, elements which can help campaigns manage candidate's political and personal images. For instance, the interjection of personal narratives from average Americans into campaign videos may provide characters with whom voters can more strongly identify with. This strategy can also help voters gain a better understanding of what certain issue-positions may mean for them personally. While seen as informative, Clinton's "Let the Conversation Begin" series was criticized for its incongruent messaging. The videos depicted Clinton at home, in her living room, talking informally to potential voters. However, even though the scene was relaxed and conversational, her dialogue was perceived as being clinical, with her language and tone being more indicative of legal discourse rather than someone having a "conversation" with friends.[48] When the campaign shifted focus and allowed individuals to share their own personal narratives of what Clinton's election to the presidency may mean and how various policy initiatives may impact them, both the political and personal image of the campaign changed. When Clinton was able more effectively align the message and the context of her campaign, she began to be seen as more politically attuned to her audience.[49]

YouTube also provides campaigns a valuable luxury that mainstream media outlets do not: infinite time and space through which to disseminate campaign messages. In early 2012, the Obama campaign stepped outside of traditional political communication structures and produced a seventeen-minute-long, online documentary written by award-winning director Davis Guggenheim and narrated by Tom Hanks titled "The Road we've Travelled." The production included a compilation of video clips and interviews documenting Obama's first term in office. It discussed both the perceived problems the president inherited from former administrations and also the major successes of his first term, such as the recovery of the automobile industry. The video served to illustrate for the public the work and success of the Obama administration, but it also served secondary purposes, to jumpstart fundraising and public engagement for the upcoming election. The video was released both online and in over 300 premier screenings in offices and supporters' homes across the country.[50] The online video was distributed through a new YouTube platform which enabled the campaign to embed fundraising links directly into the video, allowing supporters to donate without having to navigate from the Obama YouTube channel.[51] Prior to YouTube, a campaign would have never be able to distribute a video of this length through such a highly trafficked outlet; it would have only been possible to distribute such a video via email directly to supporters, where sharing and linking would have been more difficult. The campaign counted on the video being shared through social media and worked to leverage the inherent credibility that comes from videos that are shared with others by friends and family to elevate the video beyond political propagandizing.

YouTube has forced successful candidates to show a critical adaptation in online political campaigning. Candidates are able to reach out directly to their voting constituencies, target messages for differing voting blocs, and more effectively manage their political and personal images. Additionally, campaigns are able to more strategically disseminate their messages directly into digital communities where individuals are accustomed to sharing, discussing, and debating political messages. However, this environment can also prove challenging for candidates as often campaign's use of technologies, or in some cases lack of use, provide important communication cues for the public. For example, the commenting functionalities on many candidates' official YouTube channels have been disabled by the campaigns. In the YouTube environment, this simple lack of access can make a campaign appear unwilling to use the platform to connect with, and hear from, potential voters. Politicians and campaigns must find an effective balance between traditional political communication and online platforms that will allow them to most effectively create and distribute messages that resonate with the audience and motivate them to share campaign information with others.

THE MULTI-VOICEDNESS OF YOUTUBE

YouTube flourishes as a Web 2.0 medium that provides not only substantial benefits, but also serious challenges for political candidates. There is a mulit-voicedness to this medium that is not present in other types of media. This multi-voicedness can both enhance political message dissemination and make it more challenging. Campaigns must consistently contend with the ability of third parties — other campaigns, individuals, or organizations — to produce and disseminate politically oriented videos with the same freedom as the campaigns themselves enjoy.

In March of 2007, the multi-voicedness of YouTube emerged with ferocity. Phil de Villas, a then anonymous YouTube user, created a mash-up of Apple's 1984 Super Bowl commercial in which he cast presidential candidate Hilary Clinton as Big Brother and encouraged viewers to defy the political establishment and to "Vote Different" by supporting Barack Obama. In the mash-up, de Villas replaced the talking head of actor David Graham in the original video with clips from Clinton's "Let the Conversation Begin" video. The mash-up alluded to Clinton's campaign videos as attempts at political brainwashing. The video was viewed 3 million times in the first month,[52] which was 500 times as many views as Clinton's original campaign video generated.[53] Although the Obama campaign did not have any part in the creation or distribution of the video, it was able to reap the benefits of a video targeting one of Obama's staunchest opponents that generated millions of views at no cost to his campaign.

In June 2007, a YouTube user by the name of "Obama Girl" posted a video titled "I Gotta Crush . . . on Obama." The video, produced by the website BarelyPolitical.com, featured a pretty young woman seductively singing about her love for Obama. The video generated thousands of views in its first five hours online and garnering the attention of the mainstream press by its second day; it had amassed over twenty-six million views as of April 2014. It was also named by *Newsweek* as one of the top ten memes (a concept that spreads from person to person via the Internet) of the decade.[54] While Obama was not necessarily thrilled with the fact that the video had upset his daughters, he did acknowledge that in the "fertile imagination of the Internet," videos like this will occur.[55]

The 2008 election cycle saw the generation of thousands of YouTube videos, posted by the campaigns, mainstream media, and the public. A music video created by singer will.i.am, titled "Yes We Can," generated a substantial online following during the election. Reportedly feeling captivated and inspired by then-Senator Obama's speech after his defeat in the New Hampshire primary, the singer gathered a group of thirty-nine celebrities, singers, and songwriters and in a matter of just two days turned the words of Obama's speech into an online video sensation. The song, which will.i.am. felt was reflective of Martin Luther King Jr., John F. Kennedy, and Abraham Lincoln, was a product of the songwriter's desire to become involved and advocate for positive change.[56] In response to the video, Andrew Rasiej, a co-founder of the website techpresident.com, stated that "it was the perfect melding of Obama's political message with a desire for more engagement by the American public manifested in a simple video instantly viewed by millions without any influence by the mainstream media and the political parties themselves."[57] The video, which generated over twelve million views in its first weeks, had generated over twenty-four million views as of April 2014, was adopted by the Obama campaign as its official theme song, and was honored with the first-ever Emmy Award for Best New Approaches in Daytime Entertainment.[58] Once again, although the Obama campaign had no hand in the creation or distribution of the video, it was able to reap the benefits of a viral video espousing the themes of its campaign and to capitalize on the multi-voicedness of YouTube.

While campaigns can clearly benefit from multi-voiced third parties on YouTube, user-generated content can also prove challenging, and in some cases impossible, for political campaigns to overcome. In August 2008, American soldier and Iraq war veteran Joe Cook, who had served a tour in Iraq during which he lost a leg, posted a personal message to then-candidate Obama on YouTube. Cook's video was a response to comments made by Obama about his opposition to the Iraq war. In the video, Cook tells Obama, and other politicians who spoke out against the war, that their positions were disrespectful to the service and sacrifices of those who had died promoting freedom. Cook stated, "Dear Mr. Obama, having spent twelve months in the Iraq Theater, I can promise you this was not a mistake. I witnessed firsthand the many sacrifices made for the people of Iraq. Those sacrifices were not mistakes." The video was a clear illustration of how an individual who disagrees with a politician's stance or statements has the ability for their message to reach a mass population. While the video was not necessarily overwhelmingly detrimental to the Obama campaign, it did became one of the most popular non-campaign affiliated videos of the election, generating over fourteen million views, thousands of comments and shares, and being rated by the British Broadcasting Corporation as the number one political advertisement of 2008.[59]

However, not all YouTube moments are inconsequential. In June of 2010, while running for reelection in North Carolina, Democratic Congressman Bob Etheridge was recorded being approached by two students who asked him if he "fully supported the Obama agenda." The Congressman responded by physically accosting one of the students, first grabbing his arm and then his neck, and shoving his camera down while demanding to know the students' identities, to which one student replied "we're just here for a project . . . we're just students." The video, posted to YouTube shortly after the encounter, quickly went viral, amassing nearly three million views and gaining the attention of the national mainstream media. The incident was a boon for Etheridge's relatively unknown opponent, Renee Ellmers, who, in the twenty-four-hour period after the video's posting received nearly 25,000 dollars in donations and enough of a bump in her polling numbers to push her ahead of Etheridge. Responding to the race's rapid change in direction, an Ellmers' consultant stated that the video had ". . . changed the politics in the district. It is now one of the most competitive races in the country."[60] While no legal ramifications came of the incident, the video generated a substantial number of online calls for the Congressman to be charged with assault for his actions. Etheridge did eventually apologize for his combative behavior stating,

"No matter how intrusive and partisan our politics can become, this does not justify a poor response. I have and I will always work to promote a civil public discourse."[61]

Videos of this ilk gave rise to an interesting narrative regarding political uses of YouTube: the video-stalker as a partisan attack. In the video, the students' faces were blurred out, leading some to speculate that they were not students, but rather staffers from the opposing party attempting to capture a "gotcha" moment on video. Addressing this criticism, Brad Woodhouse, the Democratic National Committee spokesman at the time stated that, "Motives matter, and I think you can see who was behind this. This was a Republican party tracking operation . . . Republicans know if they admit their involvement in this game of gotcha it will undermine their credibility."[62] Although it is not possible to assess any level of causality between the video and Ellmers' eventual defeat of Etheridge, even seasoned political commentators noted that while Etheridge should have still won the race because of his fundraising prowess, the video provided a "pretty clear scenario to see how he loses."[63]

In 2012, *Mother Jones*, an independent news organization, released a video of Mitt Romney's "47 percent" comments,[64] providing yet another example of how a third party's YouTube video could substantially upset and alter a campaign's focus. The video, recorded by Scott Prouty, a bartender at a closed-door fundraiser for the Romney campaign, captured the candidate seemingly derogatorily discussing the "47 percent of the people who will vote for the president no matter what." Following the event, and offended by Romney's dismissal of middle-class voters like himself, Prouty wanted to let the public hear Romney's private words and decide for themselves how concerned he was for their well-being. Prouty connected with *Mother Jones* and it posted the video online, where it quickly went viral, generating over 3.3 million views, and dominating mainstream media commentary for weeks. While the Romney camp attempted to mitigate the fallout of the video, Prouty had expanded the reach of the video by exercising a substantial level of technological savviness and maximizing the number of links to the video on *Mother Jones*, YouTube, Twitter, Facebook, and other social media, making the video the first homespun Internet campaign to discredit a candidate with their own words.[65]

Online parodies and satirical videos, which generate, in some cases, astronomical viewership numbers, are additional YouTube voices that can have an impact on political communication. During the 2012 election, a video from the *Epic Rap Battles of History* channel titled "Barack Obama vs. Mitt Romney," in which Obama and Romney characters, with a cameo by Abraham Lincoln, rap their grievances towards one another, generated over 68 million views and over half a million comments. Other videos, such as a compilation of President Obama's public speeches into a video mash-up of the popular song "Call Me Maybe" by Carly Rae

Jepsen, reached nearly 38 million views, generating twenty-four million of those views in just a few months. A Mitt Romney "Gangnam Style" parody video reached 48.3 million views, a video endorsement for Romney by the Simpson's Mr. Burns generated over nine million views, and a mash-up of Obama and Romney speeches titled, "Will the Real Mitt Romney Please Stand Up?," based on the Eminem song "The Real Slim Shady," generated over 8 million views. Although campaigns do not respond to or engage with videos of this nature, these videos quite often contain some level of accurate political information and frequently unfavorably mock the candidates. Accumulating research indicates that younger voters are increasingly turning to nontraditional media sources, such as late-night television comedy programs, for political information.[66] As this trend is likely to continue and the amount of multi-voiced political information on YouTube increases, the impact of parody and satirically-driven videos, with regard to both the political content they provide and the number of views they collectively accumulate, will be interesting to assess during future campaigns.

The multi-voicedness of YouTube functions in two important ways: it generates a great deal of online, and often, mainstream media attention and upsets the historical balances of finances and control in political campaigning. A video, such as "Vote Different," that had the ability to generate millions of viewers (over 6.3 million as of April 2014) and cost relatively little to make upsets the economics of traditional political television advertising production and distribution.[67] These videos also change the primary parties who have traditionally been the principal creators and distributors of political and campaign information. Historically, political media advisors have been able to judge the pulse of elections and craft and dispense appropriate messages through proven distribution channels. Now, YouTube has subverted the traditional gatekeeping protocols of both the mainstream media and political campaigns, forcing campaigns to be consistently aware and reactive to what is happening not just in their opponent's campaigns and the mainstream media, but also in the vast Internet environment.

CONCLUSIONS AND CHALLENGES

Although television and official campaign websites still remain central platforms in the distribution of campaign messages, YouTube has become an platform where serious political campaigning, message development and management, and political and personal image control occurs. In 2010, none of the top political videos on YouTube were produced by a political campaign or politician. In 2011, 40 percent of the top political videos were campaign advertisements and an additional 20 percent were of Obama giving public presentations. As a platform, YouTube is an appealing venue for political campaigning because it provides candidates a historically sought after source-controlled medium for campaign communication.

In 2012, among the list of the top political videos were Obama's complete acceptance speech and a video of Obama thanking his staff following end of the campaign. While it did not rank as one of YouTube's top political videos, Mitt Romney's "binders full of women" comment,[68] part of a debate answer regarding pay equality for women, quickly went viral and became the subject of much political punditry amassing well over half a million views across various YouTube channels and posts. Between the beginning of the presidential primaries and the end of August 2012, official presidential candidate videos had been viewed over 100 million times and between the end of July and the end of August users spent more than 20 cumulative years viewing Obama's and Romney's official videos on YouTube.[69] Campaigns' video uploads consistently gain online traction, with many receiving hundreds of thousands of views within a few days and others generating hundreds of thousands of views within hours. Following the announcement of Paul Ryan as his running-mate, Romney's official YouTube channel saw a 300 percent increase in subscribers and views and their first official video together generated over 1.1 million views in just two weeks.[70] Voters are clearly using YouTube as a source of political campaign information and the political information that individuals are choosing to view on YouTube is evolving. While parodies, satire, and gotcha moments do generate substantial viewership numbers, so too do political advertisements and speeches.

However, campaigning on YouTube also brings with it inherent challenges. While YouTube gives campaigns an unlimited platform through which to speak to potential voters, it also gives opponents, mainstream media outlets, and the public full access to campaign materials. Because of this, campaigns must be conscious of what is posted to YouTube, how messages are framed, and be able to quickly respond to the ways in which opponents, the media, and the multiple voices on YouTube may mash-up and redistribute campaign messages. There are also historic criticisms waged primarily at televised politics that can be aptly applied to YouTube and political videos in general. For instance the concern that images, supplant meaningful discussion of issues in contemporary campaigns[71] and that campaigns encourage candidates to act more like beauty contestants than politicians, introducing themselves, offering standardized statements, explaining their vision for America, wearing appropriate costumes . . . and consistently endeavoring not to offend.[72] If these criticisms are valid and the public indeed has a "limited capacity for dealing with information,"[73] as other critics lament, then the future of YouTube as a medium for sustained campaign communication may be inconsequential.

Future research on YouTube as a platform for political message development and image control could investigate the ways that campaigns strategically use YouTube for important political functions such as political branding, message development, and in the creation of audience-identification. Other research could strive to connect the viewing of campaign content, such as speeches and press conferences, to voter intentions and mobilization. Finally, some interesting research investigating what legitimate political information the audience may learn from viewing parodies and satires and how that may connect to voting decisions could also be conducted.

YouTube has a profound power to help shape the public's political conversation. The platform allows campaigns to play to their strengths with regard to message development and image management and the ability to reach an incredibly broad audience. In order to capitalize on this environment, and increase the viralability of their messages, campaigns must understand how messages that align with their initiatives can best correlate with video content that has proven attractive to a YouTube audience. YouTube provides campaigns many varied options for engaging with the American public through political videos. Future elections will likely provide even more varied and novel political communication options through which candidates can effectively and creatively court the voting public.

NOTES

1. Chapman Rackaway, "Trickle-Down Technology," *Social Science Computer Review* 25, no. 4 (2007): 466–83.

2. John Tedesco, "Changing the Channel: Use of the Internet for Communicating about Politics," in *Handbook of Political Communication Research* (Mahwah, NJ: Lawrence Erlbaum Associates, 2004), 507–32.

3. Morley Winograd and Michael Hais, *Millennial Makeover: MySpace, YouTube & the Future of American Politics* (New Brunswick, NJ: Rutgers University Press, 2008).

4. Ibid.

5. Josh Wolford, "Note to 2012 Presidential Candidates: Your Social Media Presence Is a Big Deal," *WebProNews*, November 1, 2011, http://www.webpronews.com/note-to-2012-presidential-candidates-your-social-media-presence-is-a-big-deal-2011-11.

6. Gerald Holubowicz and Jean Guillo, *Moneyocracy: The Rise of the United Corporations of America*, Documentary (Insomnia World Sales, 2012), www.moneyocracy-project.com.

7. Ibid.

8. Wolford, "Note to 2012 Presidential Candidates: Your Social Media Presence Is a Big Deal."

9. Ibid.

10. Amanda Michel and Ed Pilkington, "Obama Passes YouTube Milestone as Online Videos Remake Campaigning," *The Guardian*, July 24, 2012, http://www.theguardian.com/world/2012/jul/24/obama-youtube-milestone-online-videos.

11. Thomas Hollihan, *Uncivil Wars: Political Campaigns in a Media Age* (Boston, MA: Bedford/St. Martins, 2009).

12. Churchill Roberts, "From Primary to the Presidency: A Panel Study of Images and Issues in the 1976 Election," *Western Journal of Speech Communication* 45, no. 1 (1981): 60–70.

13. Kathleen Kendall and Scott Paine, "Political Images and Voting Decisions," in *Candidate Images in Presidential Elections* (Westport, CT: Praeger, 1995).

14. Paul Sniderman, James Glaser, and Robert Griffin, "Information and Electoral Choice," in *Information and the Democratic Process* (Urbana, IL: University of Illinois Press, 1990).

15. Howard Fineman, "Many a Hurdle for Hillary," *Newsweek Magazine*, February 5, 2007.

16. Samuel Popkin, *The Reasoning Voter: Communication and Persuasion in Presidential Campaigns* (Chicago, IL: University of Chicago Press, 1994).

17. Jonathan Karl, "Newt Gingrich Announces 2012 Presidential Campaign via Twitter," *ABC News*, May 11, 2011, http://abcnews.go.com/Politics/newt-gingrich-announces-2012-presidential-campaign-twitter/story?id=13578139.

18. Lynda Lee Kaid and Mike Chanslor, "Changing Candidate Images: The Effects of Political Advertising," in *Candidate Images in Presidential Elections* (Westport, CT: Praeger, 1995), 83–97.

19. Pamela Benoit, *Telling the Success Story: Acclaiming and Disclaiming Discourse* (Albany, NY: State University of New York Press, 1997).

20. Kathleen Kendall and June Yum, "Persuading the Blue Collar Voter: Issues, Images and Homophily," in *Communication Yearbook 8* (Beverly Hills, CA: Sage, 1984), 702–22.

21. Tedesco, "Changing the Channel: Use of the Internet for Communicating about Politics."

22. Hollihan, *Uncivil Wars: Political Campaigns in a Media Age.*

23. John Tedesco, Jerry Miller, and Julia Spiker, "Presidential Campaigning on the Information Superhighway: An Exploration of Content and Form," in *The Electronic Election: Perspectives on the 1996 Campaign Communication* (Mahwah, NJ: Lawrence Erlbaum Associates, 1999), 51–63.

24. William Husson et al., "An Interpersonal Communication Perspective on Images of Political Candidates," *Human Communication Research* 14, no. 3 (2006): 397–241.

25. Ibid.

26. Dietram Scheufele, "Agenda-Setting, Priming, and Framing Revisited: Another Look at Cognitive Effects of Political Communication," *Mass Communication and Society* 3, no. 2–3 (2000): 297–316.

27. Lynda Lee Kaid and Monica Postelnicu, "Political Advertising in the 2004 Election: Comparison of Traditional Television and Internet Messages," *American Behavioral Scientist* 49 (2005): 265–78.

28. Shyam Sundar, Sriram Kalyanaraman, and Justin Brown, "Explicating Web Site Interactivity: Impression Formation Effects in Political Campaign Sites," *Communication Research* 30, no. 1 (30-59): 2003.

29. Kathryn Montgomery, "Youth and Digital Democracy: Intersections of Practice, Policy, and the Marketplace," in *Civic Life Online: Learning How Digital Media Can Engage Youth* (Cambridge, MA: The MIT Press, 2008), 25–50.

30. Jay Samit, "All Politics Is Social: Social Media Engagement Will Decide Election 2012," *SocialVibe*, June 2011, http://advertising.socialvibe.com/political_solutions.

31. Linda Witt, Glenna Matthews, and Karen Paget, *Running as a Woman: Gender and Power in American Politics* (New York, NY: The Free Press, 1995).

32. Amber Davisson, "I'm In!": Hillary Clinton's 2008 Democratic Primary Campaign on YouTube," *Journal of Visual Literacy* 28, no. 1 (2009): 70–91.

33. Ibid.

34. Michel and Pilkington, "Obama Passes YouTube Milestone as Online Videos Remake Campaigning."

35. The Pew Research Center, *How the Presidential Candidates Use the Web and Social Media* (Pew Project for Excellence in Journalism, August 12, 2012), http://

www.journalism.org/analysis_report/
how_presidential_candidates_use_web_and_social_media.
36. Ibid.
37. Hollihan, *Uncivil Wars: Political Campaigns in a Media Age.*
38. Michael Gurevitch, Stephen Coleman, and Jay Blumler, "Political Communication – Old and New Media Relationships," *The ANNALS of the American Academy of Political and Social Science* 645 (2009): 164–81.
39. The Pew Research Center, *Obama Speech on Race Arguably Biggest Event of Campaign* (Pew Research Center for the People and the Press, March 27, 2008), http://pewresearch.org/pubs/777/obama-wright-news-interest.
40. Ibid.
41. Hendrik Hertzberg, "Obama Wins," *The New Yorker*, November 17, 2008.
42. Chris Cillizza and Aaron Blake, "Mitt Romney's $10,000 Mistake," *The Washington Post*, December 12, 2011, http://www.washingtonpost.com/blogs/the-fix/post/mitt-romneys-10000-mistake/2011/12/11/gIQA9aEQpO_blog.html.
43. Jon Ward, "Mitt Romney's First Direct-To-Camera Ad Comes At Make-Or-Break Moment In Campaign," *Huffington Post*, September 26, 2012, http://www.huffingtonpost.com/2012/09/26/mitt-romney-ad_n_1915665.html.
44. Sniderman, Glaser, and Griffin, "Information and Electoral Choice."
45. Kendall and Paine, "Political Images and Voting Decisions."
46. Aaron Smith and Maeve Duggan, *Online Political Videos and Campaign 2012* (Washington, DC: Pew Internet & American Life Project, November 2, 2012), http://www.pewInternet.org/~/media//Files/Reports/2012/PIP_State_of_the_2012_race_online_video_final.pdf.
47. LaChrystal Ricke, "YouTube and the 2012 Presidential Election: An Examination of How Obama and Romney's Official YouTube Channels Were Used in Campaign Communication.," in *Presidential Campaigning and Social Media: An Analysis of the 2012 Election.* (New York, NY: Oxford University Press, 2014), 246–58.
48. Davisson, "I'm In!": Hillary Clinton's 2008 Democratic Primary Campaign on YouTube."
49. Ibid.
50. Sam Stein, "Obama Campaign Releases Full 17-Minute, First-Term Documentary," *Huffington Post*, March 15, 2012, http://www.huffingtonpost.com/2012/03/15/obama-campaign-documentary-release_n_1350070.html.
51. Ibid.
52. Winograd and Hais, *Millennial Makeover: MySpace, YouTube & the Future of American Politics.*
53. Davisson, "I'm In!": Hillary Clinton's 2008 Democratic Primary Campaign on YouTube."
54. Julia Allison, "Internet Memes," *Newsweek*, 2010, http://2010.newsweek.com/top-10/Internet-memes/obama-girl.html.
55. John Clayworth, "Obama Responds to 'Crush,'" *Des Moines Register*, June 19, 2007, http://web.archive.org/web/20080211114524/http://blogs.dmregister.com/?p=6506.
56. will.i.am, "Why I Recorded Yes We Can," *Huffington Post*, February 3, 2008, http://www.huffingtonpost.com/william/why-i-recorded-yes-we-can_b_84655.html.
57. Nikki Schwab, "In Obama-McCain Race, YouTube Became a Serious Battleground for Presidential Politics," *U.S. News and World Report*, November 7, 2008, http://www.usnews.com/news/campaign-2008/articles/2008/11/07/in-obama-mccain-race-youtube-became-a-serious-battleground-for-presidential-politics?page=2.
58. Reuters, "Will.i.am's 'Yes We Can Song' Video Awarded Emmy for New Approaches in Daytime Entertainment," *Reuters*, July 16, 2008, http://www.reuters.com/article/2008/06/16/idUS145884+16-Jun-2008+MW20080616.
59. Rajini Vaidyanathan, "Top Hits of the YouTube Election," *BBC News*, October 30, 2008, http://news.bbc.co.uk/2/hi/americas/us_elections_2008/7699509.stm.

60. Rob Christensen, "Etheridge Slip Puts Foe on Map," *News & Observer*, June 16, 2010, http://www.newsobserver.com/2010/06/16/535042/etheridge-slip-puts-foe-on-map.html.

61. Nick Wing, "Bob Etheridge Attacks Student: North Carolina Congressman Gets Rough with Interviewer," *Huffington Post*, June 14, 2010, http://www.huffingtonpost.com/2010/06/14/bob-etheridge-attacks-stu_n_610978.html.

62. Ibid.

63. Sean Trende, "Is Etheridge in Trouble?," *Real Clear Politics*, June 15, 2010, http://www.freerepublic.com/focus/news/2534891/posts?page=57.

64. David Corn, "Secret Video: Romney Tells Millionaire Donors What He REALLY Thinks of Obama Voters," *MotherJones*, September 17, 2012, http://www.motherjones.com/politics/2012/09/secret-video-romney-private-fundraiser.

65. Tim Carmody, "Mitt Romney's Damning '47 Percent' Video and the New Politics of Privacy," *The Verge*, March 14, 2013, http://www.theverge.com/2013/3/14/4103184/romney-prouty-47-percent-video-new-politics-of-privacy.

66. Lauren Feldman and Dannagal Young, "Late-Night Comedy as a Gateway to Traditional News: An Analysis of Time Trends in News Attention Amongh Late-Night Comedy Viewers during the 2004 Presidential Primaries," *Political Communication* 25 (n.d.): 401–22.

67. Patrick Goldstein, "Network Fear: The Net as Copilot," *Los Angeles Times*, March 27, 2007, http://articles.latimes.com/2007/mar/27/entertainment/et-goldstein27.

68. Suzi Parker, "Mitt Romney's 'binders Full of Women,'" *The Washington Post*, October 17, 2012, http://www.washingtonpost.com/blogs/she-the-people/wp/2012/10/17/mitt-romneys-binders-full-of-women/.

69. YouTube Trends Team, "Videos Mentioning Obama or Romney Top 2 Billion Views," *YouTube Trends*, August 27, 2012, http://youtube-trends.blogspot.com/2012/08/videos-mentioning-obama-or-romney-top-2.html.

70. Ibid.

71. Hollihan, *Uncivil Wars: Political Campaigns in a Media Age*.

72. Dan Nimmo and James Combs, *Mediated Political Realities* (New York, NY: Longman, 1990).

73. Pamela Conover and Stanley Feldman, "How People Organize the Political World: A Schematic Model," *American Journal of Political Science* 28, no. 1 (1984): 95–126.

THREE

Political Advertising and Fundraising via YouTube

YouTube's large and ever-increasing audience, targeting technologies that enable strategic placement of videos based on geographic location and video-content type, and prevalence of young users make YouTube a vital platform for the dissemination of political advertisements and fundraising videos.[1] Effectively conceptualized and situated videos can stimulate interest in political campaigns, increase issue knowledge, effect audiences' attitudes towards candidates, potentially influence the agenda of the mainstream media,[2] influence vote choice, and generate substantial fundraising capital. However, critics postulate that politicians fail to embrace all that YouTube has to offer, instead most often using the platform simply as an alternative venue for the redistribution of televised advertisements.[3] This chapter examines how YouTube has evolved as a medium for political advertising and fundraising and aims to assess whether campaigns have used the platform as a way to move beyond political advertising and fundraising of the past or instead as a digital repository for campaign material originally generated for other forms of media.

POLITICAL ADVERTISING VIA YOUTUBE

YouTube allows campaigns to expand the repertoire of their political advertising arsenal. By utilizing YouTube as an integral advertising hub, campaigns can capitalize on the growing number of political Internet users to engage Americans of all demographics and across all levels of democratic interest and engagement. With more than 45 percent of YouTube's users being over the age of thirty-five, YouTube provides a ripe environment for campaigns to engage with users across key voting blocs.[4] Video viewership data indicates that the YouTube audience is attuned to and highly interested in watching online political advertisements. With 98 of *Advertising Age*'s top 100 marketers having run advertisement campaigns through the site,[5] the YouTube audience has become accustomed to viewing advertisements embedded in videos and campaigns can effectively interact with people who are more highly engaged with advertising content and not flipping channels or fast-forwarding through advertisements on their DVRs.[6] In 2011, of the top ten political videos on YouTube, which in sum generated over fifty million views, four were campaign advertisements. This demonstrated that the YouTube audience held significant interest in political advertisements before the presidential primaries had even begun. One of the top advertisements was for Texas Governor Rick Perry's campaign, which focused on ending "Obama's war on religion" and asserted that "faith made America strong and it can make her strong again." It generated over seven million views within the first month of being uploaded to YouTube and 8.7 million total views during the primary season.

Research on live television estimates that as many as 45 percent of potential voters in key political states no longer regularly consume live television.[7] This has required campaigns to utilize new technological platforms in order to best reach some voter demographics with political advertisements. Because of this, in each subsequent election cycle, larger portions of campaign advertising expenditures are being spent on online video initiatives and advertising. During the 2012 presidential election, candidates collectively spent 159 million dollars in online advertising, representing a 588 percent increase between 2008 and 2012 on online video advertising expenditures.[8] These increased expenditures have, in turn, helped candidates reap substantial savings. Through YouTube, campaigns can upload and distribute as many video advertisements as they care to produce no cost.[9] In 2008, the contents on Barack Obama's YouTube channel was watched for a collective 14.5 million hours; in terms of paid broadcast hours, this amount of time was worth approximately 47 million dollars to the campaign.[10]

Online advertising offers distinct advantages to traditional media advertising. For offline media, campaigns must focus on a one-to-many communication format and gear their advertisements to simultaneously reach and persuade the broadest base of individuals possible. Campaigns must create advertisements that universally discuss broad political issues and are often financially forced to put more money into creating fewer advertisements.[11] Following candidacy announcements, campaigns have a finite window of time through which to engage in the two most important functions of political advertising: to define (or redefine) a candidate's image and clearly develop campaign issues.[12] Properly conceptualized online advertising campaigns can increase interactivity, accountability, iterability, and targeting, making them an attractive compliment to mainstream campaign advertising strategies.[13] Strategic online advertising can expand the time and space for campaigns to develop these functions and dynamically increase the audience's attention. These campaigns can be more specific in their messages, more precisely target voter demographics, and can simultaneously harness complex and multidirectional relationships with multiple audiences. Additionally, because unlike traditional display ads, which interrupt the attention of the audience to make an impression on them,[14] the viewing of political advertisements on YouTube are often user-initiated, they are nondisruptive to the users' typical behavior, and can be perceived to be more effective.[15]

Just as televised political ads have been frequently discussed in newspapers and local news broadcasts,[16] online political advertisements can also impact the agenda of the mainstream media.[17] Sophisticated online political advertisements are crafted in such a way that they are intended to generate airtime on news programs, essentially allowing campaigns to generate free airtime for their commercials. The interest generated by media coverage can then entice technologically savvy audience members to hopefully share the advertisements via social media platforms. This behavior may be quite contrary to the ideals of the Internet as a democratizing entity[18] and instead provides additional evidence that the actors who influence news media and elections offline are the ones influencing it online as well.[19] Campaigns can also greatly extend the reach of traditional media advertisements by buying television spots to gain the attention of the mainstream audience and then moving the ads to YouTube where they can generate more traction and viewers. For example, during the 2012 election, the Mitt Romney campaign mashed-up a statement that President Obama had made during a press conference into an attack ad.[20] The advertisement, titled "Doing Fine?," was originally released on television, then it was picked up as news story by CNN, and uploaded to YouTube where it generated over 1.4 million views.

YouTube has fundamentally changed many aspects of political advertising. The next sections will discuss how YouTube has altered the political advertising landscape, offered enhanced strategies for targeting voters, and how sometimes messages crafted for an online audience can get lost in translation.

CHANGING POLITICAL ADVERTISING LANDSCAPE

There many ways that YouTube enhances the functionalities of political advertising. The platform has enabled lesser known candidates, with limited political coffers, to reach vast audiences, expanded options for third-party political engagement, and increased the role of the online political influentials.[21]

The 2006 U.S. Senate race between Jon Tester and incumbent U.S. Senator Conrad Burns in Montana provides an example of the early prowess of political advertising on YouTube. During the election, staffers from the Tester campaign recorded Burns at various political engagements in hopes of generating attention in the local media. While some of the footage was picked up and made its rounds through local and national media, it was an advertisement consisting of mashed-up videos, set to music, and posted to YouTube that gained the most traction for the Tester campaign. Brushing off its significance, Burns spokesman Jason Klindt stated that "I don't think Montanans are voting based on a YouTube ad. I don't think it has a big impact." However, the advertisement generated over 75,000 views, five times the number of views than any of the canned commercials that either candidate posted to YouTube received.[22]

While there exists no causal data indicating why Tester was victorious over the three-term Senator Burns, it is likely that without Tester's use of YouTube to circulate campaign advertisements, we wouldn't be discussing this race in terms of its political posterity.

YouTube as a platform for online advertising allows lesser known and less well-funded political candidates the opportunity to reach a large number of potential supporters.[23] Such candidates need to use media like YouTube in order to broadly, and affordably, circulate advertisements and increase their political branding.[24] The 2010 campaign for the Alabama Agriculture Commission nomination is a clear example of how a local candidate can utilize YouTube advertisements to gain national exposure. In May 2010, candidate Dale Peterson gained online momentum and mainstream media attention following the posting of a campaign advertisement titled "We are Better than That" to YouTube. In the ad, Peterson equates the sitting elected officials to thugs and criminals who ignore the problems of illegal immigration, high unemployment, and the consistent loss of family-owned farms. He calls out his opponent for bragging on Facebook about receiving illegal campaign contributions and asks the audience "who on Earth would support such a dummy?" While Peterson did not win the nomination, his campaign video generated over 2.6 million views and thousands of comments; providing proof that a gun-toting, tough-talking candidate in a relatively obscure state race could gain national attention with the strategically crafted YouTube video.

IMPACT OF THE THIRD PARTY

The rise of YouTube for political advertising has also enabled the elevation of third-party voices. As previously discussed with regard to the "Yes We Can" and "Obama Girl" videos, third parties, who tend to have no official affiliation to political campaigns can easily construct and disseminate political advertisements. The Internet gives anyone practically instantaneous interaction capabilities with political content, providing anyone, be it candidate, campaign, individual, or organization the ability to flood the nation's political conversation with their own, unfiltered ideas.[25] While a democratic society lauds the ability of the public and other third-party entities to have an open and accessible venue through which to participate in political discourse, advertisements crafted outside of the purview of official campaigns can be misleading and difficult for campaigns to combat.

Through YouTube, advertisements created by third parties have the potential to quickly generate a substantial audience and can easily detract from campaigns' official messages. While third-party interaction with political content is nothing revolutionary in political campaigning, the speed at which these parties can create and distribute political advertisements is vastly accelerated because of the YouTube environment. For example, during the 2008 presidential election, precisely eleven minutes after an Obama-McCain debate had ended on broadcast television an advocacy group posted a pro-Obama advertisement to YouTube that compared video clips of McCain's responses from the recently completed debate to clips of his responses in a previous debate. The ability to compile and distribute an advertisement so quickly and using such timely media footage proves how different the YouTube environment can be versus that of traditional media, where creating and distributing a similar advertisement via television would be expensive and likely take weeks to develop.

The YouTube environment can also make it difficult for undiscerning audience members to know exactly who is responsible for the creation of political advertising content. In 2011, one of the most highly viewed political advertisements on YouTube appeared on the surface to be an ad created by the Obama campaign. However, the advertisement was in fact created by an unaffiliated third party who by titling its advertisement "President Barack Obama's First Ad of 2012," may have seemed to the less discerning viewer to be an advertisement for Obama's reelection created by the campaign. In actuality, the video, which generated over two million views, was a partisan representation of Obama's first term in office that was produced and distributed by the National Republican Senatorial Committee. While there is a small disclaimer, available only if one expands the video's information section, stating this is not an actual Obama advertisement, it is evident from the supportive messages for Obama in the comment thread that perhaps not all viewers of the video understood its satirical intentions.

The vastness of the YouTube environment makes it exceptionally difficult to track, categorize, and in some cases, even find political advertisements created by third-party entities. Because of this, it is nearly impossible to gain any accurate idea of how many other-generated political advertisements are circulating YouTube. Research indicates that advertisements created by interest groups, citizens, and other political actors only accounted for about 3 percent of the political advertisements posted to YouTube during the 2008 election.[26] However, these videos attracted markedly higher views than the advertisements sponsored by the political parties and the candidates. The average number of views for a citizen-created ad was 807,000 versus just over 60,000 for candidate-sponsored advertisements.[27] This indicates that while some assessments argue that content produced outside of the traditional political realms was "rare and undistinguished" in 2008,[28] third-party voices matter substantially because often they are being listened to at a higher frequency than the official voices of the parties and candidates.

ADVERTISING INFLUENTIALS

As previously discussed, the Internet environment has paved the way for the emergence of online political influentials.[29] Personal influence has long been known to enhance the power of persuasion.[30] Therefore, it is reasonable to assume that a link to a political advertisement sent or shared by a friend will be highly influential because it comes with the added credibility of the sender.[31] As advertisements are passed virally from person to person, they gain a level of credibility over ads distributed through direct campaign marketing.[32] Research indicates that the level of sharing for politically-themed advertisements often doubles the average rate of sharing of non-political advertisements.[33] This dramatically enhances the reach and resonance of political advertisements beyond what could be achieved strictly through traditional media. With traditional media advertising, public dialogue about political commercials only occurs when viewers have direct connections to one another. In the YouTube environment, the commenting functionalities provide anyone who views an advertisement with a forum through which to discuss the ad with anyone else who has viewed the ad. This may lead to online influentials having a more substantial impact upon the dialogue surrounding political advertisements. Campaigns can also capitalize on these comments, benefiting in many ways from the direct feedback provided by the audience in the comment threads.

Hoping to capitalize on the interactivity of political influentials and their knack for viral sharing, the 2008 Obama campaign developed a creative end-of-election advertising strategy. To get influentials to encourage their networks to vote, the campaign created the ability for users to embed their friends' names into customized individual videos of fake news clips that "blamed" the friend for not voting, thus costing Obama the election by only one vote.[34] Strategies such as these encouraged interaction with political advertising messages and promoted the widespread sharing of campaign content. By creating ads with viralability in mind and emphasizing one-click sharing options across social media platforms, campaigns have been able to use online political influentials to spread their messages and increase the audiences of their political advertisements.

ENHANCED AUDIENCE TARGETING

While traditional advertising strategies are still vital to the effective spread of campaign messages, YouTube has provided campaigns tools to enhance their audience targeting strategies. Microtargeting techniques and engagement-oriented advertising have helped augment campaigns' effectiveness at reaching specific voter blocs and engaging more efficiently with the constituency. YouTube's analytical tools give campaigns the ability to easily and quickly collect large-scale video viewership data and use this information to produce coordinated and targeted campaign communication.

MICROTARGETING

Through microtargeting, the analysis of cross-sectional information embedded into users' social media profiles, campaigns can easily determine and target specific audiences that are highly likely to engage with and share videos in the manner that campaigns desire and anticipate. For example, during the 2012 election interested individuals were invited to join "Pet Lovers for Obama" via advertisements featuring photographs of the Obama's dog, Bo. This type of microtargeting reaches a very specific and strategic population with the anticipation that audience members will share advertisements with like-minded users in their social network. YouTube also allows campaigns to effectively target demographics through geolocation techniques, the targeting of potential voters based on their geographic location. This audience targeting technique, which allows campaigns to reach only the most relevant viewers for specific videos, is particularly useful in key swing states.

ENGAGEMENT-ORIENTED ADVERTISING

As viewing campaign advertisements is one of the main reasons that individuals report watching online political videos,[35] it is vital that campaigns are strategic in what they request of their audience. The purpose of many advertisements is simply to distribute candidate information. However, engagement-oriented ads are created with the strategic purpose of getting the audience to take some type of action. Engagement advertising has proven to be a highly effective strategy across social media platforms because it efficiently targets viewers and engages potential supporters within the platforms that they are already frequenting in regular intervals. As a strategy, engagement advertising asks users to interact directly from their current digital location at the moment that they are watching the ads and are the most likely to be interested in interacting with campaign messages. For example, campaigns can use YouTube advertisements to combine geolocation targeting with engagement-oriented advertising strategies to mobilize potential volunteers through click-to-call techniques. This strategy asks users to click links embedded in the advertisement to directly connect with volunteer centers in their geographic location.[36] Political advertisements on YouTube are more likely to incorporate engagement-oriented strategies than advertisements placed in other media formats. YouTube ads are much more likely than television advertisements to ask viewers to register to vote, volunteer, donate money, or take some other type of action.[37] Interestingly, candidate-sponsored ads are more likely than citizen-generated advertisements to call the viewer to action.[38]

Through microtargeting and engagement-oriented advertising, YouTube has made it easier for campaigns to specifically target precise demographics and to put engagement tools at the audiences' fingertips. Effectively leveraging these strategies can create a "share-ripple" among individuals who feel motivated to share advertisements and participate in the engagement-oriented activities requested by the campaigns. The enhanced audience engagement strategies enabled by YouTube allow campaigns to capitalize on advertisement viralability and to quite often increase the circulation of advertisements well beyond the reach and expanse of paid media strategies.

ADVERTISING: LOST IN TRANSLATION

YouTube can provide candidates with an effective platform through which to effectively distribute campaign advertisements. However, not all candidates have been successful at translating their political messages effectively in the YouTube environment. Some campaigns have successfully capitalized on the lessons learned during the previous election cycles regarding how to most effectively reach constituents with advertisements. Yet, other candidates have fallen victim to ill-conceived strategies or inappropriate personal actions, which, on YouTube, can be difficult to overcome.

In October 2010, Republican Senatorial candidate Christine O'Donnell's official YouTube channel became the most watched channel of any 2010 candidate[39] following the posting of a campaign advertisement titled "I'm You." The ad was produced in response to a video clip from a 1999 appearance on the television show *Politically Incorrect* with Bill Maher during which O'Donnell stated she had "dabbled" in witchcraft. Unfortunately, her response became bigger news than the video clip and proved to be an ill-fated attempt to overcome the minor controversy that the video had caused her campaign. O'Donnell began her first television advertisement for Delaware's general election Senate race by stating, "I'm not a witch. I'm nothing you've heard. I'm you." While the campaign potentially benefited from the increased exposure generated by widespread mainstream media circulation of the advertisement, it also suffered from sharp mockery. It became heavily parodied, ridiculed on late-night comedy shows, and even scoffed at by mainstream news anchors who joked about her choice to wear all black during the statement. Even O'Donnell herself thought that the advertisement, which generated nearly 850,000 YouTube views, was a mistake and hurt her on the campaign trail.[40]

Other campaigns have used YouTube to circulate allegorical advertisements that would likely be inappropriate for traditional media. For example, in August 2011, as part of his bid for a Congressional seat representing Texas's 33rd district, Roger Williams posted a video to YouTube titled "The Donkey Whisperer." In the staunchly anti-Obama and anti-government commercial, Williams metaphorically fused Democrats with welfare recipients and compared them to donkeys, all while interacting on screen with actual live donkeys. Williams talked to the live donkeys using language targeting welfare recipients with phrases such as "I know you're embarrassed because you are part of the problem" and "all these guys want is more shelter, more feed. [. . .] You want a handout." The advertisement, which had been viewed over two million times as of April 2014, received a moderate level of support from conservative voters on Twitter; however, its prominence and viral sharing via YouTube has forever linked the name Roger Williams with the moniker "Donkey Whisperer." While perhaps potentially poignant at the time, this video, like George Allen's "macaca moment"[41] may be difficult to overcome if Williams chooses to engage in future political elections.

Herman Cain's 2012 campaign advertisement "Now is the time for action," was considered by many pundits to be unconventional. The ad featured Cain's Chief of Staff, Mark Block, smoking a cigarette while stating his belief that Cain would "put the united back in United States." Although the advertisement generated substantial online attention, generating nearly 400,000 views in just one week, it was considered "bizarre" by a majority of the people who viewed it. It was theorized to be an attempt by the campaign to get a viral video hit versus to provide potential voters with any real political substance.[42]

These advertisements are a good example of campaigns attempting to capitalize on viralability rather than thinking through the elements requisite to effectively disseminate a campaign's message. While these videos,

which are just a small sampling of the ways in which political ads on
YouTube have has gone awry, were successful in reaching substantial
audiences, they seemingly negated the fact that advertisements, no matter where they are placed, must still maintain a level of credibility and
substance in order to be politically effective.

YOUTUBE ADS IN THE 2012 OBAMA/ROMNEY RACE

YouTube provides campaigns with the ability to expand the reach and
function of political advertising. However, are campaigns fully utilizing
YouTube's political functionalities or is campaign advertising still stuck
in the "prehistoric age"[43] of advertising?

YouTube during the 2008 and 2010 elections, was still in a state of
relative infancy. By 2012, YouTube had been integrated by many candidates as a fully functional element of campaign communication strategies. The 2012 campaign therefore provides a good case through which to
analyze how campaigns use YouTube for advertising.

Both the Obama and Romney campaigns heavily used the candidates'
dedicated YouTube channels for campaign advertisements. Each campaign used their channels in ways that were both similar and markedly
different. Both embraced YouTube's video-on-demand strategies, a tactic
where users are presented with an advertisement before their selected
videos begins, to reach specific voters. It is estimated that strategic buying of video-on-demand space could reach up to 165 million viewers a
week through the Internet and mobile devices.[44] Use of this strategy
allowed the campaigns to potentially reach voters who no longer frequently watch live television.[45] It also allowed the campaigns to use
microtargeting techniques to target specific voting demographics, with
precise messages, in a manner that was cheaper to distribute and easier to
track than broadcast advertisements.[46]

The types and quantities of advertisements that the campaigns elected
to distribute through the candidates' YouTube channels, however, dif-
fered substantially. Roughly 54 percent of the content on Obama's You-
Tube channel was composed of political advertisements, the remaining
videos were a collection of many different campaign communication
strategies.[47] The advertisements were a mixture of informational advertisements, focusing primarily on Obama's agenda and his policies, and
traditional political attack ads. Attack ads were the most prominent type
of advertisement on the channel, representing roughly 32 percent of the
channel's advertising content, and focusing on concepts such as Romney
and the Republican Party's gluttony and greed.[48] Romney's YouTube
channel also offered viewers a variety of video types; however, well over
90 percent of the videos on the campaign's channel were advertisements
with few other communication strategies being utilized. Attack ads were

the most prominent type of advertisement on Romney's channel as well, comprising roughly 57 percent of the site's content and focusing on the need for renewed political leadership and the development of a financially productive country.[49] The Romney campaign attempted to use You-Tube as a platform to repair the candidate's perceived inability to connect with voters by reposting a television advertisement where Romney connected his policies to measurable changes for poor and middle-class families. However, critics argued it did little to address the perception that Romney was not connected to the average American voter.[50]

While over half of the content on Obama's YouTube channel was comprised of advertisements, the campaign also included informational videos about the candidate's platform videos, user-generated content, candid videos of Obama and his staff on the campaign trail, and other engagement-oriented videos, such as videos encouraging unregistered voters to register online.[51] Conversely, Mitt Romney's YouTube channel functioned primarily as a repository for campaign advertisements. Despite uploading an average of one new video each day, by the end of the election, only 4 percent of the channel's content was composed of anything other than reposted television advertisements.[52] While the Romney campaign did try its hand at a few engagement-oriented videos, such as an introductory video of Mitt Romney that discussed his life, upbringing, and career, overall, the videos were highly scripted and polished.

Although YouTube has opened the door for new voices to participate in political advertising and has offered campaigns enhanced audience-targeting methodologies, in general, campaigns seem to still be heavily reliant on advertising strategies prominent in mainstream campaign communication. It appears as if online political advertising via YouTube still closely mirrors that of off-line political advertising,[53] especially the heavy reliance on and dominance of attack advertisements. Collectively, it appears as if the major party campaigns missed the opportunity to use YouTube to break out of the traditional confines of political advertising. Instead of capitalizing the unlimited virtual space of YouTube to create longer, more critically developed and perhaps more targeted advertisements, most online campaign advertisements conform to the standard thirty-second or one-minute ad.[54] As of yet, we have not seen much of the unbridled creativity and expression that many speculated YouTube would unleash[55] and although tactics are maturing, there has yet to be a breakout moment of social discovery or adoption of YouTube-specific advertising strategies.[56]

POLITICAL FUNDRAISING VIA YOUTUBE

The ability to raise funds through digital platforms has been perhaps one of the crowning achievements of online campaigning. In 1998, Barbara

Boxer's Senatorial campaign was the first campaign to successfully launch an online fundraising campaign, netting 25,000 dollars through Internet pledges.[57] Contemporarily, campaigns raise hundreds of millions of dollars online and routinely break fundraising records through new, inventive, and sometimes gimmicky methods for reaching donors. Digital fundraising is substantially more cost efficient than traditional methods of fundraising because the solicitation of donations cost campaigns very little and often result in large numbers of small donations. Online videos have proven to entice donors, with 5 percent of small online donors in 2004 and 2 percent of large political donors noting that online advertisement videos prompted their donation.[58] In examining audience response to online political advertisements, video ads generate double the response rate (measured in clicks) as standard image advertisements.[59] Digital donors often include people who have never given to political campaigns and those who are willing to give small donations repeatedly.[60] It is estimated that, over time, it is possible that digital fundraising strategies will make campaigns less beholden to wealthy donors or private interest groups.[61] The use of the Internet to solicit donations is quickly surpassing traditional methods of fundraising and the use of traditional media for fundraising appeals.[62]

Historically, the Democratic and Republican parties have approached social media networking and online fundraising with differing levels of tenacity. The Republican Party did, and to some extent still does, not believe that their constituency will be heavily invested in engaging in online social networking and fundraising activities. Mike Turk, eCampaign Director for the Bush-Cheney 2004 campaign discussed the differences between Republican and Democratic campaign and fundraising strategies by stating, "First, and most important, is the fact that we simply do not engage in the same type of activities online. . . ."[63] The disparity in these strategies was evident after the first fundraising reports of the 2008 election indicated that Democrats had raised 78.1 million dollars to the Republican's 50.6 million dollars, with one-third of the Democratic contributions being the product of small donations generated from online fundraising efforts.[64] During the 2008 election, Barack Obama raised roughly 500 million dollars from three million donors who made a total of 6.5 million online donations.[65] This campaign saw the first substantial fundraising impact made from small online donations and saw a greater number of people making donations than had ever before donated to political campaigns.[66] While the Republican Party has become more adept at using online fundraising initiatives, members of the party still rely more heavily on email campaigns than social media in its fundraising strategies.[67]

As with advertising, YouTube has provided campaigns with innovative ways to solicit fundraising dollars from the constituency. Through utilization of similar microtargeting and engagement-oriented strategies, campaigns can use data mining technologies to discover information in users' profiles that they can use to more effectively encourage donor participation. YouTube-derived fundraising campaigns focus on the personal, often presenting the viewer with similarly situated individuals supporting the candidates and by empowering the audience to be an integral part of the campaigns through donations. Through emphasizing participation and creating the feeling of personal efficacy, campaigns can substantially benefit from focusing on small donations rather than traditional big donor strategies.[68] Just like brand advertising strives to develop consumer loyalty, political campaigns can persuade and engage potential supporters through capitalizing on feelings of personal connectedness and engagement.[69]

While stand-alone fundraising videos have not been highly prevalent on political YouTube channels, advertising videos have emerged to serve a dual purpose as fundraising videos as well. Many candidate advertisements began with a superimposed dialogue box that encouraged viewers to contribute small amounts to the candidates. These fundraising strategies enabled donors to contribute in multiple ways, for example, through one-click donation widgets and options for contributions to be charged directly to viewers' cell phone bills, meaning there was no immediate out-of-pocket expense to the donors. Many campaigns implemented a one-stop-shopping approach to fundraising by providing ways for donors to contribute without needing to navigate away from political advertisements. For example, the 2012 Obama campaign encouraged viewers to donate via text messaging by superimposing "to contribute 10 dollars to Obama for America, text OBAMA to 62262" at the beginning of a majority of the advertisements on Obama's YouTube channel. Understanding the importance of maintaining a captive audience, the 2012 Mitt Romney campaign also embedded options for visitors to donate without leaving the candidate's dedicated YouTube channel.[70] By implementing YouTube-based fundraising strategies, campaigns have been able to economically reach a vastly larger number of potential donors than through traditional fundraising mechanisms. Campaigns have been able to generate substantial donations via small one-time donations and reach a population of donors who have likely never contributed to a political campaign before, but who are willing to give small donations repeatedly.[71] Online fundraising strategies have also been successful at engaging a younger demographic, with the mean age for online donors being twelve years younger than offline givers.[72]

It is important in the increasingly competitive digital campaign environment that campaigns work to become more adept at engaging potential donors via social media platforms like YouTube. Campaigns that are able to develop appropriately situated online videos can generate substantial funds by requesting small donations and reaching thousands more potential donors than through other fundraising strategies. Campaigns can also use YouTube videos to create sustainable relationships with supporters and mobilize demographics, such as younger voters, who that have historically not responded well to offline fundraising methods.[73]

CONCLUSIONS AND CHALLENGES

With more than 200 million Americans online, political information is frequently and regularly distributed outside of mainstream media channels.[74] YouTube allows campaigns the ability to easily, effectively, and affordably target and distribute advertisements and fundraising videos and reach demographics who are no longer profoundly reliant on mainstream media. Heavy reliance on the Internet for political advertising and fundraising purposes will persist in contemporary political campaigning.[75] Although political consultants postulate that email will remain a key source of online political fundraising strategies in future elections, these initiatives will work better when tied to overall broader social media campaigns and initiatives.[76] However, as the public becomes more accustomed to viewing online advertisements in general, online political ads and fundraising videos will play increasing large and important roles in future political campaigns.

Advertising and fundraising via YouTube does, however, present some challenges. Similar to other areas of online political engagement, getting viewers to take concrete and measureable actions after watching advertising and fundraising videos can be difficult. As most political advertisements focus on shaping public opinion, list-building, and raising funds, connecting with a viewer at the precise moment that they are primed for political action can be complicated.[77] Although campaigns have become more adept at embedding one-click engagement functions into their YouTube channels, creating sustainable and repeated interaction with the campaigns can be difficult to encourage. Research suggests that the more a viewer is exposed to a candidate's messages the more likely they are to vote for that candidate.[78] However, just as it is with mainstream media tactics, it is difficult to correlate the impact of exposure to a candidate's online advertisement and citizens' mobilization behaviors, such as donating, volunteering, and voting.[79]

Tracking unique video views and gaining a truly accurate portrayal of the actual reach of advertisements and fundraising videos can also be a challenge. While a video may have hundreds of thousands of views, it is conceivable that viewers return more than once to watch the same videos, equating to video viewership numbers being overstated. There is also some credence to the thought that politicians' online videos may be "preaching to the choir" by primarily reaching individuals already invested enough in the candidate to seek out and view their advertisements or fundraising videos.[80] Additionally, because most individuals tend to engage in a more than one activity at a time online, there is a question as to whether users are closely watching YouTube ads because they may be simultaneously engaged in other online activities.[81] Finally, although YouTube users have become increasingly accustomed to viewing embedded advertisements with video-on-demand, the potential exists that users will grow wary of these intrusions and figure out technological ways around watching ads, meaning the circulation and reach of online political ads may potentially suffer.

In a constantly evolving digital environment, it will become even more incumbent upon campaigns to develop videos with viralability in mind and to consistently present information to supporters in a manner that encourages the creation of share ripples. As political communication via YouTube continues to advance during future election cycles, it will be interesting to see the ways in which the platform develops as a conduit for political advertising and fundraising. Future research in this area will be necessary to understand how and why campaigns use YouTube for political advertising and fundraising, what role third-party and influential voices will play in the future of political content creation, and to discern if campaigns continue to use YouTube as a digital repository for televised advertisements or begin to more fully embrace the medium to break the confines of traditional political advertising. If previous election cycles are any indication, campaign communication technologies will continue to advance and evolve. This will likely heighten the role that YouTube will play in the creation and distribution of political advertisements and fundraising videos, leading to both interesting political content and a broad landscape for new political communication research.

NOTES

1. Ryan Lawler, "Political Ads Find Their Way onto YouTube," *Gigaom*, November 1, 2010, http://gigaom.com/2010/11/01/political-ads-find-their-way-onto-youtube/.

2. Doris Graber, *Mass Media and American Politics*, 8th ed. (Washington, DC: CQ Press, 2009).

3. Travis Ridout, Erika Fowler, and John Branstetter, "Political Advertising in the 21st Century: The Rise of the YouTube Ad" (presented at the American Political Science Association, Washington, DC, 2010).

4. YouTube, "Why Use YouTube?," n.d., retrieved from http://www.youtube.com/yt/politics101/.

5. Ibid.

6. James Peters, "With Video, Obama Looks to Expand Campaign's Reach through Social Media," *The New York Times*, May 14, 2012, http://www.nytimes.com/2012/03/15/us/politics/with-youtube-video-obama-looks-to-expand-social-media-reach.html?_r=0.

7. Sarah Stirland, "New Digital Targeting Helps Romney Campaign Reach Voters," *Tech President*, December 22, 2011, retrieved from http://techpresident.com/news/21546/youtube-facebook-romney-digital-ad-targeting.

8. Jen Christensen, "Obama Outspends Romney on Online Ads," *CNN*, June 2, 2012, http://www.cnn.com/2012/06/03/politics/online-campaign-spending/index.html?hpt=hp_bn5.

9. Vassia Gueorguieva, "Voters, MySpace and YouTube: The Impact of Alternative Communication Channels," in *Politicking Online: The Transformation of Election Campaign Communication* (New Brunswick, NJ: Rutgers University Press, 2009), 233–48.

10. Claire Miller, "How Obama's Internet Campaign Changed Politics," *The New York Times*, November 7, 2008, sec. Technology, http://bits.blogs.nytimes.com/2008/11/07/how-obamas-Internet-campaign-changed-politics/?_r=0.

11. William Benoit, *Communication in Political Campaigns*. (New York, NY: Peter Lang Publishing, 2006).

12. Anne Johnson and Lynda Lee Kaid, "Image Ads and Issue Ads in U.S. Presidential Advertising: Using Videostyle to Explore Stylistic Differences in Televised Political Ads from 1952–2000," *Journal of Communication* 52, no. 2 (2002): 281–300.

13. Henry Copeland and Megan Mitzel, "The Huge Opportunity for Online Political Ads," *New Politics Institute*, n.d., http://ndn-newpol.civicactions.net/sites/ndn-newpol.civicactions.net/files/Advertise_Online.pdf.

14. Michael Cornfield and Kate Kaye, "Online Political Advertising," in *Politicking Online: The Transformation of Election Campaign Communication* (Mahwah, NJ: Rutgers University Press, 2009), 163–76.

15. Ridout, Fowler, and Branstetter, "Political Advertising in the 21st Century: The Rise of the YouTube Ad."

16. Erika Fowler and Travis Ridout, "Local Television and Newspaper Coverage of Political Advertising," *Political Communication* 26 (2009): 119–36.

17. Kevin Wallsten, "Yes We Can: How Online Viewership, Blog Discussion, Campaign Statements, and Mainstream Media Coverage Produce a Viral Video Phenomenon," *Journal of Information Technology & Politics* 7 (2010): 163–81.

18. Joe Trippi, *The Revolution Will Not Be Televised: Democracy, the Internet, and the Overthrow of Everything* (Harper Collins, 2008).

19. Matthew Hindman, *The Myth of Digital Democracy* (Princeton, NJ: Princeton University Press, 2009).

20. Kevin Bohn, "Romney Campaign Uses Obama's Line against Him in Attack Ad," *CNN*, June 14, 2012, http://politicalticker.blogs.cnn.com/2012/06/14/romney-campaign-uses-obamas-line-against-him-in-attack-ad/?iref=allsearch.

21. John Tedesco, "Changing the Channel: Use of the Internet for Communicating about Politics," in *Handbook of Political Communication Research* (Mahwah, NJ: Lawrence Erlbaum Associates, 2004), 507–32.

22. Amy Schatz, "In Clips on YouTube, Politicians Reveal Their Unscripted Side: Rival Posts 'Gotcha' Videos in Tight Montana Race," *The Wall Street Journal*, October 9, 2006.

23. Hindman, *The Myth of Digital Democracy*.

24. Copeland and Mitzel, "The Huge Opportunity for Online Political Ads."

25. Morley Winograd and Michael Hais, *Millennial Makeover: MySpace, YouTube & the Future of American Politics* (New Brunswick, NJ: Rutgers University Press, 2008).

26. Ridout, Fowler, and Branstetter, "Political Advertising in the 21st Century: The Rise of the YouTube Ad."

27. Ibid.

28. Robert Klotz, "The Sidetracked 2008 YouTube Senate Campaign," *Journal of Information Technology & Politics* 7 (2008): 110–23.

29. Joseph Graf and Carol Darr, *Political Influentials Online in the 2004 Presidential Election* (Institute for Politics, Democracy, and the Internet, February 5, 2005), http://www.ipdi.org/UploadedFiles/influentials_in_2004.pdf.

30. Elihu Katz and Paul Lazersfeld, *Personal Influence* (Glencoe, IL: Free Press, 1955).

31. Ridout, Fowler, and Branstetter, "Political Advertising in the 21st Century: The Rise of the YouTube Ad."

32. Peters, "With Video, Obama Looks to Expand Campaign's Reach through Social Media."

33. Jay Samit, "All Politics Is Social: Social Media Engagement Will Decide Election 2012," *SocialVibe*, June 2011, http://advertising.socialvibe.com/political_solutions.

34. Angelo Fernando, "The Revolution Will Be Mashed up (and Uploaded to You-Tube): Campaign Strategists in the U.S. Are Realizing the Power of Video Ads as Political Weapons," *Communication World* 26, no. 1 (January 2009).

35. Aaron Smith and Maeve Duggan, *Online Political Videos and Campaign 2012* (Washington, DC: Pew Internet & American Life Project, November 2, 2012), http://www.pewInternet.org/~/media//Files/Reports/2012/PIP_State_of_the_2012_race_online_video_final.pdf.

36. Stirland, "New Digital Targeting Helps Romney Campaign Reach Voters."

37. Ridout, Fowler, and Branstetter, "Political Advertising in the 21st Century: The Rise of the YouTube Ad."

38. Ibid.

39. YouTube, "The 2010 Election on YouTube: By the Numbers," *YouTube: Official Blog*, November 1, 2010, http://youtube-global.blogspot.com/2010/11/2010-election-on-youtube-by-numbers_01.html.

40. Christine Stewart, "Christine O'Donnell: Witch Ad Was a Mistake," *CNN*, August 16, 2011, http://politicalticker.blogs.cnn.com/2011/08/16/christine-odonnell-witch-ad-was-a-mistake/.

41. David Karpf, "Macaca Moments reconsidered...Electoral Panopticon or Netroots Mobilization?," *Journal of Information Technology & Politics* 7 (2010): 143–62.

42. Tierney Sneed, "Smoking Herman Cain Campaign Ad: Brilliant or Bizarre?," *U.S. News and World Report*, October 26, 2011, http://www.usnews.com/opinion/articles/2011/10/26/smoking-herman-cain-campaign-ad-brilliant-or-bizarre.

43. Cornfield and Kaye, "Online Political Advertising."

44. Stirland, "New Digital Targeting Helps Romney Campaign Reach Voters."

45. Nick Judd, "Inside Mitt Romney's Digital Mind," *Tech President*, January 19, 2012, http://techpresident.com/news/21649/inside-mitt-romneys-digital-mind.

46. Christensen, "Obama Outspends Romney on Online Ads."

47. LaChrystal Ricke, "YouTube and the 2012 Presidential Election: An Examination of How Obama and Romney's Official YouTube Channels Were Used in Campaign Communication.," in *Presidential Campaigning and Social Media: An Analysis of the 2012 Election.* (New York, NY: Oxford University Press, 2014), 246–58.

48. Ibid.

49. Ibid.

50. Jon Ward, "Mitt Romney's First Direct-To-Camera Ad Comes At Make-Or-Break Moment In Campaign," *Huffington Post*, September 26, 2012, http://www.huffingtonpost.com/2012/09/26/mitt-romney-ad_n_1915665.html.

51. Ricke, "YouTube and the 2012 Presidential Election: An Examination of How Obama and Romney's Official YouTube Channels Were Used in Campaign Communication."

52. Ibid.

53. Klotz, "The Sidetracked 2008 YouTube Senate Campaign."

54. Ridout, Fowler, and Branstetter, "Political Advertising in the 21st Century: The Rise of the YouTube Ad."

55. Klotz, "The Sidetracked 2008 YouTube Senate Campaign."

56. Cornfield and Kaye, "Online Political Advertising."

57. Thomas Hollihan, *Uncivil Wars: Political Campaigns in a Media Age* (Boston, MA: Bedford/St. Martins, 2009).

58. Institute for Politics, Democracy, & the Internet and The Campaign Finance Institute, *Small Donors and Online Giving* (Washington, DC: The George Washington University, 2006).

59. Gueorguieva, "Voters, MySpace and YouTube: The Impact of Alternative Communication Channels."

60. Institute for Politics, Democracy, & the Internet and The Campaign Finance Institute, *Small Donors and Online Giving*.

61. Costas Panagopoulos, "Technology and the Modern Political Campaign: The Digital Pulse of the 2008 Campaigns," in *Politicking Online: The Transformation of Election Campaign Communication* (Piscataway, NJ: Rutgers University Press, 2009), 1–18.

62. Meagan Dorsch, "Tweeting the Election: Facebook, Twitter and Other Social Media Sites Could Be a Powerful Force in the 2012 Election," *Technology*, April 2012.

63. Winograd and Hais, *Millennial Makeover: MySpace, YouTube & the Future of American Politics*.

64. Ibid.

65. Jose Vargas, "Obama Raised Half a Billion Online," *The Washington Post*, November 20, 2008, sec. The Clickocracy, http://voices.washingtonpost.com/44/2008/11/20/obama_raised_half_a_billion_on.html.

66. Bryan Cain-Jackson, "President Obama Has Changed Social Media Forever," *Technorati*, August 21, 2012, http://technorati.com/social-media/article/president-obama-has-changed-social-media/.

67. Winograd and Hais, *Millennial Makeover: MySpace, YouTube & the Future of American Politics*.

68. Pamela Rutledge, "How Obama Won the Social Media Battle in the 2012 Presidential Campaign," *The Media Psychology Blog*, January 25, 2013, http://mprcenter.org/blog/2013/01/25/how-obama-won-the-social-media-battle-in-the-2012-presidential-campaign/.

69. Samit, "All Politics Is Social: Social Media Engagement Will Decide Election 2012."

70. Peters, "With Video, Obama Looks to Expand Campaign's Reach through Social Media."

71. Costas Panagopoulos and Daniel Bergan, "Clicking for Cash: Campaigns, Donors, and the Emergence of Online Fund-Raising," in *Politicking Online: The Transformation of Election Campaign Communication* (Piscataway, NJ: Rutgers University Press, 2009), 127–40.

72. Ibid.

73. Hindman, *The Myth of Digital Democracy*.

74. YouTube, "Why Use YouTube?"

75. Panagopoulos and Bergan, "Clicking for Cash: Campaigns, Donors, and the Emergence of Online Fund-Raising."

76. Rob Lever, "2012 US Election Campaign a Digital Battleground," *Google News*, October 13, 2012, http://www.google.com/hostednews/afp/article/ALeqM5h-83y9eiaiOfOfwRUEOHlkqqpgPg.

77. Copeland and Mitzel, "The Huge Opportunity for Online Political Ads."

78. Nicholas Valentino, Vincent Hutchings, and Dimitri Williams, "The Impact of Political Advertising on Knowledge, Internet Information Seeking, and Candidate Preference," *Journal of Communication* 54 (2004): 337–54.

79. Rick Lau, Lee Sigelman, and Ivy Brown Rovner, "The Effects of Negative Political Campaigns: A Meta-Analytic Reassessment," *Journal of Politics* 69 (2007): 1176–1209.

80. Ridout, Fowler, and Branstetter, "Political Advertising in the 21st Century: The Rise of the YouTube Ad."

81. Ibid.

FOUR

YouTube and Political Debates

Political debates serve many important purposes in a democratic society. Debates function as a "focal point" for our nation's general elections[1] and generate more public attention and citizen-to-citizen discussion than any other single campaign event.[2] Televised political debates provide capsule summaries of campaigns' issues[3] and, as events, are capable of attracting the attention of the "marginally attentive" citizen.[4] Foundational research on televised debates suggests that viewers retain three primary motivations for viewing debate content: to learn about candidates' issue positions, compare candidates' personalities, and to gain information that may help them in their voting decisions.[5] This chapter discusses the ways that the use of YouTube, both as a platform for hosting political debates and as a forum through which televised debates are reposted and discussed amongst the citizenship, have extended the functions of national political debate. It also discusses how through extensions of asynchronous interactivity, connections to politicians, and person-to-person connectivity, the CNN/YouTube Presidential Primary debates offer insight into how YouTube can function as a political debate platform.

ONLINE POLITICAL DEBATES

Prior to the 1990s, the format of political debating in the United States had remained relatively unchanged for decades.[6] In the 90s, debate formats started to evolve and innovate through such formats as single-moderator debates, town hall debates featuring citizen questioners, and informal candidate round-tables.[7] Based on recommendations from researchers and the public, the Commission on Presidential Debates (CPD) sought to serve the public's voter education needs more effectively by excluding panels of journalists as questioners, altering candidate response sequences, and promoting the public voice and citizen interaction in debate processes.[8]

Internet-based political debating dates back to the elections of the mid-1990s, when candidates in local, state, and national elections engaged in rudimentary forms of online debate. These debates, typically organized by media outlets, were an attempt to harness the growing prominence of the Internet in politics.[9] They utilized early forms of wikis (websites that allow users to add, modify, or delete content) and other group-page technologies which allowed candidates to post their answers to questions generated by the public to the hosting organizations' websites. These early technologies did not provide opportunities for the public to engage with candidates online, rather interested individuals had to either follow debates via the organizations' websites or sign up to receive the debate via email after it was completed. These question and answer events did, however, provide some abilities for the public to discuss candidates' answers through group-page functionalities. Early e-debates illustrated a shift from a passive debate audience, one that was previously only able to consume political information via closed forms of mass media, to a more active audience who, if they chose to, could elevate their level of participation in political debates by submitting questions for candidates to answer or engaging with other members of the public through group-page communication.

As online technologies continued to evolve, organizations and media outlets continued to experiment with various types of e-debates and methods through which heightened public engagement could be captured. Historically, political debates have not overtly welcomed public interaction, with most research suggesting that debates are created for audiences only in the sense that candidates construct arguments in order to persuade them, but not necessarily to engage them.[10] In traditional debate formats, which still dominate a great deal of the nation's political debating events, the audience and the public are passive receptors of information. Often, live debate audiences are instructed to remain silent throughout the duration of a debate. For example, at the beginning of televised debates, moderators have made statements such as, "there is an audience here in the hall, but they have been instructed to remain silent throughout" and "they [the audience] are not here to participate, only to listen."[11] Although town-hall debate formats have provided some level of public participation by allowing members of the audience to directly question candidates, most often these questions are pre-screened and the audience member is not allowed to ask any follow-up questions.

As social media outlets, such as YouTube, began to play more substantial roles in political communication, the public was offered many novel ways to become involved and engaged in this traditionally closed form of political communication. Mainstream and online media outlets experimented with many methods of both hosting political debates and integrating social media functionalities into broadcast debates. The goal of many media outlets was to offer citizen participation through the interactive tools of new media.[12] These engagement-oriented methods included soliciting debate questions online, allowing audience members to submit real-time feedback via social media during live debates, offering downloadable applications for streaming presidential debates, archiving debates for on-demand viewing, and working with the Commission on Presidential Debates to develop live debate streams and live reaction platforms.[13]

The integration of social media functionalities into political debates has offered the public a level of interactivity with debates that was once reserved for the political elite. YouTube as a platform for hosting and supporting communication about political debates has capitalized on both synchronous and asynchronous interactivity to heighten the public's connection to political debates, each other, and political actors. In doing this, YouTube has provided new methods through which the audience, the candidates, and the media interact with one another via political debate.

2007 CNN/YOUTUBE PRIMARY DEBATES

The CNN/YouTube Presidential Candidate Debates offered one of the first illustrations of how YouTube could successfully be incorporated into the political debate landscape and provide a good case through which to see how YouTube debates have helped to change the political debate landscape. In June of 2007, CNN and YouTube announced a joint venture to produce and host two live candidate forums derived from thirty-second video questions submitted via YouTube. Wanting to capitalize on the growing popularity of YouTube for political content viewing and interaction, the media outlets sought to use the debates to bring a level of authenticity, transparency, and access to voters.[14] The public was challenged to embrace the "ever-increasing role of the Internet in politics" and create video questions that were creative and provocative.[15] In sum, over 7,900 videos were posted for possible inclusion in two live candidate forums; ultimately, thirty-eight were selected for the Democratic debate broadcast and 34 were chosen for the Republican debate broadcast.[16]

The broadcasts were moderated by CNN's Anderson Cooper and drew substantial debate audiences. The July 2007 debate between Democratic candidates generated over 2.6 million viewers, just shy of the 2.8 million who had tuned in to watch the traditional New Hampshire Democratic debate in June.[17] The Republican forum, in November 2007, brought in 4.49 million viewers, making it the most watched debate on cable news to that date.[18] The debates were also successful in reaching members of the highly sought-after 18- to 34-year-old voter bloc, with over 400,000 members of this demographic watching the Democratic debate[19] and around 516,000 tuning in to the Republican debate.[20] In order to extend the debates to the broadest audience possible, both debates were simulcast across all of CNN's network platforms, including CNN.com, CNN International, CNN en Espanol, CNN radio, and CNN Airport Network. The debates were also downloadable through the CNN election site. YouTube also created a sub-platform called *Face the Candidates* where videos from each of the candidates espousing their positions on significant national issues, such as Iraq, education, healthcare, immigration, and the economy, could be located, commented on, rated, and shared to further extend the reach and content of the debates.

Response to the debates was mixed. CNN and YouTube were enthusiastic about the format, feeling that the debates provided an important step toward including citizens in campaign dialogue and engaging "more viewers—and potential voters—than ever before."[21] Others also demonstrated favorable attitudes towards the debates with *The New York Times* referring to the debates as "the most earthshaking change in communication technology for presidential politics since the Kennedy-Nixon debates in 1960."[22] Andrew Rasiej, co-founder of the website techpresident.com, called the debates a "transformative moment" in American political communication.[23] Media critic Jack Muse noted that the debates deserved praise because the "citizen-interrogators" had generated the most diverse questions ever asked in presidential debates.[24]

Many media outlets, however, felt the debates were no more than "flashy political stunts" that contained no substance and did nothing to further either democratic understanding or political participation amongst the American electorate.[25] The YouTube platform was also seen as problematic, with critics arguing that the nature of YouTube put more focus on the creation of the videos and not on the development and articulation of appropriate debate questions.[26] Critics also argued that the static nature of the videos and the lack of follow-up questions made it easy for candidates to indirectly address the questions asked in the videos or to fall back on their standard talking points.[27] It was also suggested that the debates were not genuinely generated by the public as competing campaigns were accused of "stuffing the ballot box" by having campaign staff produce and upload videos for possible inclusion in the broadcasts. For example, during the Republican debate a question regarding whether or not homosexuals should be allowed to serve openly in the U.S. military was asked by a gay rights activist and retired general, who was also an adviser to Hillary Clinton's campaign.[28] Additional criticisms were waged that CNN created a specific agenda by selecting certain types of questions for some candidates and not choosing questions that were tough or pertinent enough for others.[29]

Candidates' responses to the debates were also mixed. Following the Democratic debate, most of the participating candidates responded positively to the format and acknowledged the need to successfully integrate Internet-based activities into their campaigns.[30] Republican candidates, however, were not initially inclined to participate in their own edition of the debates. For example, Mitt Romney stated, "I think the presidency ought to be held at a higher level than having to answer questions from a snowman," referencing a question about global warming that was asked by an animated snowman during the Democratic debate.[31] Other candidates simply remained quiet regarding their participation. Patrick Ruffini, a prominent Republican blogger, former eCampaign director for the Republican National Committee, and former online adviser to Rudy Giuliani, stated that Republicans' refusal to participate in the CNN-YouTube debates was symptomatic of the party's "failure to convey that the online community matters to them."[32] Andrew Sullivan, another prominent conservative blogger, stated, "ducking YouTube after the Dems did so well will look like a party uncomfortable with the culture and uncomfortable with democracy."[33] Ultimately, most of the leading GOP candidates participated in the YouTube primary debate; however, only did so after CNN and YouTube agreed to allow the campaigns to pre-screen the questions that would be asked during the broadcast. This agreement brought into focus one of the most substantial criticisms waged against CNN regarding these debates—the process used to select the broadcasts' debate questions. Those well-versed in YouTube believed the videos that generated the most "thumbs up" (i.e., votes) should have been the ones selected for the broadcasts. The videos selected for airing were instead chosen by CNN staff. Thereby, arguably undermining the user-generated nature of the debates that CNN and YouTube advertised and allowing CNN to set the agenda for the debates.[34]

CNN's perspective was that it selected debate questions that would be deemed appropriate by both journalists and candidates. In doing so, it protected citizens from being manipulated by the political campaigns by the aforementioned ballot box stuffing and also offset criticisms regarding the format's novelty.[35] Further defending its video selection process, CNN cited as examples that the two most popular videos submitted for the debates in terms of viewership data were a video questioning if Arnold Schwarzenegger was a cyborg and another asking whether candidates would convene a conference on UFOs. Host, Anderson Cooper, further defended CNN's decision by arguing that a vote-based forum for video selection would be susceptible to manipulation by the campaigns. He noted that, "you would have campaigns completely stacking the deck to try to get the questions they want asked to their candidate. And we already saw attempts at that in terms of campaigns getting particular . . . trying to get people to ask particular questions."[36] Stephanie Mackley, a heavy YouTube user whose video was one of the ones selected for the televised Democratic debate, responded to CNN's explanation for selecting the videos in-house by stating that "CNN doesn't believe in democracy. Anderson [Cooper] is cooking up a scenario here where if the selection of these questions were left to the masses, we would have a whole debate about cyborgs. So, thank goodness CNN is at the helm of this whole thing because who knows what chaos would ensue if the general public were actually allowed to choose media content."[37]

Regardless of one's interpretation of the success or failure of the CNN-YouTube debates, they provided the first measurable illustration of how the audience, the candidates, and the media interacted with online political debating. The debates were an important step in the developing collaboration between YouTube and political information dissemination. The debates laid the groundwork for other media outlets, such as *Yahoo!*, the *Huffington Post, Slate Magazine,* and *Fox News* to host user-generated political debates which have further altered the nature of political debating. The debates provided a popular political focal point where voters could quickly learn about the election, generated large broadcast audience viewership, and allowed campaign issues to be brought into sharper focus by the candidates and the media. They also provided a solid framework through which to see how future political debating either via YouTube or in conjunction with the platform could work to extend political debates, amplify debate audiences, and shift how the audience, the candidates, and the media engage with online political debates.

EXTENSION OF POLITICAL DEBATES

Historically, political debating has had a prescribed structure and has functioned as a part of a formal moment in televised politics. Traditional televised debates have had rules, both latent and manifest, and rituals that apply to the settings and audiences, as well as the candidates' speech and attitudes. This structure has given traditional political debating the impression of a representative legitimacy, where serious political discussion and opposition occurs. Televised debates are seen as information-rich sources of communication that help to facilitate the public's procurement of salient political information.[38] Contrarily, YouTube debates that have relied on the public to generate debate questions have faced substantial criticism for their perceived lack of credibility and substantiveness. Critics seemingly fail to believe that the American public is capable of constructing debate-worthy questions that substantively contribute to national political discussion.[39] However, YouTube debates have changed the nature of political debating through amplifying the size of the audience that has access to both online and traditional debates and extending debates' life-cycle.

In a continual effort to engage larger audiences and increase engagement in political debates, media outlets have developed novel interaction strategies and have leveraged the power of online collectives to not only gain the audience's attention, but to keep it invested throughout the creation, production, and distribution of the online debates. For example, in 2011 *Fox News* teamed up with Google and YouTube to host a Republican primary debate. In twenty days, over 20,000 video questions were uploaded to the *Fox News* YouTube channel for possible inclusion in the debate. *Fox News* allowed users to vote on the questions they would like to see the candidates answer and promised that users would "see a selection of these videos posed to the GOP candidates live on stage."[40] Leading up to the debate, the official YouTube blog kept a running tally of the question categories that were receiving the highest number of submissions, which candidates were receiving the highest percentage of questions, and from which U.S. cities the most questions were being submitted. Following the debate, video clips containing the answers from all of the questions asked during the broadcast debates were uploaded to *Fox News'* YouTube channel where they could be commented on, discussed, and shared. Unlike traditional broadcast debates, which generally occur around the time that a large number of citizens are beginning to earnestly follow campaigns,[41] YouTube and *Fox News* worked to maintain the attention of the audience preceding, during, and after the debate. Debates have been found to encourage viewers to seek out additional campaign information following the completion of their debate viewing.[42] By hosting debates via YouTube, viewers could fulfill their information-seeking objectives by easily linking to additional online material, including candidate's websites and other YouTube videos on similar topics. This YouTube primary debate brought in over six million viewers, easily surpassing the viewership numbers of any of broadcast primary debates of 2011, and ranked high with the key 25- to 54-year-old voter bloc.[43] The debate was illustrative of the continued interest the public has shown in user-generated debates and proved that YouTube debates can been a ratings boon for mainstream media networks.

YouTube debates utilize its multi-faceted platform for content creation and distribution options that allow amplified interaction with political debating. Historically, with televised debates individuals who did not watch live debate broadcasts were typically only able to engage with debate information through subsequent mediated commentary or mainstream media accounts of what had occurred. Contrarily, YouTube-derived debates allow the audience unlimited access to the questions submitted for debate inclusion as well as archives of candidates' answers. This provides them dynamic platforms through which to discuss, rate, share, and deliberate over candidates' answers. While most viewers are appreciative of what televised debates offer them in terms of issue-information,[44] disappointed viewers lament that exposure to debates instead raises questions and areas for which they require additional clarification.[45] Because YouTube debates frequently provide users with access to special debate coverage, such as behind-the-scenes reporting, candidate introduction videos, and on-demand videos, the audience can extend its interest in the debates well beyond the actual moment of the debate. Additionally, because YouTube has become an online political listening platform, audiences' ability to interact more fluidly with one another can enhance their understanding of debate topics and feelings of efficacy.[46] Targeted debates, like YouTube debates, have been found to enhance efficacy, decrease cynicism, and also to create heightened levels of identification between citizens and candidates.[47]

YouTube's archiving and repository functions also extend the lifecycle of political debates. Historically, televised debates did not enjoy much longevity following the original broadcasts. Aside from any lingering mediated political commentary in the days following debates, they are often shelved and only materialize again as clips in future news stories. YouTube, however, has made it possible for past debates to be uploaded in their entirety, helping to preserve them for political posterity and giving interested users free access to past debates. While it may be assumed that the general public is not all that interested in viewing political debates once they have aired, past debates typically generate a few thousand views and debates that have occurred since YouTube became part of the nation's political communication mechanism have generated substantial viewership numbers. For example, the full-length videos of the three main presidential debates and the one vice presidential debate from 2012 have each generated an average of four million viewers who posted an average of over 60,000 comments per debate.

THE AUDIENCE

Debate format matters a great deal to the viewers.[48] Citizens want to feel as if debate discussions are representative of legitimate public policy agendas and that the issues being discussed are relevant to the public and not just to campaign strategy.[49] YouTube debates offer opportunities for the audience to enhance their level of engagement with televised debate content and to become integral voices in the creation of actual debate content. In recent U.S. elections, digital communication technologies and Web 2.0 platforms have allowed for a digital agora, or electronic gathering place, to form. This space has transformed the Internet and mass media outlets from magnifiers of campaign messages into participatory spaces where individuals not only receive political information, but also engage each other in discussion and deliberation.[50] This agora encourages greater participation in the campaign and can increase the likelihood of voting.[51]

In addition to functioning as a debate-hosting platform, YouTube further engages audiences by providing a real-time, interactive forum for discussion during broadcast debates. Research indicates that different debate formats yield different communicative outcomes[52] and that debates tend to have the most significant impact upon voters who are highly interested, yet undecided.[53] Debates can also impact the voting intentions of viewers with weak or no candidate preference.[54] Televised debate audiences have used YouTube's social media functionalities to communicate with one another, the candidates, and the media before, during, and after broadcast debates. Because many viewers have become dual-screeners, who watch debates on television while simultaneously discussing them via online platforms, the digital agora of YouTube allows the audience to translate the passive activity of television viewing into a venue for deliberative discussion. This type of interactive communication can be instrumental in expanding the voters' political discussions and can exponentially expand the possibilities for audiences' engagement with debates. This interaction can also help undecided voters or those with weak candidate preferences gather important information which can be vital to their voting decisions.

By sharing opinions, fact checking, assessing diverse perspectives, and evaluating candidates' performances, viewers can engage in comparative communication. This may encourage voters to overcome the exposure selectivity that can be prevalent in politics and learn more about all candidates, both those they support and those they oppose.[55] The millions of comments, posts, and shares that occur across the platform during both YouTube-hosted debates and those broadcast by other media networks are indicative that voters use the YouTube to enhance dialogue, expand their spheres of participation, exert influence, voice opinions, and become politically involved. Engagement of this nature with debate material can also help to lessen voters' political cynicism.[56] Online audience discussion also benefits political campaigns and mainstream media outlets by providing them easy-to-access focus groups through which they can instantaneously assess the public's thoughts, perceptions, and opinions.

Audiences have also used YouTube debates to personalize their debate experiences. The posting of questions and video responses embedded with personally important and relevant information, emphasizes a direct and personal connection between the public and political issues that objective questions asked by journalists cannot convey. For example, questions from a lesbian couple asking about gay marriage, a bald cancer patient asking about rising health care costs, and a refugee worker surrounded by orphans asking candidates about their commitment to helping end ethnic cleansing, add a level of sincerity and intenseness and put a human face to political issues in ways impossible via other forms of political debate.

Citizens have high expectations for political debates and democracy benefits from political leaders' willingness to meet and discuss issues of public salience.[57] YouTube debates have both changed and increased the audiences' expectations. Prior to this type of debate access, the collective public had never possessed much ability to engage in unfettered discussions about political debating; at least not in a form that the mainstream media or political campaigns had given much credence to. With the emergence of these debates, the constituency has begun to relish their ability to converse as a collective with the candidates and have begun to expect more from candidates during debates. The public desires debate responses that move beyond traditional political stumping. A young man featured in the opening video from the CNN-YouTube Democratic primary debate summed his up by asking, "Since this is such a revolutionary debate would you as politicians do something revolutionary and that is to actually answer the questions that are posed to you tonight?"

Contemporary audiences can leverage YouTube functionalities to insert themselves into political agendas, and on occasion, to upend political messages that had been carefully crafted by the political and media elite. Savvy dual-screeners can fact check any statement made by a candidate or pundit, identify misinformation, find the correct fact(s), and link their followers to the accurate information almost instantaneously. This pushes campaigns to be more responsible in their distribution of facts during political debates. In this online, user-empowered environment, where political moments can quickly be turned in to popular culture fodder, the audience has become a more relevant and substantial factor in political debates.

THE CANDIDATES

Debates provide voters with the most direct and convenient access to political candidates.[58] While debates help to facilitate information acquisition, they also influence voters' perceptions of candidates' character and image traits.[59] Many YouTube debates have posted candidate introductions or bio videos prior to the debates as a method for better connecting with the constituency. Often these videos are humorous or self-mocking and focus on the candidates' personal image, which for some voters can be more persuasive than issue-oriented debating points.[60] YouTube debates provide the perfect medium for candidates to engage in dual-strategy communication with voters that focuses on both highlighting issue stances and emphasizing a positive self-image.[61] However, YouTube can also be a double-edged sword in this regard; candidates must be consistently cognizant of how they represent both themselves, and their agendas, because of the speed and ferocity with which YouTube clips, especially political gaffs, will spread across social media.

YouTube can also be a very helpful campaign tool. Now that a majority of televised debates are simultaneously streamed on YouTube, campaigns can quickly gauge the audiences' reactions to candidates' debate performances and prepare appropriate and timely media responses. You-Tube's community and crowdsourcing functionalities during debates may help to activate voters' democratic tendencies.[62] This constituency conversation provides candidates practically instantaneous debate feedback. Campaigns can analyze the public's rapid-fire online chatter and judge, in real-time, the audience's responses to debate questions, candidates' answers, and their opinion of the campaign in general. Campaigns can also benefit from geolocational data, the real-world geographic location of an Internet connection, attached to users' profiles to identify important patterns and trends in the public commentary. This information is invaluable in vital battleground and swing states because it allows campaigns to better understand how candidates are being received and what topics or concerns are trending in varying geographic regions.

Through linking and video sharing, campaigns now have the ability to extend the life-cycle of political debates by pushing communication and commentary about televised political debates out to potential voters who did not watch televised debates. Campaigns that strategically engage in the practice of social media listening, the real-time monitoring and analysis of social media traffic, are able to more effectively gauge the topics and issues creating salience amongst their dedicated constituents, as well as undecided and oppositional voters. These technologies allow campaigns to best strategize how to effectively communicate with these voters during future debate opportunities. Through utilizing these methods to monitor voters' opinions and commentary, campaigns are often discovering that the issues that they have attached the most significance to are not necessarily the precise issues that their constituencies find to be of highest importance.

YouTube has also altered how candidates engage their opponents in online debate. Campaigns are not only using YouTube to enhance messages about their own positions and initiatives, but also to attack the credibility, stance, and statements of their opponents. YouTube allows candidates to quickly rebut claims made by opponents and to use their opponents' own words and videos against them to effectively frame talking points for their own campaign. For example, John McCain's 2008 campaign created a political attack ad by mashing-up various video clips of opponent Barack Obama's responses during the CNN-YouTube primary debate with clips of vice-presidential candidate Joe Biden during a debate with opponent Sarah Palin to provide evidence that Biden had misrepresented Obama's stance on an important foreign policy issue. This strategy, while a somewhat common tactic in political attack advertising, allowed the McCain campaign to use Obama's and Biden's own political performances against them in an effort to more effectively situate the claims of its own campaign.

YouTube has also become a repository for previously televised political debates. This has provided the public, the media, and future oppositional campaigns with unfettered access to previous debate material. This allows the public to see first-hand how candidates answered questions during previous political bouts, the media to pull clips for news stories and commentary, and opposing campaigns the opportunity to re-appropriate debate material for use in future debates and advertising.

While YouTube provides numerous opportunities for candidates to engage in conversation or debate with potential voters, more often than not, campaigns only use YouTube, specifically their dedicated YouTube channels, to push direct messages about their own campaigns, to rebut opponent's negative messages, and to discredit opponents. As YouTube continues to play a substantial role in both the creation and distribution of political debates, it will be interesting to see how and if campaigns develop novel and effective ways to integrate audience engagement strategies into their political debating strategies.

THE MEDIA

Increased audience engagement in YouTube-derived debates has also pushed mainstream media outlets to continually search out and develop new ways through which to successfully integrate what occurs online into broadcasts about debates. Historically, although issue discussion makes up the crux of political debates, these issues are often not the primary focus of media reports following debates.[63] The fast-paced nature of the Internet means that audience members are no longer reliant on the media's interpretation of debates. The audience can easily gather reactions and commentary from pundits, independent journalists, bloggers, citizens, and other politicians that unfold in real-time before, during, and after debates.

YouTube allows a wider range of political voices from a broader population to be heard. Often, the press' interpretation of debates can become more important in determining the public impact of debates than the actual content of the debates.[64] The digital agora has given the audience the ability to participate in shaping political debate narratives. Contemporarily, it is not uncommon for media report to incorporate audiences' reactions that have been gathered from social media into news stories.

Members of the media have also asserted the desire to reassess the ways that debate content and debate questions are generated. In 2008, just prior to the last round of presidential debates before the election, the Open Debate Coalition, a diverse group of individuals, including university professors, Internet strategists, website founders and directors, and media professionals, called upon candidates Barack Obama and John McCain to insist on a new method for choosing debate questions. The Coalition asserted that although some debates during the primary season selected public questions that had been submitted through various online forums, the selected questions, which were often chosen by the media outlets hosting the debates, were "gimmicky and not hard-hitting enough."[65] The Coalition requested that instead of relying on media hosts to design or choose debate questions, they should instead come from bubble-up Internet technologies, where online users vote and the most popular questions get pushed to the top and addressed by candidates. Although bubble-up technology is the essence of social media, many media outlets and candidates are against reliance on it because frequently questions that candidates do not want to address, such as the legalization of marijuana, or questions crowd-sourced by opposing campaigns, frequently rise to the top of the bubble. However, Coalition member, Craig Newmark, founder of Craigstlist, asserted that the country is undergoing a "great movement towards networked grassroots democracy" and incorporating citizens in this evolving form of democracy is "good for the country."[66]

During the 2008 primaries, the Coalition also requested that media outlets release the copyrights to debate videos so that debates could be legally shared on YouTube without fear of legal repercussion. Citing a situation where candidate John McCain was threatened with legal action by a media outlet for using a debate clip as part of a campaign message, the Coalition asserted that if the presidential debates were for public benefit, the right to share and speak about them afterward should not be controlled by the media. The Coalition requested that both candidates committed to dedicating the raw footage of any public political debates they participated in to the public domain; thus, ensuring audiences' rights to share, discuss, and mash-up the footage without fear of copyright infringement. While the Coalition circumvented the Commission on Presidential Debates by sending its letter directly to the candidates, both the Obama and McCain campaigns subsequently called on the Commission to more effectively use Internet technologies to generate debate questions that better reflected the public's concerns.[67] The campaigns also collectively supported the dedication of debate footage to the public domain, with the McCain campaign stating that "We also believe that Americans—including the campaigns themselves—should be able to 'debate the debates' using all available tools on the Internet and elsewhere, including blogs, webvideo services and other means."[68]

YouTube has helped to change online political debates. Through providing new opportunities for debate engagement, it has collectively, changed the expectations that the audience, the candidates, and the media should have for the future of political debates. As YouTube continues to develop, it will likely continue to grow in importance as an increasingly active channel of political debate and allow for a more robust and accountable discussion of key issues facing the constituency.[69] Political debates are positioned as a national conversation about salient political issues and YouTube has opened the door to allow all interested parties to be a part of that discussion.

CONCLUSIONS AND CHALLENGES

Political debates are a vital part of the U.S. election system and process. They provide an important opportunity for citizens to learn about candidates and help them decide for whom to vote[70] and produce a better-informed constituency.[71] While the 2007 CNN-YouTube Primary Debates occurred at a stage of infancy for online political debating, they were a strong, early indicator of the potential future power that YouTube would hold in online political debating. YouTube debates regularly draw large audiences, are attractive to key voting blocs, and have ignited a trend across media outlets to more heavily incorporate both the public and YouTube in the creation of debate content. YouTube debates help to reframe politics as a venue for deliberative discussion and not only an arena of gamesmanship, failure, scandal, and gaffes.[72]

YouTube has created a space for the public to engage substantively in political debates. It has altered the interactivity, vernacular, and tone of debates, encouraged proactive involvement by the public, and allowed lay voices into traditionally highly exclusive political discourse. There appears to be substantial and continued interest in YouTube-based debates, which indicates that the Internet, in general, and YouTube specifically, have the necessary credentials to support online debate and participatory democratic engagement. The changing nature of the technological environment has created more opportunities for citizen-driven agenda control, which has decentralized the prominence of journalists in political debate reporting, encouraged more active participation by citizens, and begun to reverse the passiveness of tele-democracy; all of which then serves to potentially enhance the political efficacy of the constituency. YouTube has also promoted the growth of Internetized television, the incorporation of Internet technologies, such as live online polling, into televised debates, that provide the audience with a sense of unrestrained action and interaction.[73] Internetized television has helped mainstream televised media to overcome the handicap of being seen as a one dimensional communication medium and has begun to further stimulate the audiences' role in the political debate process.

YouTube as a conduit for generating debate questions, streaming, and archiving debates also brings about some important points of concern. Debates that are both configured through and broadcast via YouTube can serve to reinforce concerns of the digital divide and to further emphasize socioeconomic barriers that are often related to democratic engagement and voting practices by specific demographics. Even minor technological requirements, such as broadband Internet access, exclude some socioeconomic populations from being able to fully participate in the online debate experience.

Although YouTube debates have created and opened up channels of dialogue that have not been previously accessible to the public, the long-term use and acceptance of such formats is tenuous at best. While the public consistently submits vast numbers of debate questions when the opportunity arises for them to do so, the mainstream media and political campaigns seem reluctant to fully embrace these formats. Although journalists, and their questions, rarely represent the larger public's concerns, critics suggest that the intensity of the questions asked by the public are not substantive enough to generate the level of political discussion warranted by political debates. Because citizens' questions tend to be broader and include a level of vagueness, candidates can capitalize by directing their answers to advantageously selected elements of the question rather than the specific point of the question.[74] The idea of crowdsourcing questions has begun to be quietly dismissed by some political correspondents. For example, during a presidential debate for the 2012 election, moderator Candy Crowley, CNN's chief political correspondent, elected not to accept questions from the public via any online sources, despite a Google Moderator page announcing that they were soliciting questions from the public for the debate. Even Barack Obama, despite appearing very accessible across social media platforms, quit taking questions from YouTube after questions for a White House online chat were dominated by questions about the legalization of marijuana. He has since only elected to answer questions from formats through which he can decide which questions he wants to answer.[75] Critics of crowdsourcing questions also cite concerns of up-voting, where activists and advocates will saturate YouTube debate platforms with specific veins of questions, and of an Internet bias towards a more tech-savvy generation. Finally, the generation of debate content via YouTube must also be approached cautiously. A difficult balance between media and public creation and control of debate content must be struck. Voters want to be a primary contributor to debate content, however, media entities are responsible for ensuring that all candidates during a debate are addressed and that questions legally suitable for broadcast are generated. It is doubtful, that because of media concerns such as these, that we will ever see a truly user-generated debate make its way onto broadcast media.

Despite these issues, targeted debates, such as those generated and hosted via YouTube are important for the furtherance of the United States' political communication spectrum. Future YouTube debates will also provide for interesting new veins of debate research to emerge. Future debates will provide data that could expand theoretical discussions usually reserved for televised debates. Researchers may also be able to expand on normative theories and draw new theories regarding the relationship between debate content generation, media agenda setting functions, and audience's uses and gratifications behaviors. Future research could also enhance the literature on effects of debate viewing, media coverage of debates, and discussions on the short and long term impact of debate formats. Televised debate research has limited knowledge on the long-lasting effects of debate exposure.[76] YouTube debates, with the ability to track audience members' responses through comment threads may offer an effective platform for examining audience effects by looking at the longevity of interaction and impact through an entire debate series. Whether YouTube continues to be a platform for hosting debates, or in the future becomes more prominently a platform for Internetized debate discussion, there will be expansive options for academic investigations during future elections. As the future of online political debating continues to evolve and the public's desire to participate is fueled by online platforms, the mainstream media and campaigns will be best served by finding a representative balance between controlling the creation of political debate content and engaging with the audience in ways beyond those of traditional political debating.

NOTES

1. Diana Carlin, "Presidential Debates as Focal Points for Campaign Arguments," *Political Communication* 9, no. 4 (1992): 251–65.

2. Thomas Patterson, *The Vanishing Voter: Public Involvement in an Age of Uncertainty* (New York, NY: Knopf, 2002).

3. Mitchell McKinney and Diana Carlin, "Political Campaign Debates," in *Handbook of Political Communication Research* (Mahwah, NJ: Lawrence Erlbaum Associates, 2004), 203–34.

4. Michael Pfau, "The Changing Nature of Presidential Debate Influence in the Age of Mass Media Communication" (presented at the 9th Annual Conference on Presidential Rhetoric, TX A&M University, 2003).

5. Steven Chaffee, "Presidential Debates: Are They Helpful to Voters?," *Communication Monographs* 45, no. 4 (1978): 330–46.

6. Sidney Kraus, *Televised Presidential Debates and Public Policy*, 2nd ed. (Mahwah, NJ: Lawrence Erlbaum Associates, 2000).

7. McKinney and Carlin, "Political Campaign Debates."

8. Alan Schroeder, *Presidential Debates: Forty Years of High-Risk Television* (New York, NY: Columbia University Press, 2000).

9. LaChrystal Ricke, "Debates via Social Media," in *Encyclopedia of Social Media and Politics* (Thousand Oaks, CA: Sage, 2014).

10. Jack Blimes, "Questions, Answers, and the Organization of Talk in the 1992 Vice Presidential Debate: Fundamental Considerations," *Research on Language and Social Interaction* 32, no. 3 (1999): 213–42.

11. Commission on Presidential Debates, *Debate Transcript: October 13, 2004* (Commission on Presidential Debates, 2004), http://www.debates.org/pages/trans2004d.html.

12. Caroline McCarthy, "MySpace, MTV Team up for One-on-One Presidential Dialogues," *CNET*, August 22, 2007, http://news.cnet.com/8301-13577_3-9764866-36.html.

13. Caroline McCarthy, "MySpace Gets Official Presidential Debate Deal," *CNET*, August 5, 2008, http://www.cnet.com/news/myspace-gets-official-presidential-debate-deal/.

14. Eric Deggans, "YouTube Users to Feed CNN Presidential Debate Questions," *St. Petersburg Times*, June 15, 2007.

15. YouTube, "CNN, YouTube Team up to Host First-Ever Voter-Generated Presidential Debates.," June 14, 2007, http://www.youtube.com/press_room?morgue=yes.

16. LaChrystal Ricke, "A New Opportunity for Democratic Engagement: The CNN-YouTube Presidential Candidate Debates," *Journal of Information Technology & Politics* 7, no. 2–3 (2010): 202–15.

17. Benjamin Toff, "Debate Ratings Lag," *The New York Times*, July 27, 2007, http://www.nytimes.com/2007/07/27/arts/27arts-YOUTUBEDEBAT_BRF.html?_r=0.

18. Anthony Crupi, "CNN's YouTube GOP Debate Draws Record 4.49 Million Viewers," *Mediaweek*, November 29, 2007.

19. Mark Raby, "CNN Youtube Debate a Hit among Young Viewers," *TG Daily*, July 25, 2007, http://www.tgdaily.com/content/view/33075/113/.

20. Crupi, "CNN's YouTube GOP Debate Draws Record 4.49 Million Viewers."

21. YouTube, "CNN, YouTube Team up to Host First-Ever Voter-Generated Presidential Debates."

22. The New York Times, "Changing the Terms of the Debate," *The New York Times*, August 17, 2007.

23. Ken Dilanian, "YouTube Makes Leap into Politics: Debate Will Include Q&A from Internet," *USA Today*, July 23, 2007.

24. Jack Muse, "The Consensus on Last Night's Debate Format," *Huffington Post*, July 27, 2007, http://www.huffingtonpost.com/jack-muse/the-consensus-on-last-nig_b_57608.html.

25. Joshua Levy, *The CNN/YouTube Debate: Make It Truly Open* (techpresident, June 14, 2007), http://techpresident.com/blog-entry/cnnyoutube-debate-make-it-truly-open.

26. Patrick Healy and Jeff Zeleny, "Novel Debate Format, but the Same Old Candidates," *The New York Times*, July 24, 2007, http://www.nytimes.com/2007/07/24/us/politics/24debate.html.

27. Ibid.

28. Fox News, "Democratic Backers Question GOP Candidates in YouTube Debate," *Fox News.com*, November 29, 2007, http://www.foxnews.com/story/2007/11/29/democratic-backers-question-gop-candidates-in-youtube-debate/.

29. Jennifer Stromer-Galley and Lauren Bryant, "Agenda Control in the 2008 CNN/YouTube Debates," *Communication Quarterly* 59, no. 5 (2011): 529–46.

30. Caroline McCarthy, "YouTube, CNN Aim to 'Revolutionize' Presidential Debate Process," *CNet News Blog*, June 14, 2007, http://news.cnet.com/8301-10784_3-9729506-7.html.

31. Jose Vargas, "YOUTUBE, TAKE TWO Few GOP Candidates Commit to Debate," *The Washington Post*, July 27, 2007, http://www.washingtonpost.com/wp-dyn/content/article/2007/07/27/AR2007072700283.html.

32. Katharine Seelye, "U.S. Politics to Draw All Eyes to YouTube; Debate May Start a New Phase in Web Campaigning." *The National Herald Tribune*, June 14, 2007.

33. Ibid.

34. Stromer-Galley and Bryant, "Agenda Control in the 2008 CNN/YouTube Debates."

35. Ibid.

36. Deggans, "YouTube Users to Feed CNN Presidential Debate Questions."

37. Stromer-Galley and Bryant, "Agenda Control in the 2008 CNN/YouTube Debates."

38. William Benoit, Mitchell McKinney, and Michael Stephenson, "Effects of Watching Primary Debates in the 2000 U.S. Presidential Campaign," *Journal of Communication* 52, no. 2 (2002): 316–31.

39. Ricke, "A New Opportunity for Democratic Engagement: The CNN-YouTube Presidential Candidate Debates."

40. YouTube, "Fox News/Google Debate: Digging into Your Questions," *YouTube Official Blog,* September 19, 2011, http://youtube-global.blogspot.com/2011/09/fox-newsgoogle-debate-digging-into-your.html.

41. McKinney and Carlin, "Political Campaign Debates."

42. James Lemert, "Do Televised Presidential Debates Help Inform Voters?," *Journal of Broadcasting and Electronic Media* 37, no. 1 (1993): 83–94.

43. Alex Weprin, "Fox News/Google Debate Most-Watched GOP Primary Debate Yet," *TVNewser,* September 23, 2011, http://www.mediabistro.com/tvnewser/fox-newsgoogle-debate-most-watched-gop-primary-debate-yet_b89147.

44. David Sears and Steven Chaffee, "Uses and Effects of the 1976 Debates: An Overview of Empirical Studies," in *The Great Debates, 1976: Ford vs. Carter* (Bloomington, IN: Indiana University Press, 1979).

45. McKinney and Carlin, "Political Campaign Debates."

46. Sears and Chaffee, "Uses and Effects of the 1976 Debates: An Overview of Empirical Studies."

47. Mitchell McKinney and Mary Banwart, "Rocking the Youth Vote through Debate: Examining the Effects of a Citizen versus Journalist Controlled Debate on Civic Engagement," *Journalism Studies* 6 (2005): 153–63.

48. Diana Carlin, "Watching the Debates: A Guide for Viewers," in *Televised Election Debates: International Perspectives* (New York, NY: St. Martin's Press, 2000), 157–77.

49. McKinney and Carlin, "Political Campaign Debates."

50. Rita Kirk and Dan Schill, "A Digital Agora: Citizen Participation in the 2008 Presidential Debates," *American Behavioral Scientist* 55, no. 3 (2011): 325–47.

51. Patterson, *The Vanishing Voter: Public Involvement in an Age of Uncertainty.*

52. Michael Pfau, "A Comparative Assessment of Intra-Party Political Debate Formats," *Political Communication Review* 8 (1984): 1–23.

53. Chaffee, "Presidential Debates: Are They Helpful to Voters?"

54. Susan Hellweg, "Introduction," *Argumentation and Advocacy* 30 (1993): 59–31.

55. Chaffee, "Presidential Debates: Are They Helpful to Voters?"

56. Lynda Lee Kaid, Mitchell McKinney, and John Tedesco, *Civic Dialogue in the 1996 Presidential Campaign: Candidate, Media, and Public Voices* (Cresskill, NJ: Hampton, 2000)

57. McKinney and Carlin, "Political Campaign Debates."

58. Ibid.

59. William Benoit, Mitchell McKinney, and R. Lance Holbert, "Beyond Learning and Persona: Extending the Scope of Presidential Debate Effects," *Communication Monographs* 68, no. 3 (2001): 259–73.

60. Peter Schrott, "Electoral Consequences of 'Winning' Televised Campaign Debates," *Public Opinion Quarterly* 54 (1990): 567–85.

61. Hellweg, "Introduction."

62. McKinney and Carlin, "Political Campaign Debates."

63. Kraus, *Televised Presidential Debates and Public Policy.*

64. Steven Chaffee and Jack Dennis, "Presidential Debates: An Empirical Assessment," in *The Past and Future of Presidential Debates* (Washington, DC: American Enterprise Institute, 1979), 75–106.

65. Andrew Malcom, "Diverse Web Coalition Asks McCain, Obama to Alter Debates," *Los Angeles Times,* September 25, 2008, sec. Nation, http://latimes-blogs.latimes.com/washington/2008/09/debates-mccain.html.

66. Ibid.

67. Sarah Stirland, "McCain and Obama Campaigns Call for Change in Debate Format," *Wired.com,* October 7, 2008, www.wired.com/threatlevel/2008/10/mccain-and-obam/.

68. Ibid.

69. Ricke, "Debates via Social Media."

70. William Benoit and Glenn Hansen, "Presidential Debate Watching, Issue Knowledge, Character Evaluation, and Vote Choice," *Human Communication Research* 30, no. 1 (2004): 121–44.

71. Arthur Miller and Michael MacKuen, "Informing the Electorate: A National Study," in *The Great Debates: Carter vs. Ford, 1976* (Bloomington, IN: Indiana University Press, 1979).

72. Michael Gurevitch, Stephen Coleman, and Jay Blumler, "Political Communication – Old and New Media Relationships," *The ANNALS of the American Academy of Political and Social Science* 645 (2009): 164–81.

73. Anastasia Deligiaouri and Panagiotis Symeonidis, "'YouTube Debate': A New Era of Internetized Television Politics?," *International Journal of E-Politics* 1, no. 2 (n.d.).

74. Stromer-Galley and Bryant, "Agenda Control in the 2008 CNN/YouTube Debates."

75. Gregory Ferenstein, "No Online Questions for the next Debate: Tired of Pot and Snowmen?," *TechCrunch*, October 12, 2012, http://techcrunch.com/2012/10/12/no-online-questions-at-next-debate-tired-of-pot-and-snowmen/.

76. McKinney and Carlin, "Political Campaign Debates."

Part II

YouTube and In-Office Communication

Technology occupies a permanent space in terms of the public's information-seeking behaviors, especially when related to the desire to access political information. While the ways in which politicians communicate with the public during campaigns generates a great deal of scholarly attention, the body of literature regarding how politicians utilize Internet technologies to communicate with and engage their constituents after they have been elected is limited. There is a great deal of political activity that takes place in the intermediary between elections. Yet, it is frequently difficult for the public to gain access to much, if any, information regarding what their elected officials are doing to serve them while in office that is not facilitated by the mainstream media.

Political YouTube channels provide a platform through which elected officials can share the day-to-day occurrences of political office with their constituents and work to keep those who elected them engaged in between election cycles. Much like political campaigns have utilized new methods to inform voters during elections, sitting politicians have devised novel strategies for keeping their constituency apprised of and interested in their time in office. Strategically, YouTube allows elected officials to be the agenda builders of their tenure and potentially, build and maintain a committed voting base long before the next election cycle beings.

An examination of the official YouTube channels of members of the United States' Senate and Congress provide interesting insights into how elected officials are choosing to use YouTube to amplify attention to the activities and obligations they undertake in office. Much like they do during campaigns, elected officials use communication strategies to reach out to their constituents. Similar also to campaigns, these online strategies help to increase authenticity, transparency, and access for constituents. As part of its promise for a more open and transparent government, the Obama administration maintained daily updates on the official White House YouTube Channel. This is perhaps one of the most measurable and consistent methods of direct-constituency communication and engagement since politicians began to use the Internet for these activities.

The ways that elected officials inform and engage their constituents through YouTube will inevitably evolve and provide for the expansion of interesting new veins of research. The information and examples contained within this section will hopefully provide the framework upon which some of these future discussions may be built.

FIVE

Elected Officials and YouTube

YouTube provides elected officials with the ability to easily, consistently, and effectively communicate with their constituencies. While campaign communication generates a substantial amount of research, the communication patterns and habits of elected officials tends to draw less investigation. However, the integration of communication technologies, such as YouTube, into in-office political communication allows elected officials to keep their constituency up-to-date with information about themselves, their work, and their future initiatives through dynamic and interactive public engagement.

Since the late 1990s, when the Internet became an evolving platform for political communication, the public has sought new ways through which to gain political information and novel methods for engaging with elected officials.[1] The continual expansion of the political Internet brings with it growing citizen expectations regarding accessibility to elected officials and transformative online political opportunities.[2] YouTube offers politicians new ways to increase the public's access to information and to enhance person-to-person connectivity with their constituents. This chapter explores how citizens benefit from increased access to elected politicians, how YouTube's communication structures enable more effective politician-constituent communication, and provides examples of how elected officials are using YouTube to enhance their accessibility to and communication with the public.

CYBERDEMOCRACY AND YOUTUBE

Successful politicians know that by affording media the status it deserves, they can increase their popularity with the public.[3] Politically, the public has specific needs and motivations for using the Internet to access

information, including seeking guidance (help deciding on important issues), information or surveillance (actively searching for political information or keeping an eye on the political landscape), entertainment, and
social utility (using information to reinforce decisions).[4] The Internet
satisfies many of the public's diverse political needs[5] and research indicates that contents' characteristics and mode of transmission can greatly
influence users' gratification with political content.[6] By participating in
instrumental media viewing, the audience intentionally seeks out specific
information to satisfy certain needs.[7] In doing so, the audience fulfills its
media needs by exerting self-awareness in active and goal-directed
searches for media content.[8] As the Internet continues to offer more access to information for the audience, the constituency can become better
informed, participate more in political life, and have a greater influence
on the political process.[9]

The wide range of political information on the Internet makes it easy
for individuals to satisfy the gratification needs they seek to fulfill.[10]
Because Internet users frequently access political sites specifically to learn
about the viewpoints of politicians, YouTube's wide range of political
information allows it to effectively function as a cyberdemocracy platform. YouTube enables elevated communication and interaction between
elected officials and the constituency, enhances both the access to and
delivery of political information, and provides an opportunity to build a
more effective relationship between the political establishment and the
polity. These attributes can enhance political attitudes, including political
interest, strength of affiliation, efficaciousness, and likelihood of voting in
future elections.[11] Additionally, as the Internet-savvy public desires more
accountability and transparency from pubic officials, the structural transformation of political information dissemination that occurs through
YouTube can help to mobilize opinions and offer interested citizens an
effective way to participate in politics. YouTube lets users exercise greater control of their political media choices, which can amplify citizens'
purposeful use of political media[12] and the effects of user-centered media.[13]

Strategic use of YouTube by politicians can reverse the indexical model of elite political communication structures. In the indexical model,
mainstream news often emphasizes political conflict, divisions between
political parties, or disparities between one party and the White House
and/or Congress.[14] Through YouTube, politicians can alter the audiences'
dependence on this communication model by providing the public with
videos that specifically illustrate what they are doing while in office.
Because political staff are the primary authors of YouTube content, they
can steer the political audience away from such conflict when appropriate and gear the political discussion in the direction that is most beneficial
to their position on an issue or legislative act. This allows the constituency a method for evaluating the credibility of political actions first-hand

and offers the public a democratic experience independent of traditional mainstream media. By structuring information on YouTube to set the agenda for political and media elite, savvy political strategists can potentially reverse media influence which often frames politics through personalization, dramatization, fragmentation, or normalization.[15] Politicians now possess the ability to function as their own agenda-builders, versus allowing the mainstream media to function as the primary agenda setters of political actors.[16] This direct information exchange can also help to facilitate a higher level of interpersonal trust between politicians and the public and heighten users' desires to engage democratically.[17] Mainstream media outlets have tried to combat this new information exchange by using their own new media strategies to engage online audiences with traditional media fodder on nontraditional platforms.[18]

Posting information generated directly by politicians allows citizens options for information consumption beyond the narrow range of issues and viewpoints frequently offered through mainstream media, which can help to alleviate an anemic public sphere. On-demand mediated communication gives the audience the ability to share and discuss political content with others.[19] Politically interested individuals access political sites in order to discover information about politicians and key issues and are often eager to share the information they have found with others.[20] In this sense, YouTube can provide an important correlation between the audiences' ability to access information and the political efficacy of its users. However, in order to enact the truly direct democracy that YouTube enables, politicians must focus on avoiding repetition of topics and providing enough new and interesting information as to sufficiently attract a wide range of viewers and to entice return viewership.

YouTube as a platform for political information dissemination also allows for an interesting model of three-way communication to occur. The traditional structure of political websites provides the perception of two-way communication between politicians and the public. Political websites are structured to provide information and responsive dialogue, where the public has options to communicate with the politician, usually via email, but do not provide a venue that encourages broad-based interaction or deliberation.[21] Conversely, YouTube provides an environment where a higher level of cyber-interactivity and highly active political discourse can take place. Three-way communication, between politicians and constituents, media and constituents, and constituents and constituents, offers an interesting mechanism for political discourse where each of the three parties may be intentionally or unintentionally influencing the other communicative parties. In the YouTube environment, those who are not necessarily a message's intended audience, or are an unknown audience, can quickly become the party that most clearly receives a political message. This communication between a sender, an intended audience, and an unknown audience is one of the elements that makes

YouTube such an interesting and viable platform for political communication. While YouTube viewers typically begin their communicative interactions as receivers, they can quickly and easily become the creators and distributors of political information.

Forums through which audiences can voice their views to government officials and which offer opportunities for likeminded individuals to both articulate their political positions and hear those of individuals like themselves can heighten users' political efficacy.[22] YouTube's comment thread functionalities give content recipients a high level of discussant power and can allow them to dictate the direction of online discourse. The configuration of comment threads allows receiver-participants to enter or leave online discussions at their leisure, to acquire information from others purely through surveillance, and for the content and quality of the discussion to be dictated and monitored by the receiver-participants. This type of receiver-participant interaction serves an important social utility function, where individuals arm themselves with information to reinforce their political decisions and to use in discussions with others.[23] Comment functionalities also offer new ways for politicians to seek citizen input, exponentially expanding on more traditional input-seeking methods such as community surveys, public meetings, and radio or television addresses. The connectivity offered through YouTube is essential to informed democratic engagement. It can enhance governmental support of public deliberation[24] and provide citizens with relevant information that may inform their policy understanding and encourage deliberative decisions.[25]

Collectively, YouTube's political functionalities allow the public to essentially watch politics in action. This can foster greater citizen interest in public issues, improve political representation, increase governmental effectiveness and competitiveness, and enhance the citizenry's feelings of efficacy. While the mere existence of YouTube technologies do not necessarily revolutionize the typical citizen's experience with politics, they do offer interested citizens a wide array of information-seeking and communicative opportunities. As the next sections will discuss, through Political YouTube channels, YouTube Town Halls, and enhanced constituency engagement methods, the platform's communicative structures have replaced the traditional one-to-many communication structure prevalent throughout historical political communication discourse with many-to-many formats of communication.

POLITICAL YOUTUBE CHANNELS

YouTube channels, or curated lists of videos connected to a specific YouTube member, have always been embedded in the technical fabric of the platform. However, because early YouTube channels were not fluid channels of communication, they were not easily integrated into politicians' overall communication strategies. Subsequent structural changes in YouTube made it easier for both politicians and the public to use YouTube channels lithely. In November 2011, YouTube was integrated into the Google Chrome web browser and into the Google+ social networking site, which allowed users the ability to view YouTube videos without having to leave a social media platform.[26] This function was important for politicians because it allowed them to more effectively retained users' attention and keep them on the channel for additional video viewing. In December 2011, YouTube focused its attention on enhancing its video channels by redesigning the site's interface to be more reflective of the news feeds on other social networking sites.[27] This redesign made it easier for similarly situated YouTube channels to be cultivated for users and integrative features made it easy to see what users' friends were watching and sharing without leaving the site.

Politicians use their dedicated YouTube channels to engage audiences in a variety of ways, including posting speeches, debates, media appearances, behind-the-scenes footage of their campaigns or day-to-day work, and advertisements. YouTube channels provide politicians with a vast amount of analytic data that they can use to assess the types of content most useful and relevant to their audience. This analytical data makes it possible for politicians to see who is watching their videos, where the channel's traffic is coming from, and deliver their audience timely and relevant political content. Much like YouTube in general has provided political campaigns with a way to more effectively engage potential voters, dedicated political YouTube channels provide engagement data that enables the efficient tracking of channels' subscribers through following what they are liking, "favoriting," commenting on, and sharing. Collectively, these tools make it easy for elected officials to know who is watching their videos, what topics are resonating with viewers, how to best keep their constituency informed about political issues and events, and allows them to direct political communication in ways that are most likely to reverberate with their viewers.

Cultivating a strong YouTube presence can increase the credibility of political communication, generate engagement and fundraising opportunities, and establish vital communication channels between politicians and voters. Subsequent to elections, politicians are using YouTube in a variety of methods in order to communicate with their constituencies. The channels are being used to disseminate information, illustrate what elected officials are working on in office, explain policy and voting decisions, and communicate directly with supporters—all in hopes of creating and sustaining a dedicated broad constituent base that is likely to vote for them in future elections.

THE YOUTUBE TOWN HALL

In May of 2011, YouTube launched the YouTube Town Hall (YTTH), an online platform through which members of Congress virtually debated and discussed important national issues. The YTTH offered viewers a snapshot of U.S. political opinions by posing questions to members of Congress and posting their short video responses elaborating on the issues or discussing how issues could be effectively managed for the good of the public. Viewers had the opportunity to select videos covering a wide range of topics and affirm their opinion of which Congressperson's answer offered the best solution by clicking to "support" the answer after watching the video. In an interesting strategy to encourage viewers to focus on the videos' content versus party affiliation, YouTube did not reveal the Congressperson's party alignment until after a viewer supported or declined to support the video. Following the selection of the Congresspersons' answer they preferred, a pop-up box with their state and party affiliation became visible. The videos that generated the highest numbers of views and supporting votes were then tracked on the YTTH Leaderboard where the top-supported video responses of each month and throughout the history of the YTTH were available for easy viewing, linking, and sharing.

Initially, YouTube selected six topics for discussion in the town hall—budget, energy, economy, health care, education, and Afghanistan—based on the public salience of these topics in Google News and Google searches the year prior. However, in its ongoing effort to make politics and political information more accessible to the public, YouTube subsequently launched an option for the public themselves to ask questions of members of Congress. YouTube users were encouraged to post questions and vote on which queries they wanted to hear answered. Each month, members of Congress then answered a selection of the top-rated questions from the page. Members of Congress addressed a variety of topics, such as:

- Do you believe that voters should show their ID before voting as a way to stop fraud?
- What do you think about the Wall Street protests?
- There are millions of undocumented individuals living in the United States, many of whom were brought to the U.S. as children. Is enacting the DREAM act a viable way for these individuals to be granted citizenship? If 5–10 percent of spending was cut from the anticipated 2012 federal budget and matched with an equivalent amount in tax increases we'd cut the federal deficit in half. Why not do it?
- Can basic information on legislators' productivity be measured and reported in an accessible, comparable format? Categories for work-

ing hours could include: Dialogue with constituents, dialogue with peers, campaigning, legislating.
* Why are we spending billions in Iraq and Afghanistan to build up their infrastructure when we could be using that money to convert our own infrastructure?

The video responses from Congress communicated answers through a variety of strategies. Many videos were simple direct-to-camera statements about the topics addressed. However, others utilized news clips, photographs, and infographics to better orient the audience with the topic. Some also directed viewers to websites where they could find additional information about the issue or participate in related initiatives. In sum, over 100 video responses were offered by over fifty members of Congress. Collectively, these videos have been viewed over 1.3 million times. Republicans' videos have received the most views, racking up over one million video views, but Democrats' videos have received the most votes from YTTH visitors, receiving over 129,000 supporting Town Hall votes. The five topics that generated the highest number of video views relate to the economy (over 645,000 views), energy (over 216,000 views), Afghanistan (over 244,000 views), education (over 90,000 views), and immigration (over 60,000 views). The video receiving the overall highest number of views was of Kansas Republican Senator Jerry Moran's answer about the industries he believed were the most important for American's economic growth and the governmental policies he thought would best encourage U.S. companies' success in those industries; the video generated over 346,000 views. The next four most popular videos were from: former Texas Republican Senator Kay Bailey Hutchison discussing gas prices and clean energy initiatives; Arizona Republican Senator John McCain's position on troop withdrawals from Afghanistan; Kansas Republican Senator Pat Roberts noting his belief that governmental regulations are harmful to business and the economy; and California Democratic Representative Mike Honda discussing the importance of strengthening the middle class while addressing the national budget and deficits.

The three topics in which the public showed the greatest interest through supporting votes were Afghanistan, education, and the economy. When breaking these three topics down according to audience votes by party, YouTube was able to generate interesting metrics that illustrated which party received the most support per topic. They were also able to highlight the words and ideas within each topic that were most frequently used by Congresspersons when discussing the issues. These metrics served as important information points for the public as they allowed them to see how the politicians' answers were being ranked by other constituents and what concepts or words the politicians were using to explain issues of public interest.

On the topic of Afghanistan, 62 percent of participants favored videos produced by Democratic members of Congress. The most frequent words Democrats used to discuss the topic were security, war, and mission; the most prevalent words in Republican videos were progress, withdrawals, and success.[28] The top voted video on the topic of Afghanistan was from New Mexico Democratic Senator Tom Udall discussing his support of President Obama's accelerated timetable to transition troops out of Afghanistan; the video generated over 14,000 views. On the subject of education, Democrats received 52 percent of the supporting votes. The most utilized words in videos by Democrats were technology, teachers, and schools; the most common words in Republican produced videos were best, schools, and states (often relating to states' responsibilities regarding education).[29] The video with the most votes on this topic was of Tennessee Republican Senator Lamar Alexander discussing strengthening the K–12 education system by modeling schools after universities to create a stronger education system; his video generated 8,000 views. Regarding the economy, Democratic videos again received the highest number of supporting votes, with 58 percent of viewers supporting these videos. The most common words in Democratic videos were tax, American, and jobs; the most prevalent words in Republican videos on this topic were work, jobs, and budget.[30] The most supported video on this topic was from California Democratic Representative John Garamendi advocating for job growth through supporting the *Make It in America* plan focused on jobs in the areas of clean energy and transportation; this video generated 6,000 views.

Looking at the topics that generated the most substantial public interest and the ideas that the political parties used when discussing specific topics provides interesting insight into political discourse in the United States. From YouTube's measurements, it is possible to gain a better understanding of the issues that most concern the American public and how the parties most frequently contextualize these important issues for the voters. These metrics are also interesting because they provide insight and information about the topics and ideas resonating across both the public and Congress that may not be possible to clearly ascertain without the type of interactive political communication that YouTube can provide.

The YouTube Town Hall provided an interesting communication platform between elected officials and the American public. It can be difficult for the public to know or gain access to information regarding members of Congress and their stances on specific topics and issues. The YTTH provided a way for the American public to hear first-hand from members of Congress regarding important issues facing the country and to participate in the creation of national political discussion. This type of content can heighten efficacy by allowing the public to benefit from material that was not filtered, edited, or scrutinized by traditional media.[31] It could also heighten the relationship between individuals' motivation for using the Internet for political information and their political attitudes.[32] The creation of the YTTH also illustrates YouTube's continued efforts to develop novel online platforms through which the constituency can be more effectively connected to elected officials and participate in the nation's political discourse.

CONSTITUENCY ENGAGEMENT VIA YOUTUBE

YouTube channels allow elected politicians to communicate with the constituency in a variety of ways. However, there is a small percentage of elected officials who appear to only post videos to their YouTube channels during elections. The information detailed in the following sections was ascertained following a content analysis of the types of videos that are posted to the active (i.e., still being used) YouTube channels of sitting Senators and Congresspersons. The investigation found that almost every elected national politician has an official YouTube channel and the channels are heavily used for information dissemination. While the vast percentage of officials post at minimum one new video to their channel each week, collectively the number of videos posted to political YouTube channels varies widely, with some politicians posting as few as just one video and other politicians posting well over 700. Channel subscriptions and viewership numbers also vary widely with subscribers ranging between eight and over 32,000 and video views ranging from as few as ten to nearly eight million. The degree to which the public comment functionality is used by both politicians and the public also varies substantially. Roughly 38 percent of politicians have disabled the ability for the public to comment on their channels, bringing into question if elected officials are using their channels as a means to engage constituents, or rather just to inform them.

FLOOR SPEECHES AND CONGRESSIONAL HEARINGS

The most prominent manner in which sitting politicians utilize their YouTube channels is for information dissemination. Politicians enhance and affirm their political brand by demonstrating for the public via video the activities that they are undertaking while in office. Politicians who frequently post to their channels rely heavily on them to post clips of policy speeches they have given on the floor of either the House or Senate and videos of their involvement in Congressional hearings. Every political official who has a YouTube channel has posted at least one video of a floor speech or Congressional hearing to their channel. As a great deal of what members of Congress do on a daily basis is never seen by the broader public, posting videos of their floor speeches allows politicians to provide their constituents with direct evidence of their work while in Washington. Typically, floor speeches are given in an almost empty chamber and remarks from speeches are seldom televised.[33] Although the public can view some floor speeches and hearings on television networks like C-SPAN, it can be difficult to know when a specific piece of legislation will be discussed or when a specific politician will be speaking. Additionally, C-SPAN is not necessarily readily available to all members of the public as it is usually part of cable packaging and not broadcast television. Posting these videos to YouTube allows for the asynchronous viewing of political content and gives constituents the opportunity to see and assess for themselves if their elected officials are representing them effectively.

Videos of these speeches can also enlighten the public to the wide variety of issues and legislation that sitting politicians work on every day. The videos illustrate a wide range of activities, including voicing support or concern for specific legislation; discussing how legislation may be beneficial or detrimental to constituencies or the American public in general; providing validity or objection to funding initiatives; and discussing other issues that officials believe to be of importance to the American public, such as the role of federal regulations. Elected officials also use videos of floor speeches to demonstrate their support for other politicians, for example, speeches honoring retiring colleagues, to pay tribute to Americans for their contributions to movements, such as civil rights leaders, and to memorialize members of the American armed forces from their states who died during combat.

Elected officials also post videos depicting their roles in Congressional hearings with a relatively high frequency. These videos, which encompass a wide range of topics, such as hearings on specific legislative acts (like health care legislation reform), emerging threats against the U.S. military, and the intricacies online gambling, allow the constituency to both access the inner workings of national politics and to see how elected officials serve them while in office.

NEWS CLIPS

Reposting televised news clips is the second most prominent type of video that appear on elected official's YouTube channels. This is a method of communication utilized by most elected officials and is most heavily utilized by senior elected officials who frequently appear on national news programs. For example, Congressman Mike Rogers, Chairman of the House Intelligence Committee, posts on average one to two videos clips each week of news interviews. In Rogers' position of power within the House, he is likely to have many more opportunities to contribute to news programs than a junior congressperson; therefore, he has many opportunities to illustrate for his constituency the actions he is taking while in office. Sitting politicians take to mainstream media airwaves for a variety of reasons. The most prominent of these reasons are to discuss proposals being talked about on Capitol Hill; explain how bills and legislation will impact Americans both now and in the future; outline specific details of legislative acts; argue for their perspective or the perspectives of their party on issues of national importance; and to discuss American's opinions on certain political issues or situations.

Politicians frequently use videos of news interviews to establish an "us versus them" relationship between the parties, between one party and the president, and between one party (or politician) and the media. The reposting of news clips can serve to illustrate the difficulties that face politicians as they are attempting to accomplish tasks while in office and can positively or negatively illustrate the "winning" and "losing" mentality that typically frames political news stories. If used strategically, the reposting of news clips, especially from reputable news sources, can allow a sitting politician to frame for their constituency the legislative actions they are fighting for or against while in office and can help serve to reinforce the political image they want their constituents to believe in.

IN-OFFICE ACTIVITIES

While floor speeches and news clips are the most prominent types of videos found across elected officials' YouTube channels, many post other types of videos that illustrate the wide range of activities in which political officials engage. Videos of politicians' participation in ceremonies permeate many officials' YouTube channels. For example, Alabama Representative Terri Sewell posted a video of her presenting at the Congressional Gold Medal Ceremony honoring the four young girls who perished in a church bombing in Birmingham, Alabama, in 1963. Videos like this allow the public to see the other responsibilities that elected officials undertake while in office, provide an opportunity for nonpartisan rhetoric to be shared with the public, and allow politicians to managing their personal image.

Elected officials also utilize their YouTube channels to provide responses to the president regarding legislative decisions and to encourage the public to take action. For example, in 2007 John Edwards posted a response to President George W. Bush's desire to extend military occupation in Iraq and urged the American public to tell Congress to use their power to end the war. In another example of this strategy, former Representative Ben Quayle of Arizona took to YouTube following the Supreme Court's decision on the constitutionality of the Affordable Care Act. In his video, Quayle noted that despite the Supreme Court ruling, he believed that the Act was unconstitutional and that President Obama had lied to the American public by enacting a tax via the Affordable Care Act. Quayle used this platform to explain how he was working to combat the "deceptive labeling" of legislation through the introduction of a constitutional amendment that would allow the public to understand the full intent of legislative acts passed by Congress. While the video did not generate a substantial number of views, Quayle utilized the YouTube platform to speak directly to his constituency and relay to them the specific efforts he was undertaking on their behalf.

INFORMATION AS ADVERTISEMENTS

Another interesting information dissemination strategy that has emerged across political YouTube channels is the use of advertising strategies for information distribution and policy discussion. While many politicians use their YouTube channels as a method to redistribute political advertisements from their campaign, some are using the platform to create commercials supporting legislative initiatives. For example, Senator Jerry Moran of Kansas used his YouTube channel to bolster support for *The Startup Act*, which he proposed to bring attention to the role that entrepreneurs and their start-up companies play in the U.S economy. In a series of commercials, the stories of various American entrepreneurs, and their fears, struggles, and accomplishments, were recounted for the viewers and the need to support American innovators was emphasized by Senator Moran. The commercial-like videos provided both precursor and follow-up support for *The Startup Act*, which was further discussed and promoted via a press conference video on his channel. YouTube videos like these tell the constituency about the legislation sitting politicians are promoting while in office and serve to generate support among the public for policy that a majority of the public would likely never know existed without YouTube videos.

TALKING TO THE CONSTITUENCY

Elected officials also use their YouTube channels as a method to "talk" directly to their constituencies in ways that are perhaps not as formal as those mentioned above. Many politicians have embraced their YouTube channels as points of direct communication with their voters. Some have envisioned stand-alone videos and ongoing webcasts that allow them to show their constituents how they are serving them while in office and answer specific questions or concerns their voters may have. In a video titled "21 days and 1,000 miles," Illinois Senator Mark Kirk created a behind-the-scenes look at how his work in Congress impacted the members of his state's constituency. The scenes, which embody all of the qualities of a promotional video, narrate Kirk's travels through the state where he met with corporations to discuss ways to encourage more public/private partnerships, discussed how he was attempting to expand resources for agricultural exportation on the Mississippi River, and how he was working at the federal level to help combat specific issues facing his constituency, such as gang violence in Chicago. Videos like these serve to illustrate for the public the multitude of ways that politicians are consistently working for them. Often constituencies only hear of the work that their elected officials are contributing to on their behalf when it relates to more substantial legislation or when they are speaking for or against federal initiatives. Videos like the one compiled by Kirk help to give an everydayness to the work that politicians accomplish on behalf of their states.

Other politicians have used their YouTube channels to more personally connect with constituents through various types of question-and-answer sessions. Some politicians have posted videos of their participation in interview sessions where they provide information that may be of interest to their constituencies, such as where they were born, their family, what motivated them to get into politics, and their goals while in office. Other officials have implemented systems for directly answering questions from the public in reoccurring weekly or monthly YouTube segments. In a series titled "From the Mailbag," Senator John Boozman of Arkansas provided short video answers to questions submitted to his office via email. In these videos, he addressed his role in pending legislation, the outcomes he anticipated achieving on committees he was assigned to, and his perceptions of the impact that legislative acts would have upon the American public. For example, regarding a question about his role in reconciling the differences between Farm Bills in the House and Senate, Boozman explained that his goal was to recommend an outcome that best served the taxpayers as a whole. He then elaborated that his goals for the legislation were to protect the food industry, control against American dependence on food importation, assure that farmers could utilize the insurance programs they were dependent upon, and ensure that the food stamp program was indeed helping the people who needed help. This level of specificity provided a clear explanation for viewers regarding precisely how the Senator was undertaking his responsibilities in office and his actions may benefit the constituency.

On her YouTube channel, Alaskan Senator Lisa Murkowski hosted a weekly webcast called "Ask Lisa" where she discussed issues of state and national concern with viewers. In questions received via email, Facebook, and Twitter, Murkowski addressed what the passing of certain legislative acts meant for the state of Alaska, explained the manner in which legislation was working its way through the Senate, and discussed issues such as the challenges facing Congress with regard to governmental reform. For example, Murkowski discussed how protocol being supported by the U.S. Fish and Wildlife commission was, in her opinion, in conflict with the state's needs and how she would work with the commission to help them better understand the needs of her constituency. Murkowski also used the "Ask Lisa" platform to elaborate upon ongoing actions she was undertaking to help repeal the Affordable Care Act and to clarify her own position on the need to fix the American health care system.

Repeated video segments, such as the ones implemented by Boozman and Murkowski, have the ability to communicate to the public that their elected officials are indeed concerned with the questions and concerns weighing on their minds. These video initiatives indicate for the constituency that elected officials are working on their behalf and demonstrate politicians' understanding that to substantiate future political support, they must be concerned with direct constituency communication.

THE PERPETUAL CAMPAIGN

Elected political officials engage in a multitude of methods for communicating with their constituencies. They use these methods for the important roles of information dissemination and to clarify, rationalize, and promote the ways in which they are consistently working to promote the welfare of and protect the interests of their voters. But, YouTube channels also serve another important political function, the ability for politicians to consistently campaign and lay necessary groundwork for potential future elections. Through the strategic use of their YouTube channels, politicians can guide future voters through the beneficial ways in which they serve their constituency and use videos to generate support well before the next election cycle is really even on the minds of the voters. For example, if a politician has a particularly strong experience speaking on the floor of the House or Senate or during a Congressional hearing, they can use that video both to demonstrate their prowess as a politician and potentially to promote their position on that topic during a future campaign. YouTube channels provide politicians the ability to frame their political performances for their audience and to provide viewers with a look at how they perform throughout their political tenure and not just during an election. This ability can give incumbent politicians a distinct advantage during political campaigns and also provide them with video footage that can easily be turned into persuasive political advertisements.

However, the public nature of YouTube channels also means that opponents, news media, and other third-party organizations also have access to these videos and can use them to spin politicians' own words and behaviors against them during future campaigns. The permanence of YouTube videos also means that it is difficult for political officials to "erase" potentially negative content which could also be used against them in future elections. Nevertheless, YouTube channels offer politicians a platform through which to consistently reach and engage current and potential supporters. If correctly utilized, these channels give politicians a direct link through which to communicate with their constituency and prime voters for future support.

CONCLUSIONS AND CHALLENGES

Although traditional media sources, such as television and the radio, often reach far more people than even highly trafficked websites, there is evidence that Internet-based politics can provide the public with two key components necessary in a functional democracy: access to unlimited political information and forums to promote deliberative interactions.[34] While some users are likely involved in online politics for social interaction,[35] there is evidence that individuals use the Internet instrumentally in the accessing of political information.[36] Online political opportunities allow ordinary citizens to create and distribute their own political content and to comment on the content created and disseminated by others.[37] Social media networks allow for rapid dissemination of innovative information[38] and can equate to a more highly informed, politically active, and influential public.[39]

YouTube plays an active and ongoing role in facilitating communication between elected officials and the constituency. Politicians are using the platform to disseminate political information, debate upon topics of public importance, answer questions from their voters, and overall engage with the populous through methods not afforded by traditional media. The public can now access high levels of specific political information that has not been filtered through the gatekeepers of mainstream media.[40] Political officials can use YouTube to improve the flow of information between themselves and their constituencies, speed up the dissemination of information, and control their political and personal images through the videos they elect to post to their YouTube channels. They can also benefit from YouTube metrics that allow them to easily assess how effectively their videos are resonating with the public.

While cyber-advocates laud the role that platforms such as YouTube now play in national political discourse, cyber-skeptics caution against the assumptions of an electronic revolution in the making. Some research has found no measurable relationship between increased access to political communication and the populous' democratic engagement.[41] Additional research reminds us that in the succession of communication technologies, including radio and television, new technologies have produced no breakthroughs in public participation nor substantial upsets in communicative power structures.[42] In order to substantiate any measurable level of change, politicians must focus on engaging constituents through methods that are most likely to evoke the public's response. Substantive interaction between politicians and voters would ideally lead to a citizenry that is more informed regarding political opinions and choices.[43] However, critics postulate that in general, it is likely that constituents respond most effectively to simple communication cues that allow them to understand candidates with minimal interpretive efforts. Therefore, to most effectively communicate with their constituencies, politicians should leverage their YouTube channels in a manner that falls between the ideals of substantive and participatory public engagement.

There is not a great deal of research regarding how politicians engage with the public on a day-to-day basis. Most research investigating political communication tends to assess communicative practices during campaigns. Future research could focus on in-depth content analyses regarding the types and reception of the information posted to the YouTube channels of elected officials. Other research could initiate audience assessment and attitude studies, perhaps investigating whether or not the public feels that this type of communicative outreach on behalf of politicians is effective, or even desired. Research could also further examine audience motivations for viewing this type of content on YouTube and perhaps linking it with political effects research.

Assessing the long-term impact and viability of YouTube as a mechanism for structural changes in the ways that elected officials communicate with constituencies will be challenging and will take time. Because YouTube is still in a stage of relative inception as a structure of in-office political communication, it may be difficult to measure and assert all of the ways in which the platform has changed and will change the distribution of political information. However, private sector research suggests that customers achieve a high level of satisfaction when they can easily connect to the products and services they desire access to. The same frame of thought can aptly be applied to the acquisition of political information. When given the ability to communicate and interact with political information in manners afforded through media like political YouTube channels, perhaps the constituency will feel a higher level of satisfaction with the political "products" whom they have elected to represent them. The public's current level of interaction with politicians and political information via YouTube channels is indicative that, at the very least, some communication patterns are being altered by YouTube's political innovations. As online political communication continues to evolve it will be interesting to see the ways that elected officials use YouTube in the future to better enhance their outreach and communication with their constituencies.

NOTES

1. Thomas Hollihan, *Uncivil Wars: Political Campaigns in a Media Age* (Boston, MA: Bedford/St. Martins, 2009).

2. John Tedesco, "Changing the Channel: Use of the Internet for Communicating about Politics," in *Handbook of Political Communication Research* (Mahwah, NJ: Lawrence Erlbaum Associates, 2004), 507–32.

3. Amy McKay and David Paletz, "The Presidency and the Media," in *Handbook of Political Communication Research* (Mahwah, NJ: Lawrence Erlbaum Associates, 2004), 315–35.

4. Barbara Kaye and Thomas Johnson, "Online and in the Know: Uses and Gratifications of the Web for Political Information," *Journal of Broadcasting and Electronic Media* 46, no. 1 (2002): 54–71.

5. Douglas Ferguson and Elizabeth Perse, "The World Wide Web as a Functional Alternative to Television," *Journal of Broadcasting & Electronic Media* 44 (2000): 155–74.

6. Elizabeth Perse and John Courtright, "Normative Images of Communication Media: Mass and Interpersonal Channels in the New Media Environment," *Human Communication Research* 19, no. 4 (1993): 485–503.

7. Alan Rubin, "Ritualized and Instrumental Television Viewing," *Journal of Communication* 34, no. 3 (n.d.): 66–77.

8. Jack McLeod and Lee Becker, "The Uses and Gratifications Approach," in *Handbook of Political Communication* (Beverly Hills, CA: S, 1981).

9. Bruce Bimber, "The Internet and Political Transformation: Populism, Community, and Accelerated Pluralism," *Policy* 31, no. 1 (1998): 133–60.

10. Kaye and Johnson, "Online and in the Know: Uses and Gratifications of the Web for Political Information."

11. Ibid.

12. Bruce Pinkleton and Erica Austin, "Media and Participation: Breaking the Spiral of Disffection," in *Engaging the Public: How Government and the Media Can Reinvigorate American Democracy* (Lanham, MD: Rowman & Littlefield, 1998).

13. Gary Hanson et al., "The 2008 Presidential Campaign: Political Cynicism in the Age of Facebook, MySpace, and YouTube," *Mass Communication & Society* 13, no. 5 (2010): 584–607.

14. Johnathan Mermin, *Debating War and Peace: Media Coverage of the U.S. Intervention in the Post-Vietnam Era* (Princeton, NJ: Princeton University Press, 1999).

15. W. Lance Bennett, *News and the Politics of Illusion* (New York, NY: Longman, 1983).

16. Dietram Scheufele, "Agenda-Setting, Priming, and Framing Revisited: Another Look at Cognitive Effects of Political Communication," *Mass Communication and Society* 3, no. 2–3 (2000): 297–316.

17. Dhavan Shah, Nojin Kwak, and R. Lance Holbert, "'Connecting' and 'Disconnecting' with Civic Life: Patterns of Internet Use and the Production of Social Capital," *Political Communication* 18 (2001): 141–62.

18. Adam Armbruster, "Local Stations Should Be Socializing; Networking Sites Can Help Viewers Connect to Community, Broadcasters," *TV Week*, April 28, 2008, http://www.tvweek.com/news/2008/04/local_stations_should_be_socia.php.

19. Lynn Spigel, "My TV Studies ...now Playing on a YouTube Site near You," *Television & New Media* 10, no. 1 (2009): 149–53.

20. Kaye and Johnson, "Online and in the Know: Uses and Gratifications of the Web for Political Information."

21. Paul Ferber, Franz Foltz, and Rudy Pugliese, "Cyberdemocracy and Online Politics: A New Model of Interactivity," *Bulletin of Science, Technology, & Society* 27, no. 5 (2007): 391–400.

22. Kaye and Johnson, "Online and in the Know: Uses and Gratifications of the Web for Political Information."

23. Ibid.

24. James Fishkin, *Democracy and Deliberation: New Directions for Democratic Reform* (New Haven, CT: Yale University Press, 1991).

25. John Gastil, "Identifying Obstacles to Small Group Democracy," *Small Group Research* 24 (1993): 5–27.

26. Lance Whitney, "Google+ Now Connects with YouTube, Chrome," *CNET*, November 4, 2011, http://news.cnet.com/8301-1023_3-57318595-93/google-now-connects-with-youtube-chrome/?part=rss&subj=news&tag=2547-1_3-0-20.

27. BBC, "YouTube's Website Redesign Puts the Focus on Channels," *BBC*, December 2, 2011, http://www.bbc.co.uk/news/technology-16006524.

28. YouTube, "YouTube Town Hall by the Numbers: It's the Economy, Stupid," *YouTube Official Blog*, August 16, 2011, http://youtube-global.blogspot.com/2011/08/youtube-town-hall-by-numbers-its.html.

29. Ibid.

30. Ibid.

31. Kaye and Johnson, "Online and in the Know: Uses and Gratifications of the Web for Political Information."

32. Ibid.

33. Hollihan, *Uncivil Wars: Political Campaigns in a Media Age*.

34. Ferber, Foltz, and Pugliese, "Cyberdemocracy and Online Politics: A New Model of Interactivity."

35. Monica Ancu and Raluca Cozma, "MySpace Politics: Uses and Gratifications of Befriending Candidates," *Journal of Broadcasting and Electronic Media* 53, no. 4 (2009): 567–83.

36. Hanson et al., "The 2008 Presidential Campaign: Political Cynicism in the Age of Facebook, MySpace, and YouTube."

37. Ibid.

38. Rachel Gibson and Ian McAllister, "Do Online Election Campaigns Win Vote? The 2007 Australian 'YouTube' Election," *Political Communication* 28, no. 2 (2011): 227–44.

39. Howard Kurtz, "Webs of Political Intrigue: Candidates, Media Looking for Internet Constituents," *The Washington Post*, November 13, 1995, sec. B1.

40. Kaye and Johnson, "Online and in the Know: Uses and Gratifications of the Web for Political Information."

41. Bimber, "The Internet and Political Transformation: Populism, Community, and Accelerated Pluralism."

42. Richard Davis, *The Web of Politics* (New York, NY: Oxford University Press, 1999).

43. Bruce Ackerman and James Fishkin, *Deliberation Day* (New Haven, CT: Yale University Press, 2004).

SIX

The White House Channel: A Case Study in YouTube Communication

The White House YouTube Channel (WHYTC) was launched January 20, 2009, the day of President Barack Obama's first inauguration. Since its launch, the WHYTC has functioned to more directly connect the Obama administration to the constituency and has furthered the administration's initiative to increase governmental transparency. The WHYTC serves as an extension of the White House website and, just as politicians' websites provide a primary gateway to them and their policies,[1] the WHYTC is the video-based postern to the Obama administration. This chapter provides an examination of the ways that the WHYTC has been used by the Obama administration to increase governmental transparency and expand communication opportunities with the constituency, and the ways in which the channel serves a public relations function for the White House.

THE WHITE HOUSE YOUTUBE CHANNEL

The WHYTC serves a few primary functions: to engage those coming to the White House website looking for information about the administration, to preserve the presidency for posterity, to depict governmental events as they actually occur, to provide behind-the-scenes moments that help the president connect with the constituency, and to entice people who would not normally visit the White House's website to do so.[2] The WHYTC was meant to transform the social media organization strategies that helped to get Obama elected into an instrument of government.[3] In 2012, the WHYTC was the seventh most trafficked news organization channel on YouTube.[4]

A vast number of videos, covering an equally vast array of topics, have been uploaded to the WHYTC. As of April 2014, the WHYTC had posted over 5,000 videos, amassed over 411,000 subscribers, and generated over 163 million video views. On average, the WHYTC uploads three new videos each day covering a wide range of topics. Strategically, because users will easily abandon websites that are infrequently updated,[5] continually posting new videos to the channel helps entice users to return to the channel often. Visitors to the site are offered easy access to the WHYTC's recent activity, featured videos, and suggested videos related to their previous viewing habits. The WHYTC is set up for easy navigation, allowing users to quickly access videos conveniently sorted into topics such as the president's weekly addresses, the daily White House press briefings, West Wing Week, and White House selects. Site visitors can also engage with content via playlists, which are sets of videos organized by the channel categorizing videos the user is likely to want to watch and which can optimize a user's experience. As users tend to engage most highly with websites that present information in a manner that is consistent with their preferences[6] and enjoy the interactivity and personalization that can occur through website attributes,[7] such as the playlists, the White House has positioned the WHYTC as a central and accessible component in its overall communication strategy.

The most viewed videos on the WHYTC are a mixture of political addresses and those with more blithe content. The two most viewed videos on the channel are President Obama's statement after the Sandy Hook Elementary shooting in Newtown, Connecticut, in December 2012, which generated over 7.7 million views; his statement on the death of Osama bin Laden in May of 2011, which amassed 6.5 million views; and Obama's 2012 State of the Union address, which generated 2.7 million views. On the lighter side, the White House's April fools' video, "Kid President," generated 3.7 million views, a video of the Obama's dog Bo inspecting the White House Christmas decorations garnered over 2.2 million views, and a video of Michelle Obama reading "'Twas the Night Before Christmas" to a group of children amassed more than 2.1 million views.

There is little argument that the White House provides the public with a great deal of information through the videos it posts to the WHYTC. However, because the White House hosting its own YouTube channel is a novel form of political communication, and because the technologies that a politician, or in this case an administration, elects to use as a means of constituency engagement can have long-reaching implications,[8] it is important, and interesting, to examine the types of videos that the White House posts to the channel as a means of constituency-based communication.

INCREASED GOVERNMENTAL TRANSPARENCY

Soon after his election, President Obama promoted the administration's commitment to creating an unprecedented level of governmental transparency. Having successfully leveraged online communicative tools during the 2008 presidential election, the Obama White House understood the Internet as a global platform for communication.[9] The administration elected to harness the power of YouTube to increase public knowledge of governmental activities, support breakthroughs in important national priorities, and substantially increase governmental transparency. The White House's initiative for transparency and open government centered on the belief that openness of communication and information would strengthen democracy, promote governmental efficiency, and encourage transparent, participatory, and collaborative government-public interactions.[10] To boost the transparency of the executive branch, Obama announced his plan to post a weekly video on the WHYTC informing the public of the government's actions and to distribute his weekly presidential address through the WHYTC in an effort to reach a broader public base.[11]

To spread this transparency initiative across governmental platforms, the administration issued directives to governmental agencies instructing them to make data and information more accessible to more the public.[12] The executive branch encouraged agencies to provide information in universally accessible formats and to seek out ways to use new media technologies to make information about governmental decisions and operations more readily available to the public. Furthering its belief that communication between the constituency and elected officials would provide for a more open and translucent national conversation, the administration encouraged executive departments and agencies to actively solicit public feedback and offer increased opportunities for public engagement in policy making.[13] The directive also encouraged agencies to actively leverage innovative tools and methods to better communicate across governmental agencies and with individuals in both the private and public sectors.[14] This initiative for transparency and open government was designed to promote accountability, collaboration, and public trust through establishing a system of more lucid communication between the government and the public. In partial fulfillment of its promise to increase transparency, the White House produced webisode (a succession of videos distributed solely online) series released through the WHYTC. These series, called the White House White Board and West Wing Week, provided specific information regarding policy initiatives and chronicled the weekly goings on of the White House.

WHITE HOUSE WHITE BOARD

The *White House White Board* (WHWB) webisodes provided elementarily explanations of policy and reform initiatives to the American public. The short videos, usually under ten minutes long, featured senior White House staff, such as the Chairman of the Council of Economic Advisors, the Deputy Director of the National Economic Council, the Director of the Office of Health Reform, and the U.S. Chief Information Officer, standing literally in front of a white board on which they explained the details of important national policy achievements and initiatives for the viewers. WHWB topics included explanations of specific policy initiatives, such as the *Startup America Program* and the *National Wireless Initiative*, and discussions of why certain initiatives, such as The Buffet Rule, were necessary. Other WHWB talks explained the president's decisions on certain issues, such as tax cuts and unemployment insurance, and detailed explanations of the president's budgets allocations.

As a primary objective of the White House is to influence public opinion,[15] the WHWBs also allowed the administration to emphasize the president's commitments and priorities and explain how the selected topics and initiatives directly impacted the American public. In the webisodes, senior administration staff spoke to the audience much like an instructor would speak to a class; they used language that was inclusive and simple, while explaining how the public would benefit from the choices that the President made on their behalf. In September 2013, the WHWB titled "What ObamaCare Means for You" was created in a specific effort to explain the Affordable Healthcare Act to young demographics. The White Board explained specifically to this demographic how they would benefit from the policy initiative and worked to dispel many of the myths regarding the legislation the viewers may have encountered.[16]

On average, WHWBs generate over 32,000 views per webisode, with the videos that most directly impact the American public, such as the Taxpayer Relief Act of 2012, payroll tax cuts, mortgage refinancing, and workforce stimulation efforts bringing in the largest number of viewers. Additionally, most WHWBs generated hundreds of comments which illustrated that the WHWBs provided both a unique opportunity for two-way communication between the administration and the public and for deliberative political discussion between viewers regarding salient political topics. For example, in the comment thread for the WHWB discussing a tax cut initiative, two users discussed the topic as follows:

> User 1: By providing companies, especially small businesses, added incentives to invest in growth opportunities is important in new job creation. This growth could greatly help this economy.
> User 2: The fact of the matter is that tax cuts do not automatically create jobs. The extra money generated by tax cuts must be spent purchasing

products or services by the recipients of those cuts in order for jobs to be created.

The WHWBs illustrated an innovative way for the Obama administration to explain initiatives and promote policy directly to the American public. The WHWBs also provided deliberative spaces where the public could discuss their opinions about the topics in the presentations.

In using this space to help the audience understand the specific impact that initiatives and legislation potentially had on their lives, the WHWBs provided an example of a dynamic, nonpartisan communication methodology that better facilitated direct communication between the administration and the nation. [17]

WEST WING WEEK

Created in 2010, the *West Wing Week,* originally conceptualized by Arun Chaudhary, Obama's New Media Road Director during the 2008 presidential campaign, and the White House's first official videographer, served an important role in Obama's commitment to governmental transparency. The short weekly videos provided a timeline of important occurrences and happenings around the White House and captured the president's official speeches and travel, as well as his political life behind the scenes. The videos aimed to present the public with a window into the presidency. [18] In an interview with the *BBC,* Chaudhary explained that his role in filming the *West Wing Week* was to document what the president does with an eye toward history. He noted that much like the White House photographer, his job was to provide the public with a level of transparency into the presidency and show the public the more regular experiences of the president. [19]

West Wing Week episodes ranged in viewership from 5,000 to 40,000 views per episode and covered a wide range of topics and themes. Part of the goal to increase the transparency of the office through the *West Wing Week* was to give the public access to events and occurrences they would not likely be able to easily access through other forms of media. These topics included the announcement and signing of treaties, acts, and other legislation; official trips abroad to meet with worldwide political leaders and American troops serving overseas; visiting different U.S. cities and states to discuss innovations and advancements that could be furthered with proper legislative initiatives; celebrating holidays; official presidential and vice-presidential addresses; and light-hearted behind-the-scenes moments, including one of the president joking with other elected officials and a clip of him mumbling to himself "I'm an old man" while filling out his census form.

While *West Wing Week* was positioned as an inventive way to digitally connect the American public with the administration, it faced criticism for propagandizing the administration. It was also criticized for being used inappropriately during the 2012 election to forward the mission of Obama's reelection campaign versus his presidential responsibilities.[20] The installments were also criticized regarding the costs associated with employing a full-time videographer and of producing weekly webisodes that critics argued were nothing more than press releases that did not provide much value to the citizens.[21] However, proponents countered that a videographer was a natural progression for a president who had created a digital tether to constituents during his election and that members of the White House press corps were resentful of Chaudhary's access to the administration.[22]

Through posting reoccurring web series, the WHYTC helped to further the Obama administration's push towards a more transparent federal government. The WHYTC effectively used innovative methods to consistently communicate the president's positions and agendas, maximize positive political content in a widely accessible manner, and help the public better understand both the presidency and the government as institutions.

EXPANDING COMMUNICATION WITH THE CONSTITUENCY

President Obama was not the first president to expand the means through which an administration communicated with the public. Franklin D. Roosevelt did so with the introduction of his famous and highly replicated Fireside Chats and George W. Bush did so through turning his weekly radio addresses into podcasts and archiving the sound files on the White House website.[23] Taking these previous successes and parlaying them with his own communicative achievements from the 2008 presidential campaign, Obama was able to harness the massive Internet-based political machine that had been built during the election and turn this audience and knowledge into an innovative method for communicating with the constituency. The Obama administration capitalized on its knowledge of how to quickly spread information to a vast audience and leveraged its online marketing and social media savviness to create the WHYTC. Through a series of weekly addresses and innovative communicative experiences, the administration devised methods for more efficiently and effectively communicating with and engaging the American public in political discourse.

WEEKLY WHITE HOUSE ADDRESS

One of the most prominent examples of using new media strategies to engage directly with the American public was the release of Obama's weekly address via video on the WHYTC and the White House website.

Historically, the president's weekly addresses had been recorded for and released to radio stations on Saturday mornings. However, understanding the importance of YouTube as a viable conduit for connecting with and keeping citizens informed, Obama elected to supplant radio addresses with YouTube videos as the default method for his weekly communication with the constituency.[24] While the addresses were still released via radio and television, they were primarily engineered to be viewed via online platforms.

Obama's first weekly YouTube address was as president-elect (briefly discussed in chapter 2). The video, during which he spoke about the economy, increased unemployment claims, and the responsibility of Congress to alleviate the economic strife of the American public, generated over one million views and thousands of comments both supporting and criticizing the newly elected president. Although not yet officially in office, Obama delivered a weekly YouTube address each week between the election and the inauguration. Obama's first weekly address as president, a five minute video in which he explained his goals for an 825 billion dollar economic plan, generated over 600,000 views and thousands of comments within twenty-four hours of being released via the WHYTC; as of April 2014, the video had been viewed over 1.2 million times. The public's reception of this new method for weekly White House communication was met with support and criticism via the video's comment thread. One user noted, "These White House vlogs [video blogs] are another milestone of the digital age. Obama is just too cool" and a self-identified Dutch user noting, "I wish our government would be this clear."[25] However, not every user felt that recording YouTube videos was the best use of the president-elect's time, commenting that, "He [Obama] has more important things to do than shoot ten takes of a weekly address."[26]

While these two addresses generated a high number of views, most likely related to their novelty and timeliness, the weekly presidential addresses averaged around 35,000 views with each generating a few hundred comments. In utilizing the multimedia opportunities offered by the WHYTC, the administration was able to reach a broader audience with the president's weekly address than it would have simply traditional radio addresses. Individuals no longer need to be in a certain place, at a certain time, engaging in a certain media to hear the president's weekly remarks, but rather were able to watch the weekly address via the WHYTC at an individualized time and place.

President Obama also used the WHYTC and the weekly presidential address in a manner not traditionally employed by other presidents. On April 13, 2013, Francine Wheeler, whose son had been killed alongside nineteen other children and six educators during the Sandy Hook Elementary school shooting delivered the nation's weekly address. Wheeler was the first person other than President Obama or Vice President Joe

Biden to give the weekly address since the administration took office in 2009. [27] In the video, Wheeler sits alongside her husband, David, in the White House Library, and states, "As you've probably noticed, I'm not the president. I'm just a citizen. And as a citizen, I am here at the White House today because I want to make a difference and I hope you will join me." Asked by Obama to deliver the weekly address, Wheeler tells of her family's personal story of loss and shares anecdotes about her slain six-year old. Wheeler implores the American public to take action with regard to gun control before the tragedy her family faced potentially impacts viewers' families by stating, "And in the four months since we lost our loved ones, thousands of other Americans have died at the end of a gun. Thousands of other families across the United States are also drowning in our grief. Please help us do something before our tragedy becomes your tragedy."

The video, which generated over 200,000 views and thousands of comments on the WHYTC (it was also posted to various other YouTube and mainstream media sites where it generated additional viewership), was delivered while a Democratic gun control bill backed by Obama was working its way thought the Senate and the House. The video, which urged viewers to call upon their representatives or join the president in working toward tighter gun control solutions, provided an interesting example of how the Obama administration used the WHYTC to influence the public, encourage specific political action, and put a human face on specific legislation supported by the president. By having the Wheelers conduct the weekly address in lieu of the president, or another elected official, Obama was able to leverage video viralability to connect the face of human tragedy with a highly politicized topic and generate a response that may not have been possible had he himself delivered a similar address and plea for action.

FIRESIDE HANGOUTS

In January 2012, President Obama hosted his first post-State of the Union *Fireside Hangout*. The *Hangout* was conducted via Google+ Hangout, a live video platform that allows up to 10 people to participate in a single conversation that can be live-streamed to the world, and streamed on the WHYTC. The hangouts were loosely based on the concept of the aforementioned Fireside Chats, even taking place in front of a fireplace in the White House, and expanded on the president's pledge for more transparency in government and his commitment to increasing communication with the American public. Following previous State of the Union addresses, Obama had engaged in post-address follow-up sessions with constituents via Facebook, Twitter, LinkedIn and YouTube during which he would answer questions that had been submitted via the online platforms. The *Hangouts,* however, were markedly different in that Obama literally "hung out," in real time, with a selected group of constituents via the Google+ platform. Since the inception of the *Hangouts* in 2012, President Obama has hosted a hangout following each subsequent State of the Union address.

To identify topics of salience for the hangouts, the public was invited to submit questions to the WHYTC that they would like to ask the president following the State of the Union. For the 2012 *Hangout,* a total of 227,000 YouTube users either submitted video questions or voted on which questions the president should answer. The best of those questions, as determined by Google, were asked during a live hangout. The event was moderated by Steve Grove, head of Community Partnerships at Google+ and YouTube's head of News and Politics, who managed the videos and flow of communication between the two men, two women, and group of students from John F. Kennedy High School in Fremont, California who were invited to participate. During the forty-nine-minute hangout, Obama answered questions about promoting a living wage for college students, American job stability, the Stop Internet Piracy Act, and the economy. The president was asked pointedly about what he would tell young people afraid to go to college because of rising student debt and a difficult job market. He was also forced to address the state of job creation and the economy with a woman who had been unemployed for five years and a mother worried about how to talk to her children about difficult times, respectively.[28] Following a question from Jennifer Wedel of Fort Worth, Texas, regarding the expansion of H1B visas for foreign workers, the president asked her to send him her husband's resume so he could look into why he had been unemployed for three years despite his background as a semiconductor engineer.[29] There were also some light-hearted moments, such as the president declining to dance because, he claimed, First Lady Michelle Obama would make fun of his moves, and a participant asking if she could introduce her children who were just off camera, which President Obama obliged.

For the 2013 *Hangout,* over 16,500 users submitted over 7,500 questions and cast over 97,000 votes for which questions the president should answer. Following the submission of questions, Google once again invited selected individuals to participate in the live hangout session. The hangout, once again moderated by Grove, featured three women and two men from a variety of backgrounds asking the president questions on topics including reducing gun violence, raising the minimum wage, limiting software patent abuses, and immigration reform. Obama was also called upon to defend his assertion that his was the most transparent presidency and to rationalize the administration's use of unmanned drone strikes.[30] Akin to the 2012 *Hangout,* the president also answered some more lighthearted questions, such as which book he would recommend the public read to better understand his political philosophy and which baby name he preferred for a participant's soon-to-arrive child.

The 2014 *Hangout* was a bit different with Obama hosting a "Presidential Hangout Road Trip." Users were asked to post a sixty-second video about themselves and the question they would like to ask the president to YouTube or Google+ and share it publically by using the hashtag #AskObama2014. During his "road-trip," Obama joined different hangouts, speaking to nine constituents, situated geographically across America to talk to people about salient issues facing the country.[31] *Hangout* participants asked the president about the minimum wage, net neutrality, protests in Ukraine, and immigration reform. However, unlike the previous two hangouts where participants asked the president some tough questions, the questions in the 2014 *Hangout* centered closely on Obama's policy agenda and did not stray into controversial topics.[32]

During the *Hangouts*, attendees were allowed to ask the president follow-up questions which lead to many substantive exchanges as questioners pushed Obama on his stances. These events featured legitimate interaction, including back-and-forth communication, between the citizens and the president with the citizens often asking tough questions and freely disagreeing with the president after some of his answers. Additionally, the hangouts featured moments where the American constituency was able to connect with the president not as Commander-in-Chief, but as a person. Remarking on the importance of the *Fireside Hangouts*, President Obama stated, "I don't know if any of this stuff affects an election, but I know that it makes our country stronger that you can make fun of the president—or anybody—and everybody can get a laugh. And that also makes sure to remind me that I work for you guys."[33]

Two other elements that increased communication between the White House and the constituency were active comment functionalities and the fact that all videos on the channel were dedicated to the public domain. While the comment function is a common feature across a vast majority of YouTube, it is deactivated on many politicians' official YouTube channels; thus, preventing the public from communicating with each other and with the politician. The public widely utilized the comment functionalities on the WHYTC to both show support for and criticism of the Obama administration and its policies. For example, one user commented on a video of Obama discussing the need for immigration reform "He listens and studies. If you disagree with him go to his website and tell him what you disagree with and why. That is what it (the website) is there for. He wants to hear all sides." Others used the comment threads to express disapproval of President Obama or the administration's policies. For example, in a video discussing tax reform, one user noted, "Obama has outsourced American jobs by borrowing trillions of dollars from China then flushing that money down the toilet, buying votes, and paying-off corrupt unions, wealthy crony socialist friends! Obama has given "stimulus" money to foreign countries like Indonesia (FACT). The so called 1 percent pays 38 percent of all income taxes while 47 percent pay absolutely no income taxes at all!" WHYTC participants also used the comment thread to show admiration for the first family. One user, commenting on a video of the Obamas surprising members of the public on a White House tour stated, "Michelle and Barrack Obama have delivered a standard for the presidency that will be hard to follow."

These events and communicative uses of the WHYTC are highly politically important. They worked to cultivate a sense of community and engagement between the public and the government and to stimulate online communication. They also amplified the interactivity of the Internet by infusing new ideas and technologies into political communication.[34] The use of the WHYTC for communication and constituent relationship building has helped to change the culture and future expectations of presidential communication.[35]

WHYTC AS PUBLIC RELATIONS

In addition to expanding transparency and communication, the WHYTC also served a public relations function for the White House. Through a series of webisodes and stand-alone videos, the WHYTC provided the public with behind-the-scenes looks at life inside the White House and the presidency.

The series titled *Inside the White House* opened the White House to the public by providing insight into the activities that take place in and around the White House. Videos in this series included a tour of the kitchen garden by Michelle Obama and the White House chef, a video about the Marine Sentries who stand guard outside of the West Wing, and exclusive discussions about the Presidential Cabinet and the Situation Room. This series also included behind-the-scenes footage and interviews from the making of the president's State of the Union Addresses, where the President's former Senior advisor and Director of Speechwriting, Jon Favreau, give the public an inside look into the process of preparing the Obama's most important speech of the year.

The two most viewed videos of this series are of the president reading letters from the public in order to stay in touch with the issues and concerns facing the constituency and of the president brewing his own homemade beer. *Inside the White House* also features a subseries of videos called *Catching Up with the Curator,* in which the official White House Curator, William Allman, discussed the White House fire of 1814, showed the audience places where the presidential seal can be found, explained the presidential portrait of Theodore Roosevelt in the White House's East Room, and talked about the Steinway Piano that has become one of the White House's most recognized artifacts. *Inside the White*

House videos averaged over 204,000 videos per webisode, generated hundreds of comments and questions from the audience, and aided in the goal of the WHYTC of better connecting the constituency with the presidency.

Other videos, cataloged in the *Behind the Scenes* series, illustrated what days were like for the president, with videos of Obama participating in an online Twitter question-and-answer session with the public, the president in his office following his second inauguration, and videos of Obama's advance team working to keep the day moving and on schedule. These videos also showed some of the fun the president has while serving his official duties, for example, one video in this series shows Obama playing basketball with members of Team USA.

Other videos, housed under the moniker *Raw Footage*, show the president shaking hands with constituents at an Iowa bookstore, surprising residents when he stops by local diners for surprise lunches while traveling, and a video titled "President Obama and the Hovercraft," where the president convinced a *New York Times* reporter to demonstrate a small hovercraft at a manufacturing company in Buffalo, New York. Other videos included the Obamas packing backpacks for the children of servicemen and women, the president playing basketball with wounded warriors from Walter Reed Army Medical Center, and Obama's surprise visits to troops serving abroad and on domestic army bases.

One of the most popular nonpolitical videos on the WHYTC is President Obama's contribution to the *It Gets Better* campaign, a movement targeted to inspire hope for young people facing harassment. In Obama's video, which generated nearly 1.5 million views and over 10,000 comments, he recounted his sadness over the recent deaths of young people who took their lives because of being bullied. He noted the importance of dispelling the myth that bullying is normal and affirmed an obligation to make sure schools are safe and young people have access to caring adults that can help. He emphasized the foundational American belief that everyone is created equal, and that we can make the most of our talents not by fitting in, but by being true to ourselves.

These videos, many of which generated hundreds of thousands of views, served the dual purpose of humanizing the administration for the public and also elevating the transparency of the government. At no point in history has the public been granted so much access into the life of a president and into the inner workings of a presidential administration.

CONCLUSIONS AND CHALLENGES

The WHYTC functioned as a platform for national political communication and was an instrumental mechanism in President Obama's attempts at creating a more transparent executive branch and elevating communication with the constituency. The channel established new and evolving methods for communication between the White House and the public and provided the administration a novel way to more effectively and efficiently connect with the constituency. Through consistently generating and uploading new and informative videos, the WHYTC made a greater amount of political information easily accessible to the public and helped to explain potentially complicated topics and initiatives to the polity. It has altered the ways that the federal government communicated with and disseminated information to the constituency and helped to effectively move the White House beyond the "electronic brochure" format of websites by incorporating interactive features and two-way communication opportunities.[36] The Obama administration effectively utilized the WHYTC as a vehicle to create open dialogue with the public. The WHYTC established a new political ecology for the digital age[37] and demonstrated the multitude of possibilities that YouTube offers for communicating with the public.

The White House's use of YouTube and the WHYTC to communicate and engage with constituents, however, has not been without criticism. Opponents have argued that the use of the WHYTC was a way for the administration to control the flow of information and was an attempt by the executive branch to manipulate the national political conversation. For example, in the 2012 *Fireside Hangout*, the question that received the most votes from the public related to the legalization of marijuana. Although the president had previously stated that his stance on that topic was clear and he would not address it during the *Hangout*, critics felt the omission of the question seemingly violated the vote-generated nature of the format and equated to agenda setting by the White House. Additional criticisms suggested that by releasing its own photos of events, video interviews, and saving information from a week's events specifically for *West Wing Week*, the White House upset the balance and role that mainstream media outlets played in the creation of national political discussion. By employing a full-time videographer, who had unprecedented access to both the president and political events, and using new media to change the reliance on old media, the White House was accused of using a federal employee to shoot, edit, and distribute political propaganda.[38] For example, during the 2012 election, the White House videographer released a video in which Obama warned that top-down economics would hurt the American middle class on the same day that Obama spoke at a rally warning about potential GOP nominee Mitt Romney's top-down economic approach.[39]

Despite these criticisms, it is clear that the Obama administration has used the WHYTC to increase, at the very least, the perception of transparency in the executive branch and used the channel as a means through which to consistently communicate with and engage the constituency. The WHYTC capitalized on the structure of YouTube and embraced its ability to provide person-to-person connectivity and asynchronous inter-activity. As different politicians assume the helm at the White House in the future, it will be exciting to see if they follow in the Obama administration's footsteps with regard to the distribution of information through the WHYTC or revert back to more traditional and closed systems of information dissemination.

NOTES

1. James Druckman, Martin Kifer, and Michael Parkin, "The Technological Development of Candidate Websites: How and Why Candidates Use Web Innovations," in *Politicking Online: The Transformation of Election Campaign Communication* (New Brunswick, NJ: Rutgers University Press, 2009), 21–47.

2. Ashley Parker, "His Job Is to Make Public Obama's Candid Side," *The New York Times*, November 11, 2010, sec. U.S., www.nytimes.com/2010/11/12/us/12video.html?_r=0.

3. Jim Rutenberg and Adam Nagourney, "Melding Obama's Web to a YouTube Presidency," *The New York Times*, January 26, 2009, http://www.nytimes.com/2009/01/26/us/politics/26grassroots.html.

4. Journalism Project Staff, *YouTube Video Creation - A Shared Process* (Washington, DC: Pew Research Center, July 16, 2012), http://www.journalism.org/2012/07/16/youtube-video-creationa-shared-process/.

5. Bruce Bimber and Richard Davis, *Campaigning Online: The Internet in U.S. Elections* (New York, NY: Oxford University Press, 2003).

6. Arthur Lupia and Tasha Philpot, "Views from inside the Net: How Websites Affect Young Adult's Political Interest," *The Journal of Politics* 67, no. 4 (2005): 1122–42.

7. Druckman, Kifer, and Parkin, "The Technological Development of Candidate Websites: How and Why Candidates Use Web Innovations."

8. Lupia and Philpot, "Views from inside the Net: How Websites Affect Young Adult's Political Interest."

9. John Hendricks and Lynda Lee Kaid, *Communicator-in-Chief: How Barack Obama Used New Media Technology to Win the White House* (Lanham, MD: Lexington Books, 2010).

10. The White House, "Transparency and Open Government," n.d., http://www.whitehouse.gov/the_press_office/TransparencyandOpenGovernment.

11. The Telegraph, "President Barack Obama's Weekly Address Posted on White House YouTube Channel," *The Telegraph*, January 25, 2009, World edition, http://www.telegraph.co.uk/news/worldnews/barackobama/4338308/President-Barack-Obamas-weekly-address-posted-on-White-House-YouTube-channel.html.

12. Jennifer LaFleur, "White House Gives Agencies Transparency To-Do List," *Pro Publica Inc.*, December 8, 2009, www.propublica.org/article/white-house-gives-agencies-transparency-to-do-list-1208.

13. The White House, "Transparency and Open Government."

14. Ibid.

15. Amy McKay and David Paletz, "The Presidency and the Media," in *Handbook of Political Communication Research* (Mahwah, NJ: Lawrence Erlbaum Associates, 2004), 315–35.

16. Arit John, "The White House Tries to Lure Young People to Obamacare with Cuteness," *The Atlantic Wire*, September 27, 2013, http://www.theatlanticwire.com/politics/2013/09/white-house-bringing-cuteness-its-obamacare-push/69947/.

17. McKay and Paletz, "The Presidency and the Media."

18. Arun Chaudhary, "West Wing Week," *The White House Blog*, April 2, 2010, www.whitehouse.gov/blog/2010/04/02/west-wing-week.

19. BBC, "West Wing Week: Producing the White House Video Blog," *BBC,* April 22, 2011, http://www.bbc.co.uk/news/world-us-canada-13166315.

20. Rajini Vaidyanathan, "Barack Obama's Shadow - the Man Who Films the President," *BBC News,* April 23, 2011, http://www.bbc.co.uk/news/world-us-canada-13148700.

21. Ibid.

22. BBC, "West Wing Week: Producing the White House Video Blog."

23. Diana Owen and Richard Davis, "Presidential Communication in the Internet Era," *Presidential Studies Quarterly* 38, no. 4 (n.d.): 658–73.

24. David Sarno, "Obama, the First Social Media President," *The LA Times,* November 18, 2008, sec. Technology, latimesblogs.latimes.com/technology/2008/11/obama-the-first.html.

25. The Telegraph, "President Barack Obama's Weekly Address Posted on White House YouTube Channel."

26. Ibid.

27. Arlette Saenz, "Mother of Sandy Hook Victim Delivers White House Weekly Address," *ABC News,* April 13, 2013, http://abcnews.go.com/blogs/politics/2013/04/mother-of-sandy-hook-victim-delivers-white-house-weekly-address/.

28. Craig Kanalley, "Google+ Hangout Puts President Face-to-Face with Americans," *NBC News,* January 30, 2013, www.nbcnews.com/technology/google-hangout-puts-president-face-face-americans-24105.

29. Erica Werner, "Obama Helps Woman with Husband's Resume," *Huffington Post,* February 1, 2012, http://www.huffingtonpost.com/huff-wires/20120201/us-obama-husband-s-resume/.

30. Meenal Vamburkar, "Obama Faces Toughest Grilling about Drones, Not from the Media, but in a Google+ Hangout," February 15, 2013.

31. Google, "Hit the Road with President Obama in the First-Ever Presidential Hangout Road Trip," *Official Blog,* January 23, 2014, http://googleblog.blogspot.com/2014/01/hit-road-with-president-obama-in-first.html.

32. Tom McCarthy, "Obama Answers Citizens' Questions in Google 'Hangout Road Trip,'" *The Guardian,* January 31, 2014, sec. World News, http://www.theguardian.com/world/2014/jan/31/obama-google-hangout-state-of-union.

33. Dan Lothlan and Becky Brittain, "Obama Hosts Google 'Hangout,'" January 30, 2012, www.cnn.com/2012/01/30/politics/obama-google.

34. David Stewart, Paulos Pavlou, and Scott Ward, "Media Influences on Marketing Communications," in *Media Effects: Advances in Theory and Research* (Mahwah, NJ: Erlbaum, 2002), 353–96.

35. McKay and Paletz, "The Presidency and the Media."

36. Paul Herrnson, Atiya Stokes-Brown, and Matthew Hindman, "Campaign Politics and the Digital Divide: Constituency Characteristics, Strategic Considerations, and Candidate Internet Use in the State Legislative Elections," *Political Research Quarterly* 60, no. 1 (2007): 31–42.

37. Jason Parham, "iPresident: How Social Media Shaped the Narrative of Barack Obama," *Complex Tech,* January 21, 2013, www.complex.com/tech/2013/01/ipresident-social-media-and-the-narrative-of-barack-obama.

38. Parker, "His Job Is to Make Public Obama's Candid Side."

39. Phillip Swarts, "Obama Videographer: Official Record or Taxpayer-Financed Politics?," *Washington Guardian,* August 8, 2012, http://www.washingtonguardian.com/obamas-video-secrets.

Part III

YouTube and Democratic Engagement

The perceived disintegration of the public sphere and the disengagement of the American populous in the nation's democratic affairs has been highly researched and much lamented. YouTube provides a platform through which the citizenship can potentially reaffirm its desires to engage democratically and through which it has a free and open forum to do so. Some research may argue that the types of engagement behaviors that the public may participate in via YouTube are not the "right" type of behaviors to sustain measurable offline democratic participation. Nevertheless, the public has found multiple and varied ways through which to engage in political action via YouTube.

Just as politicians have capitalized on technological advancements to reach voters, the public has capitalized on these advancements to more substantially engage in online politics. YouTube can offer individuals options for democratic engagement that expand levels of information and opportunities for political involvement.

Through an examination of specific YouTube events designed to encourage political participation and a broad conceptual evaluation of online democratic engagement, a discussion evolves regarding the many ways in which participation through YouTube can enhance the public sphere, encourage deliberative discussion, and strengthen the public's political efficacy. Much like politicians seek ways to enhance authenticity, transparency, and access, so too do individuals through their engagement in online communicative behaviors.

The following chapters provide an exemplar of how the public has elected to engage democratically through interactivity and person-to-person connectivity on YouTube. The discussions also provide a glimpse into the ways that YouTube helps to foster community and connectedness that mainstream media communication cannot. The chapters put forth potential future research ideas that may potentially help to legitimize the types of deliberative interactions and democratic engagement that YouTube can support.

SEVEN

YouTube and Deliberative Democracy

In traditional mainstream media environments, the creation and dissemination of political dialogue, rhetoric, and deliberation have historically been the products of those who hold power within political and media institutions. The potential impact of Internet-based political communication upon both the public sphere and deliberative democracy has been a topic of debate since the Internet began to play a significant role in politics. Assessing and measuring the democratic impact of the Internet have proven difficult and the extent to which Internet technologies enhance democracy is still somewhat ambiguous.[1] However, the integration of YouTube into political communication has initiated a shift in the public sphere and created new opportunities for the public-at-large to engage in deliberative democracy. This chapter explores the potential of online deliberative engagement, YouTube as a site for deliberative democracy, and examines the CNN-YouTube Primary Candidate Debates as an example of what deliberative public interaction looks like on YouTube.

EXPANDING THE PUBLIC SPHERE

A deliberative and functioning public sphere is vital for democracy, both for the political establishment and the efficacy of the citizenship. In order to thrive, democracy necessitates multiple, alternative, and simultaneous public spheres,[2] where strong democracy is characterized and emphasized through the participatory political behaviors of its populous.[3] In an idealized public sphere, individuals utilize broad communicative environments, which are not controlled necessarily by the state, the media, or the public, to share information, debate salient topics, discuss issues of common concern, and form public opinion.[4] The public sphere should allow individuals to act as their own social agents, access political information, and engage in robust and purposeful deliberation across multiple societal levels.[5] Ideal public spheres promote the creation and identification of multiple publics and encourage democratic sociability. These spheres should encourage discursive participation—discussion between individuals that (1) emphasizes logic and reasoning over power or coercion, (2) focuses on reasoned engagement where participants are able to identify solutions to common social or political issues, and (3) participants are open to the opinions and ideas expressed by other participants.[6]

Considering these tenets, it is possible to see the multiple ways that the Internet functions both as a public sphere and enhances the public's opportunities for deliberative interactions. The Internet contributes to the multiplicity of the public sphere and its consistently evolving technologies provide for the constitution of new social spaces.[7] Innovative and ubiquitous mass communication technologies are continually reconstructing public spaces in a manner which has revived the salon—generating new spaces where conversation about issues of national, as well as personal, interest occurs.[8] The Internet provides a platform through which the discursive interactional processes necessary to sustain a public sphere can flourish and where the citizenship can engage in dialogue and deliberation that is fundamental for an efficacious democracy. However, there is a great deal of variance among research as to what constitutes deliberative political talk. Some suggest that it is political discussion that involves the willingness to argue with a political opponent[9] or that it is instead deliberation or debate that falls in accordance with specific spatially governed rules.[10] Nevertheless, the argument can be aptly forwarded that, instead, the public sphere thrives more thoroughly upon "ordinary political conversations within the context of daily life" as issues of public importance, like political discussions, are not isolated from the functions of the public's everyday existence.[11]

The importance of this type of public-political talk makes it possible to see how the functionality of deliberation and ideas of the public sphere are amplified through Web 2.0 platforms like YouTube. The Internet provides an environment through which deliberative interaction can thrive and a reconstitution of what it means to be democratically engaged has emerged. The person-to-person connectivity and heightened interactivity that YouTube allows between the citizenship has fundamentally altered the public sphere and online deliberative interaction.

ONLINE DELIBERATIVE DEMOCRACY

The public's perceived lack of interest in politics and deliberative engagement has been framed as a failure of citizens to care about the state of American democracy. Quite often, the professed failure of the public sphere is specifically correlated to the public's failure to substantively engage in politics or its failure to participate in the "right ways."[12] Often, the everyday political discussions that citizens engage in are discounted even though research suggests that democracy can be enriched by the role of informal political communication.[13] That is, if these conversations are given as much credence as other types of political interaction and discourse. The framing of the national political atmosphere as one of "anti-politics" is quite often seen as a failure on the part of the citizenship and not as a consequence of the political system's inability to meet the social expectations of the populous.[14] Rather than a failure on behalf of the citizenship, it is arguable that individuals get stuck in the banality of contemporary formal politics and do not feel as if they are part of the greater democratic system.[15] In looking at the dominant features of the Internet, it is possible to see how the democratic ideals of the public sphere can not only function through new deliberative spaces, but thrive. Because the public sphere should function differently and separately from the "strategic actions" of the political system, including rule-based debates and formal discussions,[16] the Internet is able to shape discussion networks and influence public deliberation in different ways.[17]

The widespread adoption of the Internet, the subsequent proliferation of online literacy, and the continual development of the political Internet provide an opportunity to reflect on the changing relationships among media, communication, and deliberative engagement. New Internet platforms have given rise to new methods for widespread deliberative political discussion to occur. Chat rooms, listservs, moderated discussions, social media, and Web 2.0 platforms have all lowered the physical and fiscal barriers once prohibitive of widespread public deliberation. The Internet allows political talk to flourish within communities, across geographic boundaries,[18] and throughout the various "lifestyle enclaves" in which the online public participates.[19] Connecting citizens through various networks and communities of interest and allowing individuals to participate in collaborative platforms can improve democratic practices. These connections facilitate increased information flow and diversity of opinions, and help the public make more informed democratic decisions.[20] In order for a strong democracy to thrive, it is essential for the citizenship, not just the media and political elite, to engage in discussion on issues of public importance. Deliberative online spaces provide a decentralized many-to-many communication format that entitles each participant to comment, raise new questions, and express opinions freely.[21] Online spaces for deliberative engagement can be more beneficial to public discussion than synchronous channels,[22] like public meetings, because they provide users the luxury of time to construct messages, responses, and questions at their own pace, which can elevate rational-critical discussion.[23] Internet-based deliberation also allows participants to make use of extensive and readily available resource material which can serve to enhance the deliberative interchanges among participants.[24] Online deliberations can serve as effective tools for providing and eliciting information, understanding and appreciating differences among the polity, and arriving at collective decisions.[25] Deliberation of this nature can impact public behavior, knowledge, and attitudes and demonstrate the importance of an active citizenry to political leaders.[26]

Critics of online political deliberation assert that often the public does not possess enough knowledge to appropriately discuss topics of national importance without the priming or guidance of the information elite. This historic belief that public deliberation is the purview of those who are considered to be experts in social topics or deliberative initiatives has generated both normative and conceptual consequences. In this deliberative structure, social problems are often identified for, and not by, the public and the public's role as a stakeholder in the deliberation is undermined. What critics seemingly fail to comprehend, however, is that the point of public deliberation is the gathering and sharing of information and the open and fair discussion of salient public issues. Therefore, the public needs not possess a sophisticated understanding of the topic or issue prior to deliberation, rather, simply the willingness to engage in the reflective judgment that can come from open discussion. In deliberative processes that are broadly inclusive and focused on giving and receiving information, there is "no force except that of the better argument" to be exercised.[27]

Online deliberative participation allows citizens to constitute themselves as active agents in the nation's political process.[28] The less formalized structure of these deliberative engagements allow discussants to foster full and active citizenship by seeking and sharing diverse information, viewpoints, and forms of expression.[29] Platforms, like YouTube, which provide accessible venues for deliberative democratic discussion, allow ordinary political conversations between citizens to elevate political participation[30] and encourage other types of online political information seeking and behaviors.[31]

YOUTUBE AS A PLATFORM FOR DELIBERATIVE DEMOCRACY

YouTube is a viable platform through which the American constituency can participate in democratic engagement and has emerged as a dominant mediator of deliberative political communication. Its structure and mainstream commerciality have allowed it to become an important site of online participatory culture. The platform functions as site of cosmopolitan cultural citizenship, where cultural participation occurs through the sharing of identities and perspectives.[32] As a public sphere consisting of countless distinct but also overlapping and interconnected communicative spaces, YouTube provides a fertile environment for the type of public discussion vital for a healthy and thriving democratic state to occur. Its communicative structure, through which most individuals engage in the privacy of their homes, can promote honest discourse and encourage users to "speak up" about topics of importance.[33] While critics may assert that communicative dialogue enacted at home from behind a computer is not the most elevated level of democratic engagement,[34] research indicates that individuals are less likely to speak as freely about certain topics in public places, such as civic meetings.[35] The asynchronousity of the medium is also supportive of more reflexive, rational, and purposeful discussions.[36]

Research has cited limited opportunities for public deliberation as one factor in the perceived diminishing social capital of the United States.[37] YouTube provides enhanced opportunities for the public to genuinely engage one another in a political communication system that has enabled transnational forums, global networking, and opinion mobilization to freely develop. By connecting individuals to a large network of other users, YouTube provides a space where the cybertransformation of the public sphere can be realized. When individuals have access to a larger network of people with whom to discuss topics of national importance, their online and offline participatory behaviors are also likely to increase.[38] When citizens have access to a greater number of communicative partners, they are more likely to encounter opposing viewpoints[39] and increased interaction with new sources of information.[40] The expansive networks of individuals that one is likely to encounter via YouTube deliberation can serve to stimulate discussion as people will likely find many individuals with whom they share interests and with whom they desire to interact.

The inclusivity of YouTube nurtures participatory elements necessary to create a cultural habit of democratic talk. Participation is solely dictated by access to the platform and it is infrequent that an identifiable expert entity, like a political or media elite, can be identified formulating the parameters of the discussion. Absent key media and political stakeholders who can contribute to contrived political deliberation, public participation becomes a meaningful outcome of the political process.[41] Discussants do not have to be experts in order to participate in the communication and their involvement is enacted through the ordinary activities of the platform; users do not have to be selected or do something ancillary to engage in the deliberative communication environment. This heightens the collective capacity of citizens to discuss and act on their own behalf.[42] Transitional opinion mobilization is further achieved through flexible deliberative engagement. Participants are free to join or leave communicative situations at their discretion and can contribute to the extent that they desire. Individuals who choose to abstain from direct contribution—for example, posting comments—are still able to engage with the content by reading and obtaining information from other participants' posts. Vicariously watching the deliberative process of individuals with whom they identify allows them to, essentially, take part in the deliberative environment by proxy.[43] These interchanges simultaneously engage and educate the audience and provide a mechanism for influence beyond those interested in direct participation.[44]

YouTube has turned social media into human media[45] and has empowered new voices in the creation and distribution of persuasive political messages. Public discourse should empower citizens, provide them with a voice and collective agency, help build community, and allow them to act on behalf of their own self-interests and values.[46] It should also empower citizen's identities with a sense of belonging and perceived possibilities for participation.[47] Engaging citizens through platforms like YouTube should become a normative standard for political communication because it encourages active citizen participation in the public sphere.

Through dissemination of personal digital narratives, YouTube amplifies individuals' abilities to clearly situate themselves with regard to their personal and political stances as well as with regard to other participants. Participants can share opinions and reasons beyond their esoteric values, supply steps in arguments, and provide situated knowledge to a broad audience, all elements necessary in the creation and sustainment of healthy deliberative environments.[48] This enhances democracy at the bottom, where people are freely communicating about issues of importance amongst each other.[49] These communicative actions emphasize intersubjectivity in discussions[50] and contribute to the creation of mutual understanding, trust, and shared knowledge among the communicators.[51]

Deliberative interaction via YouTube provides a method through which to combat widespread criticism that the Internet is not capable of supporting a deliberative public sphere[52] and that, in general, the public is not capable of rational political debate and discussion.[53] YouTube has created a deliberative environment that is inclusive, voluntary, reasoned, and equal. It has also established a mechanism for educating and engaging the public in discussion of political policy and issues of public importance. These factors help to legitimize YouTube as a site of deliberative democracy and the communication that occurs through the platform serves to justify citizens' role in deliberative discussion.

THE CNN-YOUTUBE DEBATES AS DELIBERATIVE DEMOCRACY

The CNN-YouTube Primary Debates (discussed in detail in chapter 4) created and hosted by CNN and YouTube in 2007, provided an appropriate example through which to see how deliberative communication among the populous unfolds in a Web 2.0 environment. By examining user comments posted about the candidates' answers during the two live debate broadcasts it is possible to ascertain how individuals used the platform to engage one another in deliberative discussion. It is also possible to provide credence to the type of political talk the constituency is capable of engaging in when given the opportunity to do so. In sum, there were roughly 66,000 user comments, approximately 38,000 regarding the Democratic debate and 28,000 about the Republican debate, posted to the YouTube debate platform. When looking systematically at these user comments, they coalesce around specific thematic categories which are indicative of the participatory democratic platform that YouTube has become. The expressions from the participants' function as clear content typologies, illustrating the formation of collectives through shared interests, identities, and concerns.

As anyone who has ever read a YouTube comment post may expect, the range of content in the debate comment threads was broad and varied. While some of the comments may be considered mundane, and some outright offensive, there were clear deliberative themes present throughout a majority of the postings that help to advance the understanding of how deliberative dialogue may be created, sustained, and replicated in the Web 2.0 environment.[54]

DEBATE FORMAT

As evidenced by the large number of videos submitted for inclusion and the record broadcast ratings, the CNN-YouTube debates were successful in piquing public curiosity and engagement. However, a theme that ran throughout the online comments was that of frustration with the format and the limited public presence during the broadcasts. Online discussants felt as if the debates' format, moderator Anderson Cooper's frequent interjections and reframing of the public's questions, as well as CNN's process for video selection, all diminished the user-generated foundations of the debates. Discussion participants also expressed irritation with the candidates for falling back on their standard talking points and not thoroughly addressing the public's questions. In regard to both the debate format and the candidates' responses, one commenter noted, "these debates (which are really Q&A's as they don't debate) don't allow enough time to give thorough thoughtful answers." Another poster referred to CNN as the "CNN-communist news network," for dictating the direction of publicly created debate content.

CLARIFICATION AND ADVOCACY

Questions about governmental procedures and uncertainty regarding candidates' positions and voting records was another common theme found throughout the online discussions. Participants used the debate platform to ask other participants about candidates' previous voting records and to discuss among each other when candidate's answers during the debates wavered from their previous policy stances. Posts within this general theme illustrated that participants behaved deliberatively by asking questions of each other, supplying links to information regarding the topics under question, and debating both the candidates' positions and the credibility of the candidates' statements. Some of most productive dialogue found throughout the comment threads related to individuals providing clarification of candidates' voting records and participants strongly advocating for candidates. One commenter responded to another poster's question about voting records by clarifying that, "Dennis Kucinich voted against giving Bush authority to invade Iraq in 2002! He voted against NAFTA and the Patriot Act (because he read it)." Evidence of candidate advocacy is illustrated by a supporter of Democratic Senator Mike Gravel who posted,

> From my knowledge of the candidates, Mike Gravel is the most like ordinary Americans and he is the best qualified to lead the American people. It's so great that he reappeared to let us know exactly what we are missing. Now, what are we going to do about it?! He can't do everything. It's up to us to help carry the load.

In an example of less-direct advocacy, a participant noted, in regard to comments about Barack Obama's ethnicity, "Who cares if he is black? Democracy gives you a chance to vote on the 'PERSON' you like, not the ethnicity of the politician!" Affirmation of candidates' positions was also found throughout these threads. For example, in response to one candidate's answer on a controversial topic, one participant stated, "No better way to put that; hit the nail right on the head." These participants illustrated foundations of effective deliberative communication by engaging in discussion that was courteous and inclusive and by responding to disagreements constructively. Participants highlighted information that others may not have known, provided narrative-based candidate advocacy, and used language effectively to connect with other participants and promote further dialogue, all of which are important elements in deliberative discussion. This dialogue helps to typify the creation of collectives through information gathering and sharing which is foundational to sustainable deliberative communication.[55]

ESTABLISHING ARGUMENTS AND ASSESSING VALIDITY

Deliberative communication could also be seen through participants' effective establishment of arguments. By developing posts that provided the clear steps in an argument, commenters appropriately disseminated deliberative dialogue and engaged one another in persuasive political communication. The following discussion, related to the topic of gay marriage, illustrates the formation of arguments prevalent throughout many of the comment threads:

> Poster 1: Data from European demographers and statistical bureaus show that a majority of children in Sweden and Norway are now born out of wedlock, as are 60 percent of first-born children in Denmark. In socially liberal districts of Norway, where the idea of same-sex registered partnerships is widely accepted, marriage itself has almost entirely disappeared." Stanley Kurtz, research fellow at the Hoover Institution.

> Poster 2: Kurtz is a liar, plain and simple. One can view the data, ALL of it, and see that he's neglecting the decline in marriage in Scandinavian countries that has been going on since the 70s up until same sex marriage laws were passed. At which point, marriage rates went up, divorce rates dropped by around 13 percent over a ten year period. As for out of wedlock children, Scandinavia has been seeing a rise in this trend for first-born kids since the 70s. This isn't the case for second-born children.

> Poster 1: No, you are a liar. as you continue to attack traditional marriage by condoning cohabitation and out of wedlock births and same sex marriage you completely take destroy the meaning of marriage. Real people don't want that. You are plain and simple and you have just been destroyed.

> Poster 2: Sure . . . it's not Kurtz's fault that the stats don't match his conclusions. It's reality's fault for not siding with him. Is this just another part of the big gay conspiracy too? Is reality in on it?

> Poster 1: No, the stats are accurate. This is the result of the assault on marriage, and why people feel the need to defend it. People like you are willing to see children suffer for your own selfish wants. Grow up and start thinking beyond yourself.

> Poster 2: "stats are accurate" Except in the way that he misinterprets them, omits the previous years, and omits following years. Perhaps, he should have looked at the data, and then drawn a conclusion. Instead, he had a conclusion, and is looking to justify it. The two processes are completely different. In the former, you get the truth. In the latter, you're only going to look for facts that confirm your conclusion, regardless of the truth.

> Poster 1: Kurtz omits nor misinterprets nothing. You are in denile [sic] of the truth. The facts bear out his conclusions and you refuse to accept that. That is OK, there are a lot of delusional people in the world. No wonder you lose every time this issue is put to a vote.

> Poster 2:"facts bear out his conclusions". Nope. They don't. Plenty of people have shown otherwise; some more qualified, others less qualified, if that could be said in regards to Kurtz. A cursory review of the stats could reveal that Kurtz is completely omitting data from years prior that show marked trends that he is willing to ignore, and proclaim the effects of homosexuals in society.

Poster 1: Uh . . .Yup. They do. You cannot back up you assertions because you are a liar. I have given you the evidence that you asked for and the best you got is "nuh-huh". Like I said before, you are a childish lying gay propagandist, no one takes you seriously and this is why you keep losing at the poles. Pathetic, really.

Poster 2: "cannot back up". . . Look up the stats for the nations that Kurtz was looking at. Now, go ten years prior to his range of data. Go ten years prior to that. Now, since we can't fault him for not knowing the future, one can also look beyond his range, which was still five years behind the date he wrote his editorial. His conclusion has no backing. It is based upon a cherry picked set of data, and ignorant of decades of trends that moved at their steady pace. You just don't like the truth.

Poster 1: No, it is you that "don't like the truth". As these countries became progressively liberal, marriage has been destroyed and gay marriage has directly contributed to that. Its [sic] clear as a bell. You just refuse to accept the truth because it doesn't fit your agenda. Nice try, though. (as weak as it was).

Poster 2: "directly contributed to that" Then, produce the data. Put your money where your mouth is, and prove me wrong.

Poster 1: I did moron, you are too stupid to get it. You have been wrong all along and you insist on being wrong and refuse to see the light.

Poster 2: "I did . . ." No. I totally understand that the trend for the reduction in marriages, and increase in divorces, started well in advance of the granting of marriage rights for homosexuals. I've demonstrated that your sources are either woefully inept, or quote mined. If your only source for stats is Kurtz, then you are just as inept as he is, possibly even more so.

Poster 1: Look moron, just because you don't understand the science, don't call your intellectually superiors "inept". It only demonstrates your frustration at losing this debate He is an adjunct fellow of the Hudson Institute and a Senior Fellow at the Ethics and Public Policy Center, with a special interest in America's "culture wars." Kurtz writes regularly for publications such as National Review, Policy Review, The Weekly Standard, Wall Street Journal, and Commentary.

Poster 2: Looking at the statistics, one can see that Scandinavians are waiting until they actually have a child before marrying. As for Kurtz, I take back what I said. He's not a liar. That would imply that he knew better. He's just a social anthropologist. He should save the science for real scientists.

Poster 3: The quick win: 1.There is no legally significant difference between a gay couple, and a sterile or elderly heterosexual couple. 2. Heterosexuals can abuse, and even murder their children, yet do not lose their ability to get legal marriage. 3. Gay marriage does not stop heterosexuals from getting married, divorced, or having babies.

Poster 4: . . . my feelings against Homosexuality are based on much more then [sic] some petty religious beliefs. My concern is primarily for the Nuclear Family and the importance I feel it has for the U.S.A.

Poster 5: I don't understand how homosexuality in itself negatively affects the 'nuclear family'. Homosexual marriage still doesn't. Homosexual adoption? Perhaps that may affect the nuclear family. . . but you'd rather have children living without anyone than them having two parents of the same sex? I'm from Canada, where all of this is legal, and we even have more Catholic percent of population than the USA, haha. This is also how I can tell the lies about the effects of gay marriage from the truth

This thread of communication effectively incorporates logos, pathos, and ethos, the three levels of audience appeals necessary for rhetoric to be persuasive and deliberative. Presumably, this rhetoric was not constructed by individuals within positions of sociopolitical power; however, the use of audience appeals and factual evidence to advance the dialogue is indicative of a deliberative discussion between the citizenry. The primary goal within this set of comments is to provide the better argument. The evolution of this discussion thread is an excellent illustration of how deliberative communication can function in an online environment.

While this conversation initially began between just two individuals, the initial discussants could not keep other interested participants from joining the dialogue. Once additional parties joined the original conversation, the communication advanced to include multiple participants with varied viewpoints and promoted a robust discussion of a highly discussed social and cultural practice. This type of communication is an important function of deliberative engagement as it likely produces greater cognitive activity among discussants because it requests that individuals think alternatively about a topic.[56] Ultimately, this can lead to a more reflective evaluation of information.[57]

Assessing the validity of the candidates' answers during the broadcasts and discussing potential flaws with the perceived legitimacy of online discussants' posts was also prevalent throughout the comment threads. During the Democratic debate the candidates were asked, "How are you going to be different [than the current president]?" Within the various candidate answers, the issue of national debt came up, sparking significant online discussion regarding the state of the country's economy. In response to chatter about whether or not the country was in a recession, the following exchange took place:

Poster 1: FYI - a recession is a term used to show a decrease in GDP. Usually for a period of significant time (at least 2 quarters–i.e. 6 months). The US is still having positive GDP growth at the moment (which means we are still in a period of economic expansion not recession). . . so although their [sic] is a slow down in the economy, it is not even close to being classified as a recession.
Poster 2: Look around! The country is in a RECESSION the American dollar has lost 97 percent of it's [sic] value people are losing there

[their] cars, houses, and their jobs. Plus the American Government can't even fund the war in IRAQ, they are borrowing money from China. This country is printing money out of thin air, you might as well say they are printing counterfeit and they wounder [sic] why the dollar is so weak. And you talk about the Clintons! 1998 we were in a way better position than we are now so wake up dude.

This example illustrates the deliberative use of argumentation and evidence in an attempt to persuade that one position on the topic is correct and the other is not. Individuals must have the ability to read, respond, and reflect on a topic of concern in order to achieve sustainable deliberative dialogue. Posts, such as this, illustrate the deliberative nature of one poster reading the argument of another, assessing the validity of their information, and responding with an argument of their own.

REFERENT MATERIAL AND ANECDOTAL EVIDENCE

Discussants frequently invoked referent materials while debating with others. For example, in response to an individual's post against having "another" Clinton in the White House, a different commenter provided the following information, "Clinton left office with a 65 percent approval rating, the highest end-of-presidency-rating of any President who came into office after World War II." In a different discussion, an individual cited specifically proposed policy as a way to counter another posters' argument that the United States should be more connected with Christian values. The poster explaining that the U.S. is already connected to such values by noting:

In May 2004, a bill against unethical conversion was set before parliament, encouraged by the Buddhist political party, Jathika Hela Urumaya. It is based on a similar bill in the Indian state of Tamilnadu. Due to pressure from the United States the bill was abandoned.

In a discussion regarding fair tax, another discussant provided an example as to why the proposed policy was flawed:

Fair Tax: We can have a simple fair tax policy - four pages long, and clear to anyone. But the FairTax plan of a high sales tax doesnt [sic] even slow down at stupid -- it goes right to insane. It would have to be at least 40 percent—not 23 as they asdmit [sic]. So you would pay 40 percent sales tax on a new house—no one in history of the world has had a tax like that. You would have 40 percent sales tax on medical cost—no one in world has done that. Its [sic] not the rith [sic] fix.

In a politically charged discussion about gun control, many participants demonstrated their unhappiness with the anecdotal evidence provided by other discussants and instead cited the Constitution as a means of providing support for positions against tighter gun laws. In response to the subjective evidence presented in a post, one commenter noted:

> You need to read the Federalist Papers, you know, the explainations [sic] of each amendment. The 2nd is not so that we have an Army, its so that if the Fed. Gov. becomes tyrannical, we can over throw it. There is still a Fed Gov. so the 2nd Amendment still applies.

Another poster stated:

> I can only laugh at people who say the second amendment is outdated. Well, what about the first? Hell, hate speech causes more problems in domestic homes then guns do! Hell, why should we care about the 4th? The government is fully trustworthy right? Go ahead and call it an out dated piece [sic] of paper, go on, stick your head in the sand.

On this same topic, yet another participant quoted President John F. Kennedy to help solidify their perspective on the argument by posting the following quote:

> "Today we need a nation of minute men; citizens who are not only prepared to take up arms, but citizens who regard the preservation of freedom as a basic purpose of their daily life and who are willing to consciously work and sacrifice for that freedom. The cause of liberty, the cause of American, cannot succeed with any lesser effort." —President John F. Kennedy, January 29, 1961

The behavior in this discussion illustrates highly deliberative communication as it both attempts to persuade other participants to fully understand the entirety of the argument and provides specific reference(s) to information that may help others gain a better understanding of the argument. The discussion is indicative of a problem-solution oriented dialogue that should occur in deliberative environments.[58] What is perhaps most interesting about the use of referent material throughout the debates was the range of referential information that participants used to discuss topics with fellow participants. While questions related to gay rights, gun control, and abortion generated significant public dialogue, less salient topics, that received less attention in the mainstream media, also generated substantive deliberative discussions. The following is an example of how the topic of farm subsidization was discussed on the comment threads:

> Poster 1: Farm subsidies are the single largest detriment to third world development. We subsidize them far below what is competitive [sic]. Last year, we exported rice to Bangladesh. That country has a much lower oportunity [sic] cost for production. Farm subsidies should be ended as soon as possible in both the EU and the US.
> Poster 2: Economically it makes sense to just cut subsidies out, but that is short sighted. there are policy reasons at play that don't concern the immediate economic impact. if we didn't subsidize corn here, it would

go to the most efficient producer, Russia or china etc. Can you imagine if a foreign wheat cartel emerged (like OPEC does for oil) regulating our supply of wheat? Subsidies are obviously bad and contrary to a "free" market system, but the alternative is even less attractive.

Across comment threads, participants also provided personal narratives to engage others in discussion. While it is not uncommon, especially during political campaigns, to hear about how personal situations and decisions have impacted the candidates, it is somewhat rare for private individuals to be able to use their own anecdotes as a means of public persuasion. This ability serves to expand the public sphere by emphasizing the impact of public policy in discourse.[59] While personal narratives may be dismissed as inconsequential communication in deliberative dialogue, they can in fact be an effective means of persuasion, with the propaganda of one individual serving as a point of education for others.[60] Personal anecdotes also provide for a level of association and identification with other-situated individuals, allowing them to be both more persuasive and deliberative. By creating commonality and demonstrating the impact political action can have on the collective, the participatory process can be shaped.[61]

The following post, regarding the aforementioned topic on farm subsidization allowed a discussant directly impacted by such legislation to share their position with others who may not be familiar with the personal impact of the government policy:

> When you are a farmer you learn to get a thick skin about such things . . . we are one of the lucky farm families where we were able to arrange it so that we will be able to keep our head above water even with a few years of crop failure . . . most cannot . . . the family farm is the most indangered [sic] species in the country.

However, as illustrated by the following post regarding whether or not the government should help pay for private K–12 education, some participants were not persuaded by anecdotal evidence, requesting instead that individuals use referent material to support their claim:

> Poster 1: I'm a girl who went to both of private and public. I went to a private school for eight years, and I absolutely hated it. I didn't learn a lick. The teacher's method of teaching was akward [sic], and so boring. It was like living with rich spoiled kids and their parents. Soon, I went to a very good public school. The teachers were motivated, more diversity of kids, I made more friends. I even got straight A+ (Not that it was easy). Public school work was harder, and it pressured me to take more responsibility.
>
> Poster 2: You are basing your views on public/private school on experience. This experience based on a private school is very specific to the school, different private schools perform differently. Public schools work mostly on the same ciriculum [sic] but use different teaching

methods than one another. In the end, if you want to compare the public/private schools you need to use statistics NOT anectdotes [sic] (short stories).

Using referent material and anecdotal evidence allowed participants the opportunity and ability to create deliberative messages through conveying their own situated knowledge. It also provided a venue where users could attempt to intentionally change the mind of those with adversarial opinions. These discussants were allowed to exercise both freedom in message construction and regarding to whom their messages were directed to which exemplifies an appropriately deliberative environment.

CRITICIZING AND DEFENDING CANDIDATES

Throughout the debates' comment threads, individuals used the platform to criticize or defend candidates' answers as well as to express distrust and, sometimes, anger regarding candidates' answers or topic positions. Individuals expressed frustration with candidates' not answering the questions posed or falling back on standard talking points. For example, one participant noted, "Obama never answers the damn question." Discussants also frequently referenced that the debates were not the political revolution that CNN and other media outlets claimed they would be. Many participants commented that candidates seemed more interested in answering the follow-up questions posed by host Anderson Cooper than answering the questions posed in the videos by the public. Interestingly, while the criticisms of the candidates could have come across as unsophisticated public bashing, the posts instead emerged as another prevalent method of deliberative discussion where individuals were freely allowed to state and defend their opinions. The following example, directed at an answer from Hilary Clinton, illustrates how participants used the debate forum to discuss the candidate both personally and politically.

> Poster 1: Wow . . . what a nice attack on the GOP she did right there. "We'll do better then [sic] Bush, or any other Nominee on the Republican side". Ha! Dare her to say that while debating Ron Paul. Hilary is such a shill to be talking about "Change". She voted for the Iran war bill! How does another pointless, illegal, and stupid war equal change??? And we can't really say anything different with Obama, since he wasn't even there to vote on it!
> Poster 2: If the Devil offers me his support, I'd turn it down. Murdoch is the Anti-Christ to Democrats! [sic] What if Edwards ACCEPTED support from Bill O'reilly or Obama ACCEPTED support from Dick Cheney? Hillary DID ACCEPT support from the ENEMY!
> Poster 2, follow-up: "Strengthening a pragmatic rapprochement, Rupert Murdoch has agreed to give a fund-raiser this summer for Senator

Hillary Rodham Clinton, the latest sign of cooperation between the conservative media mogul and the Democratic lawmaker who has often been a prime target of his newspaper and television outlets. Asked about her relationship with Mr. Murdoch, Mrs. Clinton described him as simply "my constituent," and she played down the significance of the fund-raiser."

Personal and political support for candidates was also present in the discussions. During a question related to the reduction of energy consumption, Democratic candidate Mike Gravel indicated that he had traveled to the debate by train. To this, one online participant stated, "AWESOME!! Gravel took the train. I find it hilarious that everyone else took a jet plane. Gravel certainly has my support. He is the only candidate that makes complete sense." In relation to the question "are our troops dying in vain?" (in reference to troop fatalities in the Iraq Occupation), another participant defended Gravel's answer by posting,

I do think that Gravel's statements went over the edge, but to judge such a person like him who has served in the United States Army, only based on this one stance is either a sign of ignorance to belief, or extreme Patriotism, and I can guarantee that the majority of the people on YouTube against what he said.

Individuals who utilized the online debate comment functions to either criticize or defend the candidates engaged in a method of deliberative communication that is most often reserved for face-to-face communication. YouTube users who used the platforms to engage one another deliberatively were able to differentiate comments that offered constructive criticism from purely negative commentary and were able to engage in argumentation that may be too uncomfortable to engage in during a face-to-face setting.[62] The ability to communicate with other people in real-time about the answers and statements made by the candidates allowed for a level of deliberative debate interaction that many individuals would most likely not be able to engage in without YouTube's online platform.

CIVILITY

It is well known that online communication relaxes some of the social constraints and etiquette that are typically enforced in face-to-face communication situations. When the restrictions of communication are diminished and the topics are controversial, it is only realistic to assume that not all of the discussion occurring between online discussants would be considered civil communication. Throughout the debate dialogue, a measure of name calling, cursing, and personal attacks on adversarial posts was present. The following example illustrates a divergence from what may be considered civil dialogue in a face-to-face political discussion:

Poster 1: YOU are the government. Don't attempt to transfer your responsibilities others. All of us are in this boat together. All Americans should read the Constitution and the Bill of Rights and learn how your government functions. The presidency is only a small part of your government. Your one vote will need more help to make the changes that you want to see in your government.

Poster 2: yeah, ok, now lets [sic] get real. . .

Poster 1: What do you mean "let's get real?"

Poster 2: I mean stop spitting out lecture material from a high school government class, this is the real world, the people are barely the government if at all, the presidency is huge and bush made it much more powerful, votes hardly matter, especially with the electoral system.

The following exchange, which emerged from the aforementioned debate question regarding the death of American troops, is illustrative of the combination of anecdotal evidence and the personal attacks that occurred in many debate postings:

Poster 1: The war is a total abuse of this nation and the troops are being put through total HELL!!!! This war is in totally in vain.

Poster 2: Go tell that to all the Iraqi people that welcome us over there, thanking us every day for giving their third world country a chance to vote and choose their leader. a ticket out of poverty. a tangible hope that their family will still be alive when they get off work that day. tell that to them, and tell them that the betterment of their lives isn't worth us fighting for because we are better than them. then tell the Iraqis fighting on our side that they dont [sic] mean ****. . . uneducated sloth

Poster 3: In response to a question regarding who John McCain was trying to fool by discussing the US success in Iraq [situating the comment so that it is targeted at the correct participant]: obviously you...Have you bothered reading or paying attention to the intelligent briefings coming back from Iraq on the success of our soldiers? Or do you just spew the same old venom because that's what cool right now?

While seemingly aggressive, or uncivil, communication could be found in every comment thread across the debate platform, many participating in the online dialogue felt that this type of dialogue was unnecessary, with one poster stating, "I think it's funny that people think they can change each other's minds. Especially when they call each other idiots or scumbags."

Although some participants apparently did not mind stepping over the boundaries of what many would consider to be civil dialogue, others seemed to realize when they perhaps overstated their position or waged an attack that was too aggressive on another poster:

Poster 1: Sorry [Poster 2] if I came off a bit too strong, it just angers me to think that we are losing lives over there to give them a chance at something wholesome and they don't appreciate it. No matter when we leave it will turn ugly. Sharia law, a bigoted system of rule, will prevail. So let them have it.

Poster 2: Kinda [sic] strong, yeah. Take a breath. ;)

These communicative interactions are important when discussing deliberative public communication because they bring up an important question: must dialogue be considered civil in order to succeed at being deliberative? Online communication has given rise to higher levels of uncivil communication including that which can be perceived as hostile, insulting, and nonsensical, as well as other types of aggressive or situationally inappropriate communication. It has been argued that uncivil communication is unsuitable for deliberative dialogue and that it is unclear how such interaction and participation helps to sustain a viable public sphere.[63] Alternatively, it has also been suggested that democratic dialogue is often too civility-driven, serving to restrict robust political discussion,[64] and that often heated online debate is considered uncivil when, in fact, it could serve to highlight dissent and move the deliberative communication forward.[65]

It is, perhaps, that the ideals of civility and etiquette have been confounded and that critics who suggest that online dialogue cannot function deliberatively in the public sphere have discounted the democratic need for, and potentials of, communication that is sometimes heated and impolite and through which disagreement is discussed. When considering YouTube as a medium for democratic dialogue, it is quite possible that its free and open platform, which often does not adhere to the confines of traditional deliberative interactions, may in fact foster a more robust deliberative environment than other types of communicative media.

CONCLUSIONS AND CHALLENGES

YouTube as a platform for deliberative dialogue and engagement helps to illustrate that civic participation is alive and well[66] and that political conversation among the public is far from a dying art.[67] While the CNN-YouTube debates are certainly not inclusive of all politically driven communication that occurs via YouTube, they do provide evidence that deliberative dialogue can thrive in an online environment and illustrate what such deliberation looks like. Debate participants demonstrated high levels of engagement with the candidates' political messages[68] and used YouTube as an alternative public communication space for political discussion. The debates are also indicative of a requisite structural element necessary in the public sphere—the accessibility of a place to build on common ideals that is open to all citizens.[69]

YouTube has democratize political content dissemination and provided a platform enabling deliberative communication. Through You-

Tube, users can discuss politics, public policy, and also engage one another in purposeful interaction, both activities that are vital in deliberative democracy and the sustainment of a functional public sphere. It is, however, important to remain cautiously optimistic when discussing YouTube as a conduit for deliberative engagement as there are some inherent difficulties in using one specific case to assign overall value to online deliberative democracy. While online deliberative interaction is indeed beneficial for the populace, it must be a unitary part of an overall democratic and civic system in order to sustain an active public sphere. To achieve this, it is necessary for the citizenry to use online deliberative spaces to develop the skills and reflective abilities necessary to invite more varied viewpoints and experiences into the deliberative process. This is exceptionally important in an online environment because often the demographic and socioeconomic populations that are excluded from more traditional political communication systems fall victim to the digital divide. Online deliberation can then inadvertently serve to accentuate traditional access barriers and in turn limit exposure to the divergence of opinions necessary for truly deliberative democracy to occur.[70] Additionally, there is an inherent self-selection bias among media users. Although participants and content creators on YouTube come from diverse population with widely differing thoughts and ideas, the Internet can become a space where individuals gravitate toward like-minded individuals, providing limited opportunities for the consideration of new beliefs and ideas.[71] Finally, while YouTube broadly provides a forum for unfettered deliberative dialogue not afforded through traditional media outlets, the potential exists that this evolving public sphere is still dominated by political elites and that the platform does more to reinforce free market models of choice than democratic procedures.[72]

Nevertheless, YouTube provides a platform through which the six main conditions necessary for e-democracy to support a deliberative public sphere can be achieved: autonomy from state and economic power; reason rather than assertion; reflexivity; ideal role taking; sincerity; and discursive inclusion and equality.[73] It has been found that engagement in political discussion has an amplifying effect on political participation[74] and that when information seeking, deliberation, and participation combine, the potential of the Internet to engage citizens in political process is compounded.[75] Purposeful interaction via YouTube has allowed the constituency to innovate, create new types of public conversations, and decide for themselves how to engage deliberatively with others. All of this provides for a wealth of interesting future research options regarding how individuals use YouTube for deliberative engagement. Political videos sometimes generate tens of thousands of comments, which YouTube now threads, making it easy to follow the flow of users' conversations. While it is superfluous to assume that all of this content will be worthy of investigation, it is likely that some interesting examples of how the public engages one another, the politicians, and the media are to be found in the long-tail comment threads of some political videos.

There is evidence that YouTube can provide a broadly inclusive environment where online deliberative discussion can occur and that, when given the opportunity to engage, the public-at-large appears willing and able to do so. In sum, however, what YouTube really illustrates about online deliberative democracy is that it remains open for examination and evaluation and it will take additional research and future election cycles to truly be able to evaluate with authority YouTube's sustaining impact on deliberative democracy.

NOTES

1. David Anderson and Michael Cornfield, *The Civic Web: Online Politics and Democratic Values.* (Lanham, MD: Rowman & Littlefield, 2002).

2. Nancy Fraser, "Rethinking the Public Sphere: A Contribution to the Critique of Actually Existing Democracy," in *Habermas and the Public Sphere* (Cambridge, MA: The MIT Press, 1992), 109–42.

3. Benjamin Barber, *Strong Democracy: Participatory Politics for a New Age* (Berkeley, CA: University of California Press, 1984).

4. Peter Dahlgren, "The Internet, Public Spheres, and Political Communication: Dispersion and Deliberation," *Political Communication* 22 (2005): 147–62.

5. Tanni Haas, "The Public Sphere as a Sphere of Publics: Rethinking Habermas's Theory of the Public Sphere," *Journal of Communication* 54, no. 1 (2004): 178–84.

6. Michael Delli Carpini, Fay Cook, and Lawrence Jacobs, "Public Deliberation, Discursive Participation, and Citizen Engagement: A Review of the Empirical Literature," *Annual Review of Political Science* 7 (2004): 315–44.

7. Peter Dahlgren, "The Public Sphere and the Net: Structure, Space, and Communication," in *Mediated Politics: Communication in the Future of Democracy* (Cambridge, UK: Cambridge University Press, 2001), 33–55.

8. Robert Wyatt, Elihu Katz, and Joohoan Kim, "Bridging the Spheres: Political and Personal Conversation in Public and Private Spaces," *Journal of Communication* 50, no. 1 (2000): 71–92.

9. Elisabeth Noelle-Neumann, *The Spiral of Silence: Public Opinion-Our Social Skin,* 2nd ed. (Chicago, IL: University of Chicago Press, 1993).

10. Michael Schudson, "Why Conversation Is Not the Soul of Democracy," *Critical Studies in Mass Communication* 14 (1997): 297–309.

11. Wyatt, Katz, and Kim, "Bridging the Spheres: Political and Personal Conversation in Public and Private Spaces."

12. Roderick Hart, "Citizen Discourse and Political Participation: A Survey," in *Mediated Politics: Communication in the Future of Democracy* (Cambridge, UK: Cambridge University Press, 2001), 407–32.

13. Wyatt, Katz, and Kim, "Bridging the Spheres: Political and Personal Conversation in Public and Private Spaces."

14. Dahlgren, "The Public Sphere and the Net: Structure, Space, and Communication."

15. Don Slater, "Political Discourse and the Politics of Need: Discourse on the Good Life in Cyberspace," in *Mediated Politics: Communication in the Future of Democracy* (Cambridge, UK: Cambridge University Press, 2001), 117–40.

16. Jurgen Habermas, *The Structural Transformation of the Public Sphere* (Cambridge, MA: The MIT Press, 1989).

17. Daniel Halpern and Jennifer Gibbs, "Social Media as a Catalyst for Online Deliberation? Exploring the Affordances of Facebook and YouTube for Political Expression," *Computers in Human Behavior* 29, no. 3 (2013): 1159–68.

18. John Gastil and William Keith, "A Nation That (sometimes) Likes to Talk: A Brief History of Public Deliberation in the United States," in *The Deliberative Democracy Handbook: Strategies for Effective Civic Engagement in the 21st Century* (San Francisco, CA: John Wiley & Sons, 2005).

19. Peter Simonson, "Dreams of Democratic Togetherness: Communication Hope from Cooley to Katz," *Critical Studies in Media Communication* 13 (1996): 324–42.

20. Beth Noveck, *Wiki Government: How Technology Can Make Government Better, Democracy Stronger, and Citizens More Powerful.* (Washington, DC: Brookings Institution Press, 2009).

21. Davy Janssen and Raphael Kies, "Online Forums and Deliberative Democracy," *Acta Politica* 40 (2005): 317–35.

22. Stephen Coleman and John Gotze, *Bowling Together: Online Public Engagement in Policy Deliberation.* (London, UK: Hansard Society, 2001).

23. Dahlgren, "The Public Sphere and the Net: Structure, Space, and Communication."

24. Patricia Bonner et al., "Bringing the Public and the Government Together through Online Dialogues," in *The Deliberative Democracy Handbook: Strategies for Effective Civic Engagement in the 21st Century* (San Francisco, CA: John Wiley & Sons, 2005), 141–53.

25. Coleman and Gotze, *Bowling Together: Online Public Engagement in Policy Deliberation.*

26. Gastil and Keith, "A Nation That (sometimes) Likes to Talk: A Brief History of Public Deliberation in the United States."

27. Jurgen Habermas, *Legitimation Crisis* (Boston, MA: Beacon Press, 1975).

28. Peter Dahlgren, "Introduction," in *Communication and Citizenship: Journalism and the Public Sphere* (London: Routledge, 1991), 1–24.

29. Ibid.

30. Wyatt, Katz, and Kim, "Bridging the Spheres: Political and Personal Conversation in Public and Private Spaces."

31. Yan Tian, "Political Use and Perceived Effects of the Internet: A Case Study of the 2004 Election," *Communication Research Reports* 23, no. 2 (2006): 129–37.

32. Jean Burgess and Joshua Green, *YouTube: Online Video and Participatory Culture* (Cambridge, MA: Polity Press, 2009).

33. Robert Wyatt et al., "The Dimensions of Expression Inhibition: Perceptions of Obstacles to Free Speech in Three Cultures," *International Journal of Public Opinion Research* 8 (1996): 229–47.

34. Robert Putnam, *Bowling Alone: The Collapse and Revival of American Community* (New York, NY: Simon and Schuster, 2000).

35. Wyatt et al., "The Dimensions of Expression Inhibition: Perceptions of Obstacles to Free Speech in Three Cultures."

36. Jennifer Stromer-Galley and Alexis Wichowski, "Political Discussion Online," in *The Handbook of Internet Studies.* (Chichester, UK: John Wiley & Sons, 2010).

37. Putnam, *Bowling Alone: The Collapse and Revival of American Community.*

38. Patricia Moy, "Linking Dimensions of Internet Use and Civic Engagement," *Mass Communication Quarterly* 82, no. 3 (2005): 571–86.

39. Dietram Scheufele et al., "Social Structure and Citizenship: Examining the Impacts of Social Setting, Network Heterogeneity, and Informational Variables on Political Participation," *Political Communication* 21 (2004): 315–38.

40. William Eveland and Myiah Hively, "Political Discussion Frequency, Network Size, and 'Heterogeneity' of Discussion as Predictors of Political Knowledge and Participation," *Journal of Communication* 59, no. 2 (2009): 205–24.

41. William Gamson, *Talking Politics* (Cambridge, UK: Cambridge University Press, 1992).

42. Ibid.

43. Daniel Yankelovich, *The Magic of Dialogue: Transforming Conflict into Cooperation* (New York, NY: Simon & Schuster, 1999).

44. Bonner et al., "Bringing the Public and the Government Together through Online Dialogues."

45. Steve Grove, "Hanging Out in the Public Square," *Huffington Post*, February 21, 2013, http://www.huffingtonpost.com/steve-grove/obama-google-plus-hangout_b_2672215.html.

46. William Gamson, "Promoting Political Engagement," in *Mediated Politics: Communication in the Future of Democracy* (Cambridge, UK: Cambridge University Press, 2001), 56–74.

47. Paul Clarke, *Deep Citizenship* (London: Pluto Press, 1996).

48. Haas, "The Public Sphere as a Sphere of Publics: Rethinking Habermas's Theory of the Public Sphere."

49. Dahlgren, "The Public Sphere and the Net: Structure, Space, and Communication."

50. Ibid.

51. Johan Fornas, *Culture Theory and Late Modernity* (London: Sage, 1995).

52. Bart Cammaerts, "Critiques on the Participatory Potentials of Web 2.0.," *Communication, Culture, and Critique* 1, no. 4 (2008): 358–77.

53. Jose Vargas, "YOUTUBE, TAKE TWO Few GOP Candidates Commit to Debate," *The Washington Post*, July 27, 2007, http://www.washingtonpost.com/wp-dyn/content/article/2007/07/27/AR2007072700283.html.

54. All user comments are direct quotes from YouTube postings; they were not edited for content, spelling, or grammar.

55. Dahlgren, "The Public Sphere and the Net: Structure, Space, and Communication."

56. John Levine and Eileen Russo, "Impact of Anticipated Interaction on Information Acquisition," *Social Cognition* 13, no. 3 (n.d.): 293–317.

57. Ibid.

58. Barber, *Strong Democracy: Participatory Politics for a New Age*.

59. Gamson, "Promoting Political Engagement."

60. Garth Jowett and Victoria O'Donnell, *Propaganda and Persuasion* (Los Angeles, CA: Sage, 2012).

61. Barber, *Strong Democracy: Participatory Politics for a New Age*.

62. Patricia Lange, "Commenting on Comments: Investigating Responses to Antagonism on YouTube" (presented at the Society of Applied Anthropology Conference, Tampa, FL, 2007).

63. Cammaerts, "Critiques on the Participatory Potentials of Web 2.0."

64. Zizi Papacharissi, "Democracy On-line: Civility, Politeness, and the Democratic Potential of On-line Political Discussion Groups," *New Media & Society* 6, no. 2 (2004): 259–84.

65. Thomas Benson, "Rhetoric, Civility, and Community: Political Debate on Computer Bulletin Boards," *Communication Quarterly* 44, no. 3 (1996): 359–78.

66. Roper Center for Public Opinion Research, "A Vast Empirical Record Refutes the Idea of Civic Decline," *Public Perspective* 7, no. 4 (1996).

67. Robert Wyatt, Elihu Katz, and Joohoan Kim, "Bridging the Spheres: Political and Personal Conversation in Public and Private Spaces." (Presented at the Paper presented at the annual meeting of the Association for Education in Journalism and Mass Communication, Chicago, IL, 1997).

68. Vassia Gueorguieva, "Voters, MySpace and YouTube: The Impact of Alternative Communication Channels," in *Politicking Online: The Transformation of Election Campaign Communication* (New Brunswick, NJ: Rutgers University Press, 2009), 233–48.

69. Dahlgren, "The Public Sphere and the Net: Structure, Space, and Communication."

70. Kevin Hill and John Hughes, *Cyberpolitics: Citizen Activism in the Age of the Internet* (Lanham, MD: Rowman & Littlefield, 1998).

71. Bonnie Fisher, Michael Margolis, and David Resnick, "Breaking Ground on the Virtual Frontier: Surveying Civic Life on the Internet," *American Sociologist* 27 (1996): 11–25.

72. Slater, "Political Discourse and the Politics of Need: Discourse on the Good Life in Cyberspace."

73. Lincoln Dahlberg, "The Internet and Democratic Discourse: Exploring the Prospects of Online Deliberative Forums Extending the Public Sphere," *Information Communication and Society* 4, no. 1 (2001): 615–33.

74. Matthew Nisbet and Dietram Scheufele, "Political Talk as a Catalyst for Online Citizenship," *Journalism and Mass Communication Quarterly* 81 (2004): 877–96.

75. Rita Kirk and Dan Schill, "A Digital Agora: Citizen Participation in the 2008 Presidential Debates," *American Behavioral Scientist* 55, no. 3 (2011): 325–47.

EIGHT

YouTube and Democratic Engagement

YouTube has helped to expand citizens' political repertoire and has produced novel opportunities for engagement and participation. YouTube functions as a platform for direct democracy by offering motivated citizens a rich communication environment within which to engage in ongoing, demanding, and varied ways.[1] It can also strengthen citizenship by allowing engagement outside of the politically elite-driven discourse that tends to dominate mainstream media.[2] YouTube provides users a platform whereby many core elements necessary for sustained democratic engagement, such as political interest, knowledge, and participation are enhanced.[3] Through its structures for person-to-person connectivity and widespread interactivity, political engagement via YouTube can help citizens better understand how to think and act in a complex political world. This chapter discusses the role Internet platforms play in increasing democratic engagement opportunities, how YouTube functions as a site of participatory democracy, and provides examples of how politicians have used YouTube to enhance the public's options for democratic engagement

DEMOCRATIC ENGAGEMENT AND THE INTERNET

Since the 1960s, the level of civic involvement in terms of political participation, one of the only readily available measure of wider civic participation, amongst the American electorate has declined. Between 1960 and 2004, turnout among eligible voters in presidential elections decreased by an average of 4 percent per election.[4] In 1996, only 49 percent of eligible citizens voted, marking the lowest voter turnout in any presidential election in U.S. History.[5] According to the International Institute for Democracy and Electoral Assistance, the United States ranks 140th among the world's 163 democratically elected governments in terms of voter turnout.[6] This decline has been framed as a crisis of civic culture and citizenship,[7] with some researchers suggesting that there is evidence that people actually work to avoid allowing public issues to contextualize their lives by circumventing political conversation and participation.[8] It is suggested that by almost every measure, Americans' direct engagement in politics and government has declined steadily and sharply over the last generation, despite the fact that levels of education, one of the best predictors for political participation, has risen over this same time period.[9]

The potential for the Internet to function as an intervening mechanism in the declining engagement of the United States has been heavily theorized. Many political Internet platforms offer users online engagement and participatory opportunities. Additionally, political entities have been able to capitalize on new delivery methods to effectively communicate with supporters and recruit them into taking political action. However, gauging the true potentials of the Internet to stimulate engagement is difficult. First, the Internet is not one thing; rather, it is a multifaceted phenomenon, involving seemingly infinite websites, through which individuals can engage in multiple, overlapping, and even divergent ways. This is important in engagement-oriented research because different types of online political activities may generate different levels of engagement, which will be moderated by things such as platforms' capacity to convey information, the strength of sites' arguments, or the resources required of users.[10] Second, gathering exhaustive research on engagement is also challenging because not all research defines engagement to mean the same thing; research uses varying and widespread definitions, measurements, and conceptualizations of engagement. A substantial portion of engagement-focused research centers on the ideal of civic engagement, which is argued by many to be the driving force of democracy and assumes that the ultimate outcome of civic engagement is the act of voting. More accurately, civic engagement is defined by activities that address issues of public concern through behaviors and activities not necessarily related to political action, such as volunteerism.[11] Conversely, political engagement is characterized specifically as activities driven to influence governmental action, either through affecting policy or through the selection of governmental officials; therefore, its outcome is more closely and accurately tied to voting.[12] While voting statistics tend to be one of the most universally understood outcome measurements for both civic and political engagement, voter turnout is not necessarily an accurate assessment of a population's involvement with politics. Therefore, discussing YouTube as a platform for democratic engagement—a conceptualization that embodies elements from both civic and political engagement and considers behaviors such as public political discussion and deliberation[13]—seems most appropriate given the far-reaching engagement capacities of YouTube.

Web platforms, like YouTube, possess many attributes that are appealing and suitable for democratic engagement. These platforms offer functionalities that differ substantially from traditional mass mediated communication, therefore, making democratic engagement easier and more attractive to much of the populous. The Internet (a) increases the speed with which information can be gathered and transmitted, (b) increases the volume of information that is easily accessible, (c) creates greater flexibility for when information is accessed, (d) provides greater opportunity and mixtures of interactivity, (e) shifts the nature of community from geographic to interest-based, (f) blurs distinctions between types of media, (g) challenges traditional definitions of information gatekeepers and authoritative voices, and (h) challenges traditional definitions of producers and consumers of information.[14]

These differences, coupled with expanded opportunities for political involvement such as the potential to establish heightened feelings of connectedness in a manner that many feel has become increasingly rare in offline environments,[15] lend to the Internet functioning as a viable and thriving political sphere. The interactivities of the Internet make engagement-oriented behaviors, such as connecting with politicians and campaigns, registering to vote, communicating with like-minded and not so like-minded people, and sharing links to political content easier, less time consuming, and in some cases, perhaps more enjoyable. While different sites serve alternative audiences and appeal to different audience-gratification needs, collectively, the Internet has the capacity to lower the costs of democratic participation by making political information more easily accessible and to stimulate democratic engagement.

YOUTUBE AND PARTICIPATORY CULTURE

YouTube has emerged as a powerful democratic engagement tool and a viable epicenter of participatory culture. YouTube's prowess in these areas originates specifically from its prominent use in the everyday lives of ordinary citizens. It is a place that users voluntarily and naturally go to engage with content and with others. Because it is a diverse public space, with a vast reach, that allows a wide range of voices to be expressed, YouTube is an ideal venue for heightened democratic engagement. YouTube possesses the functionalities of politically relevant media. As a many-to-many format, it serves simultaneously as a channel for information transmission and reception, as a source of a particular kind of information exchange, and allows for the generation of communication that houses the potential for affecting democratic engagement.[16] Contrary to one-to-many media formats, such as television or radio, whose high barriers to entry can stifle individual expression and political conversation,[17] YouTube's interface highlights the potential for interaction[18] and allows for opinion and information sharing to emerge.

YouTube is a powerful political tool because it allows for behaviors important to democratic engagement, such as information seeking, participation, and deliberation, to take place in an environment where people are free to produce and engage with content in a variety of ways. Its emphasis on user control and participation allows micro-content and social connections between individuals to emerge.[19] It provides a communicative environment outside of the control of the state, is largely free of coercive or directive forces, and provides the public a place to freely engage in deliberative discourse about political matters; these factors are vital to unrestrained democratic interaction.[20] The advancement of multiple, vital, and functional public political spheres through YouTube encompass new forms and formats of democratic participation[21] which can psychologically empower the audience by fostering active discourse on issues of public concern.[22] The empowerment that emerges from sustainable public deliberation can positively impact both individuals' internal and external efficacy, as well enhance the building of political trust, interest, and tolerance amongst the citizenship.[23] By connecting citizens to others through the development of online communities, YouTube engagement can help facilitate the growth of social trust amongst the electorate and ultimately lead to a higher level of social capital.[24] These factors can ultimately lead to more sustained democratic engagement across the constituency.

YouTube's expansive network, visibility, and accessibility make it a viable platform for both increased and sustained democratic engagement. Simply put, YouTube has become the world's largest town hall meeting. Through YouTube a new meritocracy for political information, free from the gatekeepers and agenda setters of traditional media, have been able to connect people with politicians, parties, candidates, and other voters in ways that were never before possible.[25] It is a significant mediating mechanism for the cultural public sphere, where consumption of information is positively related to the platforms' functionality as a legitimate venue of democratic engagement. YouTube provides sustained opportunities for participation and dialogue, elements vital to a revived model of the public sphere.[26] Through its functionalities, it helps contribute to the notions of everyday cultural citizenship and provides for the existence of a community that highlights the privileges of democratic engagement through creative contributions, sharing, and active participation.[27] YouTube provides a platform that possesses the ability to increase the public's democratic engagement through supporting the emergence of the participatory class, functioning as a site of participatory culture, and offering new options for democratic participation.[28]

ONLINE PARTICIPATORY CLASS

With approximately one in five Internet users using a social media platform for some manner of democratic engagement, YouTube has provided
a ripe environment for an active and thriving participatory class to develop. Research indicates that 72 percent of online U.S. adults participate in
some type of social media platform (up from just 8 percent of the population who used such sites in 2005).[29] Of this user population, over one-
quarter belong to a politically or socially-oriented group or page and 20
percent have used a social media platform to follow candidates for office
or elected officials.[30] Sixty-six percent of these users, equivalent to 39
percent of all American adults, have participated in at least one of a
variety of online engagement behaviors, including: posting their personal
thoughts about political issues; encouraging friends and others to act on
issues or to vote; following, linking, or reposting political content originally posted by someone else; or posting links to political stories or arti-
cles for others to read.[31] Internet users are 53 percent more likely to vote
(or intend to vote), 78 percent more likely to try and influence someone
else's vote, and over twice as likely to attend some type of political meeting as individuals who do not use the Internet.[32] Additionally, individuals who are active online democratic participants are 73 percent more
likely to engage in offline democratic behaviors than non-users.[33] Online
users who engage democratically via social media tend to be more active
in both traditional and Internet-based political participation and are more
likely to take part in other democratic behaviors, such as joining political
or civic groups, contacting government officials, or expressing themselves in online and mainstream media.[34]

Despite conjecture that social media users are likely to only engage
within networks of like-minded individuals, there is little indication that
these users experience smaller networks or are exposed to less diversity
of thought than non-users. Research suggests that the Internet's influence
on public deliberation is in fact positive and that individuals will engage
in information exchange within wide networks.[35] Evidence suggests that
social media users: feel as if they have increasing close social ties; possess
a greater ability to consider multiple sides of an issue; are mixed along
partisan and ideological lines; and amongst those users who frequently
discuss political issues, are more likely to use social media for the purposes of democratic engagement.[36]

While the online participatory class has used the Internet to heighten
democratic engagement, research still indicates that both online and offline democratic engagement remains stratified by nearly all measures of
socioeconomic classification. For example, those individuals with higher
incomes and education tend to exhibit higher levels of online democratic
engagement, a factor which could potentially correlate to the relationship
between income and at-home broadband Internet access. However, indi-

viduals who use social media platforms, like YouTube, to engage democratically represent a more socioeconomically diverse population, with statistics indicating that democratic engagement on social networking sites is not strongly correlated with socioeconomic status.[37] When examining participation of more traditional online democratic behaviors, such as emailing a government official or making a political donation, the socioeconomic gap between individuals representing the highest and lowest income groups is 27 percentage points.[38] The variance in participation between these same socioeconomic groups drops drastically to a difference of only 3 percentage points when the democratic engagement occurs specifically through social media platforms.[39] Engagement via social media also draws in a more diverse population with regard to education. When examining engagement in traditional online democratic behaviors between college graduates and those with no college experience, the difference in participation is 28 percentage points; a number that drops to just 7 percentage points when democratic engagement takes place specifically through social media platforms.[40]

Online democratic engagement also provides increased participatory opportunities for traditionally under-engaged or disengaged demographic populations. For example, African-American users who participate in social media are 3 percent more likely to follow a public official or candidate than White users; although Hispanic social media users are much less likely than either African-American or White users to follow candidates or public officials on social media.[41] Additionally, social media platforms, like YouTube, have been found to be instrumental in mobilizing young people during elections.[42] Young adults, who have historically shown chronic levels of disengagement, who can now engage democratically through online networks have seemingly found their democratic voice through social media and have used online platforms to become democratically engaged on their own terms.[43] Young citizens, 18- to 29-year-olds, are more likely than individuals of older age demographics to use social media to "like" or promote political material, post their thoughts or opinions on political issues, repost political content, encourage the democratic engagement of others, post links to political stories, belong to political groups, and follow candidates on social media.[44] Although it is impossible to quantify how this type of online democratic engagement directly translates into offline political behaviors, such as attending rallies, volunteering, and voting, social media has proven to be a viable medium through which political dialogue amongst the constituency occurs.[45]

While a measurable online democratic participation gaps still exists, especially with regard to income and Internet penetration and differences between how older and younger demographics' use of social media, there is evidence that democratic engagement via social media platforms is decreasing some historic socioeconomic disparities. The emergence of an online participatory class through social media has created more users who more readily engage in democracy through online platforms and has begun to situate sites like YouTube as centers of democratic engagement.

A SITE OF PARTICIPATORY CULTURE

YouTube is as a site of participatory culture. In its environment, politicians, campaigns, and the mainstream media no longer have total, or quite often any, control over political messages. Through enabling the development of networks of cultural citizens, YouTube permits individuals to encounter others with cultural differences and participate in deliberative interactions across structures of belief, identity, and political orientation. Within these networks, citizens can benefit from the obtainment and dissemination of information in an efficient and timely manner[46] and the costs associated with information and communication are reduced.[47] Specifically, this participatory cost reduction paves the way for a greater proportion of minority or traditionally marginalized groups' voices to resonate in the public sphere.[48] Participation of this nature is vital for democratic engagement because discussions across these structures engage a larger number of participants that often cascade through multiple levels of nested comments. In general, these discussions tend to be wider and deeper than other types of political discussions.[49] When individuals participate in collectives formed around shared interests, where individuals from democratically marginalized groups feel free and welcome to participate, participative political spaces can be constituted.[50] When individuals feel as if they are developing a more powerful democratic voice their efficacy, and likely their sustained democratic engagement, will increase.[51]

The ability of digital natives and Netizens to create citizen-to-citizen connections is a key component to the sustainability of YouTube's participatory culture. This environment is appealing to the interested populous because it provides options for unfettered communication between citizens about issues that affect citizens. YouTube users engage other users by following and discussing on comment threads attached to political videos, such as debates or advertisements, as well as on user-generated political videos. This bidirectionality of communication increases information flow and allows for filtering and active self-selection of information by users, which can ultimately help to further individuals' engagement with both information and other constituents.[52]

Beyond a political level, YouTube allows people to connect with others on emotional levels. When individuals engage one another through YouTube, they often provide other users with intimate, emotional, and personal information about themselves or their personal situations. Generally, users divulge these personal points of information as a way to situate their own personal circumstances within the context of the video being discussed or to help substantiate their points-of-view in comment threads. This participatory citizen voice often brings others into their world, complete with their surroundings and their realities, making this type of democratic participation a powerful political experience for users.[53] The communality that is developed through this type of communication can also heighten the likelihood of sustained engagement.

Since often voters do not see the world alike, participation through YouTube also serves a political surveillance function. Participants are able to view the questions, positions, and analyses of others who may come from divergent circumstances and locations, which permits users to understand situations from a position that extends beyond that of their own self-interests. YouTube comments can serve to articulate the interpersonal and intimate identity embedded in the everyday lives of the citizenry as a voice for larger public debate and discussion around social identities and cultural politics.[54] Sometimes, the deepest, and perhaps most honest, levels of participation can often be found amongst the mundane, long-tail comment threads where users' communication works to create spaces of common participatory culture and community formation. This communication can encourage intergroup understanding and help increase political tolerance.[55]

DEMOCRATIC PARTICIPATION AND MOBILIZATION

The participatory and highly democratically communicative environment sustained within YouTube has allowed for the emergence of new types of democratic participation and has contributed to increased democratic mobilization. Mobilization theorists contend that by lowering the barriers of participation and connecting citizens to other citizens, as well as to political officials, online engagement can lead to new forms of direct democracy.[56] Amplified by "mobilizing information," or specific calls to action,[57] YouTube's social tools facilitate increases in social capital and emphasize strong links between participation and users' democratic engagement. Unlike traditional media, YouTube is a real-time media which allows for instant fact checking of political information and direct interactions with other citizens, campaigns, and mainstream media outlets. As the world's second most used search engine behind Google, YouTube makes finding and sharing information easy and fast. When taken together, these attributes contribute to an amplification effect that occurs when individuals engage collectively in three specific online activities that heighten democratic engagement (a) seeking political information, (b) contributing to online political discussion, and (c) participating in online political activity.[58] Active users likely have a reciprocal relationship with the Internet regarding their democratic engagement.[59] This means, that the more individuals are exposed to democratically engaging material through YouTube, the more likely users are to choose to participate in engagement-oriented behaviors through the site. Research indicates that political interest that can be formed and formulated within organizational membership helps motivate individuals to follow politics and public affairs[60] and that political knowledge and mobilization are important indicators of democratic engagement.[61] Therefore, "membership" in the YouTube community can provide users with the platform where both information-seeking and motivation behaviors can be fulfilled and democratic engagement can be intensified.

Since the very early studies on political participation, scholars have correlated limited access to and interest in political information to the public's collective lack of democratic engagement.[62] However, the Internet has emerged as a tool that provides information at a low cost, helping to improve the democratic process and renewing citizens' enthusiasm for political involvement.[63] Political information gathered online has been found to positively associate with citizens' civic participation, mobilization, and engagement[64] and voters who go online to seek out political information are likely to be better informed, more politically efficacious, and more democratically engaged.[65] The widespread online circulation of something as simple as a political video can help to fill political information deficiencies. For instance, if a person did not watch a broadcast political debate, but came across a video clip from the debate via YouTube, they may then attempt to find more information regarding the debate, discuss this debate clip with friends, or share the clip with others, allowing them to become politically oriented about a topic or issue they were not heavily connected to prior to their engagement with YouTube. Additionally, political discussions held through YouTube tend to cluster around topics that correspond to wider and deeper levels of information gathering. This level of engagement demonstrates a departure from the information structures exhibited in other types of political discussions and serves to further enhance individuals' political knowledge and understanding.[66]

YouTube's provision for user-generated content gives interested individuals a method of democratic engagement not available through most media. Creators of user-generated content believe that through the process of content generation, they possess the opportunity to be recognized, publicize their expertise, learn more about the world, and socialize with friends.[67] Often, individuals who are actively engaged in content generation are more focused on satisfying recognition needs than developing content for altruistic information dissemination.[68] However, both the creation and ingestion of user-generated content illustrates the role that "technicity," the creation of new kinds of social and cultural relationships formed through particular activities with specific technologies, play in the democratic engagement process.[69] User-generated content gives the audience the ability to access their world through different forms of communication, by being both a producer and consumer of media content. YouTube provides users the ability to simultaneously act upon an issue of pertinence while creating sharable content; this type of engagement is only possible in an information-rich environment like YouTube.[70] The notion of technicity could also provide an important link between content creation and external political efficacy.[71] As collective political identities are increasingly mediated through technology and online platforms progressively function as more integral parts of political communication, user-generated content, which is indicative of a higher level of democratic participation, may serve as a catalyst for the public's participatory political life.[72]

Contemporary research suggests that engagement through online video sites and social networking platforms can increase the publics' information levels and stimulate its political knowledge.[73] Engagement via YouTube provides users access to peer-to-peer communication, political information, and mobilization and organization tools, all of which can increase individuals' political knowledge and ultimately, lead to heightened democratic engagement and an elevated democratic culture. The sheer consumption of online political videos, which is practically immeasurable because of its consistent and exponential growth, indicates that the public has both a willingness and desire to engage democratically through YouTube. As citizens develop enhanced social agency and situational political involvement, YouTube becomes an efficient and easy-to-use mobilization tool that individuals use to seek out political information and participate in alternative forms of democratic engagement. As a vehicle for mobilizing constituents and reinventing how the public engages with the government, YouTube has the capacity to revitalize public deliberation and produce "strong democracy."[74]

Individuals with access are increasingly willing to engage democratically through Internet platforms and are energized by the many opportunities for them to ask questions, enter into dialogue, raise issues, tell stories, and engage in current affairs.[75] A majority of Internet users who follow politicians, campaigns, or political groups through social networking sites report increased feelings of personal connectedness with the politicians or groups they follow.[76] Because of this, YouTube offers politicians a ready-made mechanism through which to directly engage their constituency and empower them to become more democratically active through endogenous and exogenous types of engagement.[77] By providing the public with specific opportunities for democratic engagement, politicians can leverage the YouTube environment in a manner that establishes a mutually beneficial relationship for both them and the citizenry.

Beyond the posting of videos, YouTube's linking process allows the site to function as a valuable information portal.[78] By associating videos from a wide variety of sources, including users, media sources, and politicians, individuals can easily gather and process additional information related directly to the video they have watched. YouTube also functions as an important fact-checking platform for political information. If users come across information that is incorrect or misrepresented, they are highly likely to draw attention to it and discuss it virally, which essentially requires candidates or campaigns to respond almost immediately.[79] Collectively, YouTube users have demonstrated a powerful level of engagement with political messages and have used the platform to elevate their information seeking and democratic engagement.

YouTube has also shifted the power relationship between politics, media industries, and consumers. It functions as a site of cultural commons and political listening amongst its users. It is also home to many alternative or counter public spheres. The nature of its environment encourages otherness, allows for the individual representation of identities and perspectives, and offers an environment where uses can encounter cultural differences.[80] YouTube is not bound by the traditional confines of democratic engagement; instead, it functions as a mediating mechanism for cultural and political citizenship that is created and disseminated by ordinary citizens. It is a public space that cuts across typical political divisions and is inclusive of a wide range of perspectives. Through YouTube, videos passed virally between users emerge as important rhetorical and persuasive artifacts and individuals, regardless of political orientation or geographic location, can engage in boundless political discussion.[81]

ENHANCING DEMOCRATIC ENGAGEMENT

Most of the voting population is, at the very least, familiar with YouTube and can easily access political videos; thus, making the ability for politicians to reach voters via YouTube virtually limitless. While offering politicians a ready-made audience, the vast number of active YouTubers also require politicians to figure out how to strategically motivate these potential supporters to not only watch their videos, but to become participatory members of their constituency. One of the most considerable challenges of using YouTube for political information distribution is turning video viewing something actionable and giving the audience a clear responsibility to engage in after viewing the videos.[82] To combat this, politicians have focused on effectively embedding participatory tools into videos on their official YouTube channels. Campaigns have strategically linked their main campaign websites to YouTube and have worked to embed portals for sharing, donating, and volunteering directly into YouTube videos. Through the inclusion of specific content, such as candid behind-the-scenes footage, videos of rallies and campaign stops, and user-generated content, politicians promote engagement and relationship-building videos throughout YouTube. The most important strategic goals for political YouTube channels are to make it clear how the voter fits into the political environment and to make it easy for potential voters, contributors, and volunteers to take immediate and measurable participatory action without ever having to navigate away from YouTube.

Campaigns frequently use YouTube videos to make supporters feel engaged and personally connected to politicians and other voters. Political YouTube channels often include videos of average Americans discussing why they support specific politicians, videos asking supporters to stand with politicians regarding certain issues, and videos that serve to connect viewers to other supporters. For example, during the 2012 campaign, a video titled "Meet Alex," followed Alex, a father and Obama organizer, as he campaigned for the president's re-election. A different video recounted how a ten-year-old named Ian wanted to meet and thank Obama for bringing his father home from Iraq.[83] Videos containing this type of content can be vital to campaign communication as the believability in political advertising is correlated to the perceived value of the information source in the video.[84] In other words, the public attaches significance and believability to the speakers in this type of political communication. Other types of engagement-oriented videos include high-ranking political officials and celebrities endorsing politicians and videos of grassroots organizing efforts illustrating how individuals in targeted voting blocs can impact the outcome of elections. These videos allow supporters to feel involved in the political movements. These videos also help to address voters' primary justifications for watching online political videos: to gather information about candidates and campaigns, to feel more personally connected to politicians, and to find ways to connect democratically.[85]

Politicians have also capitalized on the hyperlinked nature of YouTube by directing users to specific videos where they can immediately and simultaneously become democratically engaged. For example, John Edwards' 2008 candidacy announcement video specifically directed viewers to go to the campaign's official website to become involved in his One Core organization. In 2011, candidate Tim Pawlenty actively used YouTube videos to entice his supporters to serve as his personal community advocates and ambassadors by becoming part of the "Pawlenty Action" team; members were rewarded with online "badges" for actively promoting the candidate through social media platforms. During the 2012 election, Barack Obama used YouTube videos to encourage unregistered voters to register through the website GottaRegister.com and emphasized the importance of their personal efficacy and voting.

Encouraging this type of participatory democratic behavior moves the audience from one of passive viewership into actively engaged members of the polity. Politicians that are successful at motivating supporters to a level of active participation can successfully, and inexpensively, use unofficial teams of online supporters to collect, produce, and spread videos and to combat unfavorable video comments by posting positive content ratings.[86] Politicians can easily and effectively generate an empowered army of informal spokespeople advocating on their behalf throughout the hyperlinked nature of the social media environment.[87] Creating this type of value exchange between politicians and supporters lays important groundwork for an engaged online constituency that can potentially translate online participation into important offline engagement behaviors, like canvassing and voting.

CONCLUSIONS AND CHALLENGES

The sheer number of people using YouTube to engage in politics is indicative of both the prowess and reach of YouTube as a vehicle for democratic engagement and a site of participatory culture. Politicians have been successful at not only generating substantial viewership numbers for campaign videos, but also at strategically engaging voters in and through YouTube content. These factors are illustrative of YouTube's potential as an important media for politics and government in the United States. Research indicates that media use is important in the formation and expressions of efficacy and that the more citizens connect their self-interests to politics, the more democratically engaged they will become.[88] Additionally, research illustrates that individuals who are engaged in public-affairs oriented media, which one could argue that YouTube has become, have higher levels of political interest and are more democratically active and engaged.[89] Ultimately, it is clear that Internet use and democratic engagement may be jointly determined with some correlation.[90]

Internet enthusiasts believe in what some call a "utopian view" of the ways that the Internet will bring about more a substantially democratically engaged electorate. Others lament that media platforms like YouTube fail to cultivate social capital and instead foster undemocratic ideals, such as political fragmentation and incivility.[91] For example, comments and negativity from other citizens may lead to frustration and disengagement. There is also postulation that political Internet platforms reinforce traditional mediated power relationships[92] and that established political actors project a stronger voice than citizens.[93] Critics suggest that platforms for online engagement only facilitate engagement amongst those already informed, motivated, and engaged[94] and simply reflect "politics as usual."[95] Additional concerns for the engaging power of sites like YouTube contend that the engagement and participatory actions that occurs through such sites is not legitimate democratic engagement, rather engagement without the analytic, critical, and advocacy skills that are necessary to vitalize American democracy.[96] It is argued that surface-level engagement, where social media participants are more invested in "adding glitter to pages" and poking their "friends" is not the type of civic-minded engagement that enhances democratic participation.[97]

Additionally, political fragmentation, which may be an unintended byproduct of an electoral audience overwhelmed with the wealth of on-line information, can result in the formation of public opinions within cultural enclaves, which functions conversely to the ideals of democratic engagement. Critics suggest that most users of social media are logging in for the purposes of hanging out with people that they already know and not to engage beyond their current cultural comfort zone. Despite the ability to engage with a wide range of individuals online, some research points to the tendency for users to discount opinion diversity and to instead engage within congruent communities of interest.[98] Concern is that users have a high probability of only engaging with a very similar "other," individuals whom they may not know perse, but who are very similar in demographic and ideological make up. This behavior attests to a growing tendency among the online public to avoid content that they deem undesirable.[99]

The realities of digital participation gaps must also be considered when touting the possibilities of YouTube for enhancing democracy. As with any technological medium, participation is limited to the segment of the population whose motivations, technological competencies, and site-specific cultural capital align in such a way as to make participation possible.[100] Limited digital literacies and the inclusivity of online com-munication technologies may allow established political actors to take greater advantage of online political information, subsequently widening the digital divide between information have and have-nots.[101] Despite research suggesting that the socioeconomic divisions historically linked to disengagement and disenfranchisement may be dwindling, there is still limited evidence proving that online political participation is funda-mentally altering the historical associations between offline political par-ticipation, such as voting, and socioeconomic factors.[102] Finally, evaluat-ing the virility of democratic engagement via social media platforms can be difficult because a large portion of existing research treats engagement via the Internet somewhat unidimensionally.[103]

Despite criticism that truly engaging the constituency through online and social media platforms is not possible, there is evidence that individ-uals are indeed turning to sites like YouTube for democratic engagement. There is likely some truth to the criticism that political information likely only penetrates the social networks of those who are already politically inclined. However, the configurations of YouTube allow for increases in incidental learning to occur, as one user's seeking of political information and content is likely to be seen by other users within their personal network. Future research into YouTube and democratic engagement could help to address some of these criticisms through content and descriptive analyses of democratic engagement on YouTube, the development of public involvement indices that could serve to answer whether or not YouTube is a realistic and sustainable platform for engagement, and through longitudinal survey data regarding how users are engaging democratically through YouTube.

For online democratic engagement and participation to fully help the United States' political system evolve and become more inclusive, both the public and political officials must commit to being technologically connected. Politicians and the government cannot be perceived by the public as resisting the democratic potentials of interactive communication technologies[104] and must not simply employ these platforms during elections to encourage their constituencies to help them get elected. For their part, the citizenry must commit to converting their online motivation for engagement and participation into effective and concrete political action. The attainment of an engaged and participatory democracy is dependent upon the attitudes and competencies of the electorate, its adherence to important social and political principles, and its participation in the maintenance of a vital and inspiring democracy.[105] As technologies and options for online democratic engagement further develop, YouTube will likely be employed, both by politicians and citizens, as an evolving mechanism for democratic engagement.

NOTES

1. Michael Delli Carpini, "Mediating Democratic Engagement: The Impact of Communications on Citizens' Involvement in Poical and Civic Life," in *Handbook of Political Communication Research* (Mahwah, NJ: Lawrence Erlbaum Associates, 2004), 395–434.

2. Murray Edelman, *From Art to Politics* (Chicago, IL: University of Chicago Press, 1995).

3. Delli Carpini, "Mediating Democratic Engagement: The Impact of Communications on Citizens' Involvement in Poical and Civic Life."

4. Peter Levine and Mark Lopez, *Youth Voter Turnout Has Declined, by Any Measure* (University of Maryland's School of Public Affairs: The Center for Information & Research on Civic Learning & Engagement, September 2002), http://civicyouth.org/research/products/Measuring_Youth_Voter_Turnout.pdf.

5. Michael McDonald and Samuel Popkin, "The Myth of the Vanishing Voter," *American Political Science Review* 95, no. 4 (2001): 936–74.

6. Mary Cooper, "Low Voter Turnout: Is America's Democracy in Trouble?," *Congressional Quarterly* 10 (2000): 833–56.

7. Vanda Rideout and Vincent Mosco, "Communication Policy in the United States," in *Democratizing Communication: Comparative Perspectives on Information and Power* (Cresskill, NJ: Hampton Press, 1997).

8. Nina Eliasoph, "'Close to Home': The Work of Avoiding Politics," *Theory and Society* 26, no. 5 (1997): 605–47.

9. Robert Putnam, *Bowling Alone: The Collapse and Revival of American Community* (New York, NY: Simon and Schuster, 2000).

10. Sidney Verba, Kay Schlozman, and Henry Brady, *Voice and Equality: Civic Voluntarism in American Politics* (Cambridge, MA: Harvard University Press, 1995).

11. Mitchell McKinney, Linda Kaid, and Dianne Bystrom, "The Role of Communication in Civic Engagement," in *Communicating Politics: Engaging the Public in Democratic Life (frontiers in Political Communication)* (New York, NY: Peter Lang Publishing, 2005), 3–26.

12. Verba, Schlozman, and Brady, *Voice and Equality: Civic Voluntarism in American Politics*.

13. Delli Carpini, "Mediating Democratic Engagement: The Impact of Communications on Citizens' Involvement in Polical and Civic Life."

14. Michael Delli Carpini, "Gen.com: Youth, Civic Engagement, and the New Information Environment," *Political Communication* 17, no. 4 (2000): 341–49.

15. Andrew Chadwick, *Internet Politics* (New York, NY: Oxford University Press, 2006).

16. Delli Carpini, "Mediating Democratic Engagement: The Impact of Communications on Citizens' Involvement in Polical and Civic Life."

17. Robert McChesney, *Rich Media, Poor Democracy: Communication Politics in Dubious Times* (Chicago, IL: University of Illinois Press, 2000).

18. Jean Burgess and Joshua Green, *YouTube: Online Video and Participatory Culture* (Cambridge, MA: Polity Press, 2009).

19. Bryan Alexander, "Web 2.0 and Emergent Multiliteracies," *Theory into Practice* 47, no. 2 (2008): 150–60.

20. Jurgen Habermas, *The Structural Transformation of the Public Sphere* (Cambridge, MA: The MIT Press, 1989).

21. Douglas Kellner, "Intellectuals, the New Public Spheres, and Techno-Politics," in *The Politics of Cyberspace: A Political Science Reader* (New York, NY: Routledge, 1998).

22. Louis Leung, "User-Generated Content on the Internet: An Examination of Gratifications, Civic Engagement and Psychological Empowerment," *New Media & Society* 11, no. 8 (2009): 1327–47.

23. Delli Carpini, "Mediating Democratic Engagement: The Impact of Communications on Citizens' Involvement in Polical and Civic Life."

24. Wendy Rahn and John Transue, "Social Trust and Value Change: The Decline of Social Capital in American Youth, 1976–1995," *Political Psychology* 19, no. 3 (1998): 545–65.

25. LaChrystal Ricke, "YouTube," in *Encyclopedia of Social Media and Politics* (Thousand Oaks, CA: Sage, 2014), 1411–31.

26. Nick Stevenson, *Cultural Citizenship: Cosmopolitan Questions* (Maidenhead, UK: Open University Press, 2003).

27. William Uricchio, "Cultural Citizenship in the Age of P2P Networks," in *Eurpoean Culture and the Media* (Bristol, UK: Intellect Books, 2004), 139–63.

28. Center for Information and Research on Civic Learning and Engagement, *Short Term Impacts, Long Term Opportunities: The Political and Civic Engagement of Young Adults in America*, Unpublished report (Washington, DC: Circle, 2002).

29. Joanna Brenner and Aaron Smith, *72 percent of Online Adults Are Social Networking Site Users* (Washington, DC: Pew Research Center's Internet & American Life Project, August 5, 2013), http://www.pewInternet.org/~/media//Files/Reports/2013/PIP_Social_networking_sites_update.pdf.

30. Lee Rainie et al., *Social Media and Political Engagement* (Pew Internet and American Life Project, October 19, 2012).

31. Ibid.

32. Keith Hampton et al., *Social Networking Sites and Our Lives* (Pew Internet & American Life Project, June 16, 2011), http://pewInternet .org/Reports/2011/Technology-and-social-networks.aspx.

33. Ibid.

34. Aaron Smith et al., *The Internet and Civic Engagement* (Pew Internet & American Life Project, September 1, 2009), http://www.pewInternet .org/Reports/2009/15--The-Internet -and-Civic-Engagement.aspx.

35. Eric Uslaner, "Social Capital and Net," *Communications of the ACM* 43, no. 12 (2000): 60–64.

36. Rainie et al., *Social Media and Political Engagement.*

37. Smith et al., *The Internet and Civic Engagement.*

38. Ibid.

39. Ibid.

40. Ibid.

41. Ibid.

42. Russell Dalton, *The Good Citizen: How a Younger Generation Is Reshaping American Politics* (New York, NY: CQ Press, 2009).

43. Jody Baumgartner and Jonathan Morris, "MyFaceTube Politics: Social Networking Web Sites and Political Engagement of Young Adults," *Social Science Computer Review* 28, no. 1 (2010): 24–44.

44. Aaron Smith, *Civic Engagement in the Digital Age* (Washington, DC: Pew Internet & American Life Project, April 25, 2013), http://pewInternet .org/~/media/Files/Reports/2013/PIP_CivicEngagementintheDigitalAge.pdf.

45. Rob Lever, "2012 US Election Campaign a Digital Battleground," *Google News*, October 13, 2012, http://www.google.com/hostednews/afp/article/ALeqM5h-83y9eiaiOfOfwRUEOHlkqqpgPg.

46. Hun Myoung Park and James Perry, "Do Campaign Websites Really Matter in Electoral Civic Engagement? Empirical Evidence from the 2004 and 2006 Post-Election Internet Tracking Survey," in *Politicking Online: The Transformation of Election Campaign Communication* (Piscataway, NJ: Rutgers University Press, 2009).

47. Howard Rheingold, *The Virtual Community* (Reading, MA: addison-Wesley, 1993).

48. Ibid.

49. Sandra Gonzalez-Bailon, Andreas Kaltenbrunner, and Rafael Banchs, "The Structure of Political Discussion Networks: A Model for the Analysis of Online Deliberation," *Journal of Information Technology* 25 (2010): 230–43.

50. Joke Hermes, "Hidden Debates: Rethinking the Relationship between Popular Culture and the Public Sphere," *Javnost- The Public* 13, no. 4 (2006): 27–44.

51. Russell Neuman, Marion Just, and Ann Crigler, *Common Knowledge: News and the Construction of Political Meaning* (Chicago, IL: University of Chicago Press, 1992).

52. Delli Carpini, "Mediating Democratic Engagement: The Impact of Communications on Citizens' Involvement in Polical and Civic Life."

53. Jose Vargas, "YouTube Users Will Quiz Candidates," *The Washington Post*, July 19, 2007.

54. Patricia Lange, "Publically Private and Privately Public: Social Networking on YouTube," *Journal of Computer-Mediated Communication* 13, no. 1 (2007): 361–80.

55. Vincent Price, Joseph Cappella, and Lilach Nir, "Does Disagreement Contribute to More Deliberative Opinion?," *Political Communication* 19, no. 1 (2002): 95–112.

56. Rita Kirk and Dan Schill, "A Digital Agora: Citizen Participation in the 2008 Presidential Debates," *American Behavioral Scientist* 55, no. 3 (2011): 325–47.

57. Carmen Sirianni and Lewis Friedland, *Civic Innovation in America: Community Empowerment, Public Policy, and the Movement for Civic Renewal* (Berkeley, CA: University of California Press, 2001).

58. Kirk and Schill, "A Digital Agora: Citizen Participation in the 2008 Presidential Debates."

59. Paul DiMaggio et al., "Social Implications of the Internet ," *Annual Review of Sociology* 27, no. 1 (2001): 307–36.

60. Verba, Schlozman, and Brady, *Voice and Equality: Civic Voluntarism in American Politics.*

61. Park and Perry, "Do Campaign Websites Really Matter in Electoral Civic Engagement? Empirical Evidence from the 2004 and 2006 Post-Election Internet Tracking Survey."

62. Angus Campbell et al., *The American Voter* (Chicago, IL: University of Chicago Press, 1960).

63. Anthony Corrado and Charles Firestone, *Elections in Cyberspace: Toward a New Era in American Politics* (Washington, DC: The Aspen Institute, 1996).

64. Manuel Castells, *The Internet Galaxy: Reflections on the Internet, Business and Society* (Oxford, UK: Oxford University Press, 2001).

65. Kate Kenski and Natalie Stroud, "Connections between Internet Use and Political Efficacy, Knowledge, and Participation," *Journal of Broadcasting and Electronic Media* 50, no. 2 (2006): 173–92.

66. Gonzalez-Bailon, Kaltenbrunner, and Banchs, "The Structure of Political Discussion Networks: A Model for the Analysis of Online Deliberation."

67. Leung, "User-Generated Content on the Internet: An Examination of Gratifications, Civic Engagement and Psychological Empowerment."

68. Ibid.

69. David Thomas, "The Technophilic Body: On Technicity in William Gibson's Cyborg Culture," in *The Cyberculture Reader* (London, UK: Routledge, 2000).

70. Sirianni and Friedland, *Civic Innovation in America: Community Empowerment, Public Policy, and the Movement for Civic Renewal.*

71. Jon Dovey and Helen Kennedy, *Game Cultures: Computer Games as New Media* (New York, NY: McGraw Hill, 2006).

72. Dan Gilmore, *We the Media: Grassroots Journalism by the People, for the People* (Sebastopol, CA: O'Reilly Media, Inc., n.d.).

73. Baumgartner and Morris, "MyFaceTube Politics: Social Networking Web Sites and Political Engagement of Young Adults."

74. Benjamin Barber, "Three Scenarios for the Future of Technology and Strong Democracy," *Political Science Quarterly* 113, no. 4 (1999): 573–89.

75. Michael Gurevitch, Stephen Coleman, and Jay Blumler, "Political Communication – Old and New Media Relationships," *The ANNALS of the American Academy of Political and Social Science* 645 (2009): 164–81.

76. Aaron Smith, *22 percent of Online Americans Used Social Networking or Twitter for Politics in 2010 Campaign* (Washington, DC: Pew Internet & American Life Project, January 27, 2011), http://www.pewInternet . org/~/media//Files/Reports/2011/PIP-Social- Media-and-2010-Election.pdf.

77. Park and Perry, "Do Campaign Websites Really Matter in Electoral Civic Engagement? Empirical Evidence from the 2004 and 2006 Post-Election Internet Tracking Survey."

78. Kirk and Schill, "A Digital Agora: Citizen Participation in the 2008 Presidential Debates."

79. Ricke, "YouTube."

80. Burgess and Green, *YouTube: Online Video and Participatory Culture.*

81. Ricke, "YouTube."

82. James Peters, "With Video, Obama Looks to Expand Campaign's Reach through Social Media," *The New York Times*, May 14, 2012, http://www.nytimes.com/2012/03/15/us/politics/with-youtube-video-obama-looks-to-expand-social-media-reach.html?_r=0.

83. LaChrystal Ricke, "YouTube and the 2012 Presidential Election: An Examination of How Obama and Romney's Official YouTube Channels Were Used in Campaign Communication.," in *Presidential Campaigning and Social Media: An Analysis of the 2012 Election.* (New York, NY: Oxford University Press, 2014), 246–58.

84. Aron O'Cass, "Political Advertising Believability and Information Source Value During Elections," *Journal of Advertising* XXXXI, no. 1 (2002): 63–74.

85. Aaron Smith and Maeve Duggan, *Online Political Videos and Campaign 2012* (Washington, DC: Pew Internet & American Life Project, November 2, 2012), http://

www.pewInternet.org/~/media//Files/Reports/2012/PIP_State_of_the_2012_
race_online_video_final.pdf.

86. Heather Greenfield, "YouTube Boom May Mean New Jobs on Campaigns," *E.politics*, January 30, 2007, http://www.epolitics.com/2007/01/30/tech-daily-youtube-boom-may-mean-new-jobs-on-campaigns/.

87. Jay Samit, "All Politics Is Social: Social Media Engagement Will Decide Election 2012," *SocialVibe*, June 2011, http://advertising.socialvibe.com/political_solutions.

88. Delli Carpini, "Mediating Democratic Engagement: The Impact of Communications on Citizens' Involvement in Polical and Civic Life."

89. Michael Delli Carpini and Scott Keeter, *What Americans Know about Politics and Why It Matters* (New Haven, CT: Yale University Press, 1996).

90. Delli Carpini, "Mediating Democratic Engagement: The Impact of Communications on Citizens' Involvement in Polical and Civic Life."

91. Hanspeter Kriesi et al., *Democracy in the Age of Globalization and Mediatization: Challenges to Democracy in the 21st Century* (London, UK: Palgrave Macmillian, 2013).

92. Andrea Kavanaugh, "Community Networks and Civic Engagement: A Social Network Approach," *The Good Society* 11, no. 3 (2002): 17–24.

93. Pippa Norris, *The Digital Divide: Civic Engagement, Information Poverty, and the Internet Worldwide* (New York, NY: Cambridge University Press, 2001).

94. Delli Carpini, "Mediating Democratic Engagement: The Impact of Communications on Citizens' Involvement in Polical and Civic Life."

95. Uslaner, "Social Capital and Net."

96. William Rehg, "The Argumentation Theorist in Deliberative Democracy," *Controversia: An International Journal of Debate and Democratic Renewal* 1 (2002): 18–42.

97. Danah Boyd, "Can Social Network Sites Enable Political Action?," in *Rebooting America* (New York, NY: Personal Democracy, 2008).

98. Anthony Wilhelm, *Democracy in the Digital Age: Challenges to Political Life in Cyberspace* (New York, NY: Routledge, 2000).

99. Cass Sunstein, *Republic.com* (Princeton, NJ: Princeton University Press, 2001).

100. Burgess and Green, *YouTube: Online Video and Participatory Culture.*

101. Norris, *The Digital Divide: Civic Engagement, Information Poverty, and the Internet Worldwide.*

102. Smith et al., *The Internet and Civic Engagement.*

103. Dhavan Shah, Nojin Kwak, and R. Lance Holbert, "'Connecting' and 'Disconnecting' with Civic Life: Patterns of Internet Use and the Production of Social Capital," *Political Communication* 18 (2001): 141–62.

104. Stephen Coleman, David Morrison, and Michael Syenneyig, "New Media and Political Efficacy," *International Journal of Communication* 2 (n.d.): 771–91.

105. Frans Van Eemeren, "Democracy and Argumentation," *Controversia: An International Journal of Debate and Democratic Renewal* 1 (2002): 69–84.

NINE

YouTube and Politics: The Future

YouTube Co-Founder and CEO, Chad Hurley, stated that, "at its core, YouTube is about democracy and self-expression and we're proud to be providing politicians with an environment where they can share information with voters."[1] In just a few short election cycles, YouTube has become normalized as a central platform for political communication. Through YouTube, political candidacies have been announced, mash-ups and user-generated political content have been seen by millions upon millions of viewers, the public has been invited to participate in the creation of political debates, and political speeches that may have only been seen a small audience have become some of the most viewed political moments in history. Through its ease of use, person-to-person connectivity, and asynchronous interactivity, YouTube has emerged as a centralized political communication platform that connects people to politics, and politically to one another, in ways beyond those of many other mass media technologies.

As an evolving, interactive, and media-rich site, YouTube has amplified the substantial growth of online political behavior. YouTube can harness political participation in the production, amalgamation, and exchange of information in a manner not possible through other mediated systems.[2] It has become an essential platform through which the public has chosen to become politically informed and engaged. Political videos accessed on YouTube have become invaluable components of both political communication and digital mobilization. Enhanced audience analysis and microtargeting techniques have allowed new patterns of media use with distinct sociocultural advantages to emerge.[3] YouTube has provided for the development of new communicative spaces, which have brought with them substantial benefits, recognizable challenges, and new opportunities for the future of the political Internet.

NEW COMMUNICATION SPACE

YouTube has allowed for new forms of political interaction to take place and has challenged politicians and campaigns to effectively manage new communication spaces and formations of mediation. Historically, campaigns have had a limited range of media bases to cover. Contemporarily, they are now involved in multidimensional impression management across broad, dynamic, and often unpredictable media environments.[4] Recognizing the changing face of interactive online political spaces, Democratic strategist Mary Anne Marsh stated, "You just have to assume that wherever you are . . . unless you're in your home alone, you're being recorded. Your election will be recorded from beginning to end, and so you have to be literally mindful every moment of every day, what you do and what you say."[5] While YouTube can come with inherent challenges, the political spaces created on the platform provide public spheres with constantly evolving communicative and engagement opportunities.

YouTube provides politicians with the prospect and ability to shift away from communication-as-usual and to connect new types of information seekers with political information. Through YouTube, strategic microsites of information disbursement, that amplify an authentic campaign voice, can capitalize on novel and compelling ways to inform and engage constituencies. Viewership data and user statistics indicate that the public desires to engage with political content through YouTube and that when given the opportunity it is able to substantively participate in the creation of national political discourse. Beyond functioning as a vital political tool for campaigns, that can serve as an economical alternative platform for information distribution and advertising dispersal, YouTube has the potential to help revitalized public spheres thrive through a highly democratically engaged populous. As with any evolving media platform, YouTube brings with it marked advantages and recognizable challenges.

YOUTUBE'S POLITICAL BENEFITS

One of YouTube's most substantial benefits is the opportunity for interested citizens to structure their individual involvement with the nation's political conversation in ways that feel personal and empowering. Providing the ability for the creation and sustainment of personal and effectual engagement can lead to the public retaining higher levels of participation, ownership of political ideas, and political efficacy. Political communication strategists that understand this and consistently seek ways to better engage both their current constituencies and future voters benefit from an embedded and already active populous with whom to engage.

This population then becomes easier to invigorate during future elections.

Recent research indicates that 85 percent of Americans use the Internet on at least an occasional basis and that some demographics have reached nearly universal Internet adoption rates.[6] Practically all members, 98 percent, of 18- to 29-year-olds are considered consistent Internet users, as well as 96 percent of college students, and 96 percent of individuals living in households that earn 75,000 dollars or more per year.[7] Collectively, Internet users have been found to use social media to dynamically engage in online political activism. Contrary to concerns that the Internet and social media can cause fragmented democratic engagement, research indicates that Americans are politically engaging through social media at increasing rates. Contemporarily, roughly 39 percent of American adults use social media platforms specifically for political interaction.[8] Research from the MacArthur Research Network on Youth and Participatory Politics also indicates that young people who are politically active online are twice as likely to vote as young people who do not engage with online political content. [9] Additional research from the Pew Research Center for the People and the Press discovered that 18- to 29-year-olds consistently use the Internet to access political campaign information and that they view online campaign videos at roughly double the frequency of individuals ages 30 and older.[10] Collectively, this research may position the Internet and social media platforms as key variables in the ongoing epidemic of high disengagement and low voter turnout among America's younger voter populations.

An older American demographic has also seen a rise in Internet use, with 56 percent of individuals age 65 and older reporting frequent Internet use.[11] Of Internet users who are over the age of 50 and who also participate in social media sites, 33 percent utilize social media to gather political news, post political content, and to engage in various other ways with candidates or political causes.[12] Usage patterns also indicate that the gap between younger and older demographics' use of social media for democratic engagement is shrinking. During recent elections, there was only roughly a 9 percent difference between the political social media engagement of those under 29 years of age and those over 50 years of age.[13] While younger Internet users are still the most likely population to engage in politics via social networking sites, the fastest growing segment of new social networking users is coming from those 74 and older.[14] Statistics such as these have begun to debunk the myth that political social networking is the domain of young liberals. The consistent increase in broadband access across all demographics, with broadband penetration reaching over 80 percent of the Millennial demographic (born 1977–1992) and over 70 percent of Generation X (born 1965–1976), will also likely have an impact upon the populations able to gain access to and engage with online politics during future elections.[15]

YouTube offers politicians a consistently highly-engaged population of viewers. On average, 35.4 percent of Internet users visit YouTube daily, equating to one Internet user out of every three visiting the site at least one time each day.[16] While YouTube users do not necessarily always spend a great deal of time on the site when they visit, averaging just under twenty-three minutes per visit, on an typical day, these users can visit YouTube an average of 15 times.[17] The popularity and dominance of YouTube in the online video realm has produced cultural changes in society and exemplified the potential of the Internet to be an epicenter of direct democracy. While Millennials are still the most likely demographic to watch online videos, with over 80 percent reporting having done so, older generations, specifically Older Boomers (born between 1946 and 1954), saw a 25 percent increase in video viewership behaviors between 2008 and 2010, and one in five members of the G.I. Generation (those ages 74 and up) indicate they watch online videos.[18] The political use of YouTube has broadened the cultural and sociopolitical implications of online politics. Combined with the widespread commerciality of the platform and an interactive, decentralized network of political communication that has the power to invigorate participatory democracy emerges.

THRIVING DEMOCRATIC SPACE

As more political information and communication moves online, there is growing evidence that Web 2.0 platforms, like YouTube, can have significant and measurable effects on individuals' political behavior and vote choice.[19] Interactive tools that allow users to freely discuss and see how other viewers have interpreted and rated videos have elevated YouTube from simply a site where individuals go to watch political videos to a virtual community with a thriving communal democratic space. YouTube has also produced interesting causal effects on political knowledge and participation. The viralability of political videos can create a "surprise effect," where individuals who were not necessarily seeking out political videos or content can unintentionally come across videos that individuals within their social networks have shared or commented on. In terms of campaign effects, this means that politicians are not simply drawing in existing supporters, but may also be reaching a potentially significant base of voters who are open to persuasion.[20]

The political orientations of YouTube have altered the ways that many individuals seek and gather political information. The emergence of influentials, who have emerged via the social networks of family, friends, and shared interest groups, has created a two-step flow Internet effect; whereby Web 2.0 platforms serve to promote political and campaign messages more widely and virally than candidates' official websites.[21] With direct effects from candidate websites waning, platforms such as

YouTube can serve as a source of information for influentials who in turn use this information and knowledge to mobilize others.[22] In the contemporary Internet environment, substantial and sustainable political conversation is occurring between members of the constituency on YouTube. Knowledge and opinions about candidates is no longer solidified through information gleaned directly from mainstream media sources. Instead interactions with influentials, who often possess similar socioeconomic and demographic characteristics and with whom specific interests are shared, enhance decision making.[23] Through the peer-to-peer linking of individuals, YouTube provides a venue where the type of self-organizing, exemplified by increases in both individual and collective efficacy, necessary for political mobilization and participatory democracy can thrive.

INTERACTIVE PUBLIC SPHERE

Through the empowerment of ordinary citizens and the creation of new public spaces, YouTube has enabled an evolving interactive public sphere to emerge. It has become a transformative platform where the sociopolitical power of individuals and noncorporate media entities can collectively participate in new means of organizing and mobilizing the constituency. YouTube has facilitated increased connectedness between not only politicians and the public, but between individuals and other individuals, as well as between the public and the media. This has created an environment where individuals have the opportunity to become active participants in the construction, and reconstruction, of a political culture that provides a distinct alternative to mainstream media. The platform provides a venue through which ordinary citizens can encourage and mobilize other ordinary citizens through sharing personal videos about their lives, their political decision making, and why they were ultimately compelled to vote for a specific candidate. Such engagement has the power to increase deliberative political communication amongst members of the populous with different interests, to promote human agency, and to function as distinct and alternative political moments. This interaction can have broad and beneficial sociopolitical outcomes as demographics who may have been historically less inclined to participate in top-down politics become democratically minded and politically conscious because of platform tools enabling social connections and change. This form of connectivity helps to reinvent the democratic polity as one of mutual self-organization and collective governance versus one of patronizing, top-down political elitism.[24] Individuals can tactically share information to mobilize others and increasingly capitalize on Web 2.0 activism, including developing and enacting watchdog tools which provide opportunities for ordinary citizens to scrutinize and critique political behavior.[25]

YouTube's digital revival of the public sphere is predicated on its decentralized, interactive, and participatory communication possibilities which allow for the autonomous and free-flowing discussions vital for a healthy democracy to occur. The plurality of voices allowed to engage in sustained and reflective discourse throughout the YouTube platform exemplify and amplify the ideals of a deliberative public sphere. Limited thresholds for participation invite the entire constituency to engage in the co-production of meaning and co-distribution of content that enables a spontaneous, flexible, and self-governed public sphere to flourish.[26] While some contend that the public has progressively shrunk into their respective private spheres,[27] YouTube has been able to enhance the quality of mass participation, political debate, and community development that is necessary in a representative democracy.[28]

YOUTUBE'S POLITICAL CHALLENGES

The politicizing of YouTube also comes with recognizable challenges and disadvantages. Despite the ever-growing adoption of YouTube for political and campaign communication, its role politic campaigns and communication has ignited criticism. Critics question, in this evolving and ever-expanding media ecology, if politicians have actually become more dependent upon professional campaign and image management because of the ongoing pressures to find novel ways of presenting themselves.[29] Contrary to the free flow of information and heightened connectedness to politicians for which many salute YouTube, the environment may have in fact inadvertently resulted in the death of spontaneity in political discourse. In a virally-mediated environment, such as YouTube, politicians are worried about unintentionally creating their own "macaca moment" and may be less inclined to experiment with unrefined messages or to speak unscripted at events. Online environments put even greater pressure on politicians to construct flawless political and personal images that seamlessly translate across all forms and formats of media. Increasingly, political actors also must compete with a multitude of voices also seeking public attention. Unlike campaigns of the past, where politicians generally only had to detract attention from other candidates, they must now contend with a multiplicity of social media pages, profiles, and actors all of which can easily distract the public campaigns' carefully crafted political messages. Instead of supplying a platform for spontaneous and lively political discussions and debate, these factors may ultimately contribute to more scripted discourse and the disintegration of richness in political rhetoric.

LONG-TERM RELEVANCE

The long-term political relevance of YouTube is also tenuous. Critics suggest that large video viewership numbers are not necessarily pivotal because many users are young, perhaps not highly politically engaged, and the translation of online engagement into offline behavior, specifically in the form of voting, across this demographic has been feeble at best. Campaigns often tout large viewership and "friend" numbers to exaggerate the reach of political messages; however, the sustainment of this perceived audience during non-election periods may prove challenging.[30] It is also difficult to know exactly what some of these viewership and follower numbers actually mean in terms of political engagement and message dissemination. It is hard to compare videos between campaigns and even within one campaign when the range of views can be a few hundred to multiple millions. Frequently, video views do not necessarily represent unique viewers, with users likely returning to watch the same video multiple times. Additionally, because videos can be easily linked through other pages, generating actual viewership data of YouTube videos is practically impossible. Videos can also quickly become the product of political decay, generating many views or going viral shortly after they are posted only to be quickly forgotten as the next new political moment arises. Ultimately, if politicians and campaigns are not able to entice their large numbers of viewers and followers to behave as desired, for instance through volunteering, donating, or voting, substantial online followings will likely not amass too much in the political aggregate.

LEGALITIES

Aside from political mishaps making their way to YouTube, there are many legal and ethical pitfalls that politicians must be wary of in the YouTube environment. Many campaigns and politicians freely repost interview and debate segments to their YouTube channels without first seeking permission of the media networks to which the segments legally belonged. For example, former presidential candidate Herman Cain's YouTube channel was permanently disabled by YouTube following multiple complaints from *Fox News* of copyright infringement related to the unauthorized posting of the network's news clips to Cain's YouTube channel. Many campaigns have also inappropriately used copyrighted material in advertisements, resulting in the subsequent and unceremonious removal of their political advertisements. For example, in 2008, John McCain's campaign posted two videos, called "Obama Love," to YouTube and asked supporters to vote on which one they liked the best (a strategy to encourage audience engagement). However, the McCain campaign did not acquire the rights to use the commercial's background music from its copyright holder and when the company found out, they demanded that it not be used, resulting in the commercials only being seen about 255,000 times before they were removed from YouTube.[31] Following this, the McCain campaign wrote YouTube and asked it to reconsider its video take-down policy.[32] However, YouTube maintained that any legitimate complaint of copyright infringement, such as the use of broadcast news clips in campaigns' online ads, was legal justification for YouTube to remove the videos.

During the 2012 election, Mitt Romney's campaign posted a video titled "Political Payoffs and Middle-Class Layoffs," featuring a snippet of Barack Obama singing the Al Green song "Let's Stay Together." The ad, which was intended to highlight the success and prosperity of Obama campaign donors while other Americans continued to struggle with a difficult economy, was reported to YouTube by BMG Rights Management as violating the Digital Millennium Copyright Act.[33] Although the Romney campaign claimed that use of the clips was protected under the fair use standard of copyright, YouTube removed the advertisement, as well as other clips of Obama singing the song at a fundraising event as they were found to have violated copyright protections. Following You-Tube's removal of Romney's advertisement, the campaign countered by demanding that YouTube remove a commercial circulated by the Obama campaign featuring Romney singing "America the Beautiful" also because of copyright infringement. Unfortunately, in this situation the Romney campaign illustrated its lack of understanding of copyright as unlike the Al Green song featured in the Romney advertisement, the copyright restrictions on "America the Beautiful" had expired and the song was considered public domain.

THE MULTI-VOICED CHALLENGE

The allowance for varied and multiple voices to engage in political content creation and distribution is arguably one of the most recognizable traits of YouTube. However, the ability for anyone to create, share, and disseminate political information, place viral value on their own opinions, distribute potentially uninformed political commentary, and to conceal biases or hidden agendas, is another substantial hurdle faced by politicians and campaigns in the YouTube environment. In a somewhat prophetic speech in 1970, Roger Mudd, a *CBS News* correspondent, criticized television for its tendency to "strike at emotions rather than intellect . . . on happenings rather than ideas; on shock rather than explanation; on personalization rather than ideas."[34] Mudd's sentiment exemplifies what occurs regularly in the political YouTube environment. The popularity of the platform has heightened the entertainment value of politics, as easily evidenced by the multiple millions of views generated by much of YouTube's satirically-driven political content, potentially lessening the impact of more serious political fodder. YouTube also allows individuals with limited, or sometimes no, political knowledge or credentials to participate in the creation and dissemination of political information. Any technologically savvy individual can easily capitalize on the immediacy of images and online videos, the viralability of which can easily privilege information over knowledge in the YouTube environment. A simple cursory look at YouTube's politics channel yields videos, advertisements, and mash-ups created by multiple entities, making it difficult to ascertain contents' original sources or assign credibility to the information. Additionally, while offering the public unprecedented access to information, the multiplicity of producers, sites, and distributors can overwhelm the audience with information overload[35] and create doubt about what information to trust.[36] The vast amount of inaccurate information that the constituency can now ingest can result in a pronounced knowledge gap between politically savvy and less discerning individuals. Ultimately, these factors can coalesce and create collateral damage for campaigns and politicians if they are unable to be at least one of the voices that the constituency is listening to or are unable to quickly and effectively rectify inappropriate representations or correct inaccurate information.

In what will be an ongoing battle between top-down and bottom-up political campaigning, politicians will have continued fundamental difficulties controlling content and image production and distribution in the digital world.[37] Not only is retaining control over content and images challenging, but seeking the removal or acquisition of profiles, channels, and accounts that appropriate a politician's name or image is exceptionally difficult. The best example of the challenge between command-and-control in mediated politics actually comes not from YouTube, but from a battle between the Barack Obama campaign and volunteer Joe Anthony over the Obama MySpace page. In 2004, Anthony created the Barack Obama MySpace, with no official affiliation to Obama, and grew the page into the flagship Obama destination on the MySpace platform. Fans of the page were encouraged to support the Obama campaign through donation widgets and to post the candidate's advertisements onto their own pages. Following the launch of MySpace's Impact Channel, which promoted candidate profiles and directed traffic to the candidates' sites, the page quickly grew from around 40,000 fans to over 160,000.[38] The activity on the page was so substantial, that the Obama campaign used Anthony's "unofficial" site as the campaign's "official" MySpace page rather than creating a competing Obama MySpace address. This is where previously unexplored situations considering the Internet, social media, and the organizational structure of campaigns came to a difficult and uncharted crossroad. Managing a page with over 160,000 followers was a growing challenge for Anthony, who reportedly spent between five and ten hours each day managing the page.[39] At the same time, the Obama campaign was increasingly concerned by their limited control over what someone with no official ties to the campaign was posting to and communicating through "their" site. However, since Anthony was the site's original creator, the campaign technically had no control over its contents, and when the situation between Anthony and the campaign became tenuous, Anthony changed the password, preventing the Obama campaign from accessing the page in any administrative capacity. Anthony offered control of the site to the Obama campaign, but requested to be compensated 39,000 dollars for his time and efforts and an additional 10,000 dollars in fees prior to relinquishing control.[40] However, the Obama campaign elected not to compensate Anthony and instead invoked MySpace's usage policies and claimed ownership of the page under the public figure policy. Eventually, MySpace was forced to intervene and decide who ultimately should have the right to control the page. Ultimately, Jeff Berman, MySpace's VP for public affairs, decided that "under the circumstances that Senator Obama had the right to the URL containing his name and to the official campaign content that was provided, but that the user (Anthony) should retain the basic elements of the profile, including friends who had been accumulated."[41] In the end, Anthony received no compensation and the Obama campaign was forced to work to re-establish its connections to its MySpace followers. The new site gained a paltry number of followers in comparison to the page that Antony had managed, likely because users ended up being confused by belonging to one Obama page and being courted to join another. This intervention by MySpace marked what has been, and will be, an ongoing tension between campaigns' desires to control messages about their candidates and Netizens' yearning to behave and engage in whatever manner they see fit online and through social media. As social media become even more diverse, and the explosion of content harder to track, it is likely that politicians will face ongoing battles with the tensions between retaining control over images and content the superfluidity of the Web 2.0 environment.

DIGITAL DIVIDE

As when discussing the impact of any Internet technology, the potential of that technology to amplify the digital divide, patterns of access inequality based on socioeconomic considerations,[42] must be taken into account. A marginally substantial percentage of the American population still does not have the physical access and/or the necessary technological skills to engage in online political behavior, with roughly one in nine American adults not having access to a computer and 10 percent reporting that Internet access is too expensive.[43] The concern that comes from this is that this divide, which typically accentuates patterns of social in-equalities related to income and education, is resulting in a new type of political elitism versus legitimate mass participation. Instead of online politics mobilizing a more inclusive, emancipatory, and egalitarian popu-lous, the Internet may instead be promoting the spread of viral politics that privileges an elite and competitive constituency.[44] With a few heavi-ly relied upon websites dominating a large portion of political discourse, the Internet may not be so different than historical political structures that reinforce traditional inequality in participation and societal influ-ence.[45]

A YOUNG MEDIUM

In relationship to the life-span of other media, YouTube as a site of politi-cal information, deliberative interaction, and democratic engagement is still in its infancy. The use of YouTube for political communication and campaigning has by no means been perfected and many of the potential-ities of the platform for information sharing, advertising, and engage-ment remain untapped. As with other mediated platforms, YouTube as a political vehicle faces many challenges, specifically, how to turn Internet-based activity, such as sharing videos, into real-world action, such as donating, volunteering, or voting. Measurability is challenging in the YouTube environment. It is difficult to measure the offline success of online campaigns because much of the data related to offline behavior stemming from digital engagement comes from self-report data. Addi-tionally, instead of becoming involved in traditional political behaviors, such as definitive party affiliation, many individuals are canalizing their engagement through various types of Internet activism and informal po-litical networking, all which is difficult for campaigns to track, measure, and examine. While substantial steps forward have been made through the implementation of one-click engagement functionalities, campaigns still need to take more concrete step to better translate potential support-ers' online behavior into offline action.

It is also exceedingly difficult to track the success and viralability of videos because multiple entities, including mainstream media, the pubic, and competing campaigns, can download, appropriate, and distribute videos on networks, channels, and social media platforms that politicians and campaigns cannot reliably track, or perhaps do not even know exist. For example, a video of President George W. Bush having a shoe thrown at him during a press conference in Iraq in December 2008 was posted to YouTube and quickly went viral. In just five days, "Bush vs. Shoes" had generated more than 1,150 placements, meaning that the video could be found in over eleven hundred different places on the Internet within a week.[46] Both the viralability and shareability of online videos makes it difficult to track when and where the videos are being linked, watched, and what the offline political impact of specific online videos may be. Another significant challenge of online political platforms is their constantly changing and evolving nature. YouTube is first and foremost situated as a commercial enterprise and will manage its interface in the manner that is most financially beneficial to them as a corporation. This means that campaigns must be reactive to new and trending functionalities of the platform in order to most effectively engage supporters. This will require campaigns to be vigilant to changes and trends and consistently work to sustain their relationships with their online followers. Ultimately, everyone involved—politicians, the public, and the media—is still navigating how to most effectively and successfully incorporate YouTube into their political activities.

YOUTUBE AND THE POLITICAL FUTURE

Many tend to take either a techno-utopian or techno-dystopian view when discussing the future political implications of the Internet and platforms like YouTube. The reality is, whether the Internet and social media have a beneficial or an adversarial impact on political communication, knowledge, engagement, and mobilization depends upon the active choices of the constituency. There have been, and will continue to be, mixed outcomes and perceptions regarding the perceived successes or failures of the Internet as a viable platform for politics. Some research has shown that social media has a beneficial impact on political efficacy and social capitalism.[47] Whereas, other research has found no real measurable link between political cognitions and behaviors and social media usage.[48] What is definitive, however, is that potential voters and supporters are actively engaged in a wide variety of political behaviors on YouTube. The challenge falls to politicians to consistently theorize how to effectively translate this potentially harnessable online energy into increased and sustained political behaviors, such as sharing, commenting, donating, and ultimately, voting.

Politicians and campaigns must fight the urge to simply create YouTube channels as one of their "check-list" items requisite for a contemporary political presence. It is imperative that politicians being to truly embrace YouTube strategies that will allow them to enhance democracy through important factors such as access, information and education, discussion, deliberation, and choices and action.[49] Social media users seek to make personalized connections with those that they follow via social media and desire to engage politically beyond the level of simple information-seeking. Sixteen percent of social media users have added other uses as friends because they agree with their political views and 39 percent of users see their friends talking about politics online.[50] A good example of this phenomenon can be seen in the 2010 mid-term election. On Election Day, 600,000 Facebook users were altered via Facebook message that their friends had voted. Of these users, 39 percent were more likely to vote than those who did not receive the message, translating into an additional 282,000 people casting votes that day.[51] Instances like this should encourage politicians to fully embrace platforms like YouTube and understand the abilities it gives them to fully engage the constituency in the give-and-take communication structures granted by the platform. Campaigns that successfully inspire the "FOMO" (Fear Of Missing Out) amongst their supporters, by making it easy for supporters to post their own videos and comments to their YouTube channels could potentially increase the likelihood of these supporters returning to their sites, following campaigns more closely, developing a higher sense of efficacy, and ultimately developing a level of support that translates into long-term democratically engaged behaviors.

Future campaigns should also be increasingly cognizant of the expanding role that mobile technologies will play in the upcoming lives of potential voters and supporters. There is an ever-increasing population using mobile technology as a dominant vehicle for Internet activities. Thirty-one percent of Internet users consider themselves "cell Internet users" and 17 percent of these users are considered "cell mostly" users, meaning that mobile technologies are their primary means of accessing the Internet. Additionally, 25 percent of teens, and future voters, are considered to be cell mostly users.[52] This is particularly important considering that in June of 2012, the Federal Election Commission began allowing campaigns to accept campaign contributions via text messaging; by the end of the 2012 election, 10 percent of presidential campaign contributions came from text messages or via cell phone applications.[53] As mobile devices are quickly emerging as a prominent platform through which people connect online, political strategists will need to focus on creating videos and applications that are highly accessible from mobile devices and understand the heightened role that mobile technologies will play in future political campaigns. YouTube is currently the number one mobile video viewing website, generating over one billion views a day and with over 7.1 million unique users each month,[54] making it an environment ripe with constituents that if correctly incentivized could become some savvy politician's future mobile army.

Politicians must capitalize on these trends by combining real-world experiences with online interactivity, such as embracing Quick Response (QR) code technology and other types of creative engagement methods that both appeal to supporters and encourage them to share posts, videos, and activities with those in their social networks. As entire generations of potential voters are increasingly relying on the Internet for political information, the challenge is for politicians is to find the right balance between retail politics, mass media outreach, and the power of social media to actively engage supporters of all demographics.[55] While You-Tube and Tweets will likely never replace door-knocking and other more traditional forms of political communication, YouTube and other social media platforms add exciting new elements to political information distribution and engagement. These platforms allow campaigns to court undecided voters, mobilize their support bases, and turn online support into real-world votes in novel and innovative ways. Mark Blevis, a digital public affairs strategist acknowledged the need to integrate digital campaign methodologies into broader campaign initiatives by stating, the "digital won't replace the traditional but traditional cannot exist on its own anymore because the world is becoming more digital."[56]

In order to most effectively engage the constituency in YouTube politics, politicians and campaign strategists must be willing to get out of their political comfort zone, something that so far few politicians have seemingly been willing to do. While most campaigns have some level of YouTube presence, and many have YouTube channels, very few could really be considered as having embraced YouTube as a viable and vital aspect of their political communication strategy. Whether it is concern over political message and image control or potentially a guarded understanding of the rapid ways in which the basic technological and economic organizations of political communication are changing, many politicians only engage via YouTube during campaigns and then, often only regard the platform as simply a place to publish videos and as a repository for political advertisements. So, the answer to whether or not politicians are using the tools offered by YouTube to strengthen the candidate-public relationship is, not really.

In order to grow and sustain a palpable YouTube presence, politicians can no longer simply rely on videos created for other venues and re-posted to YouTube as a sound means of political information distribution. Instead, they should focus on creating entire platforms that resonate with the audience and increase the viralability of their message. They must move beyond the narcissistic messages that are prevalent in more traditional forms of political communication, create and distribute videos that are conscious and considerate of their audiences' and potential audiences' needs, and use YouTube for what many people go there for, real information about real politics. Politicians must also understand the emotional contagion necessary to increase viralability and view YouTube subscribers as important relationships with individuals from whom they need political buy-in in order to be successful. Politicians need to look specifically at the levels of enthusiasm and Internet activity they are able to generate amongst online influentials and develop strategies that encourage these influentials to become willing distributors of their political messages. Consistently embarking on these collective efforts will allow politicians to more effectively court supporters, procure funding, and ultimately, attract voters. In sum, politicians must confidently direct their

YouTube presence, because as has aptly been stated, "Technology is a steamroller. You either drive it or it runs you over."[57]

Researchers should also begin to think differently about how they discuss the political utility of social media and YouTube going forward. The history of the political Internet has been a very short one when compared to other types of political media; however, many researchers take the position that because the political Internet has yet to substantially alter political outcomes, that its overall utility is tenuous. While important for researchers not to over-value the role of social media as a medium of mass public participation, it is equally incumbent not to downplay the importance of these platforms because they have yet to live up to some theoretically idealized version of political participation or democratic engagement. Each new era of political communication has been and will be met with a palpable level of trepidation and criticism because "anytime you fundamentally change the way you reach consumers and audiences through media, you fundamentally change the way you reach voters and constituents too."[58]

Considering that during the entire 2004 campaign season, only 10 percent of Americans consulted the Internet for political news,[59] there have been substantial strides in the populous' use of the Internet for political participation and engagement. Nevertheless, the usefulness of the political Internet is frequently downplayed as not being sufficient at engaging individuals at a high enough level that more measurable political outcomes, such as voter turnout, increase substantially. Yet, events, such as the CNN/YouTube Debates, where nearly 8,000 videos were submitted by individuals for potential inclusion in a landmark political event, indicates that the populous is willing to engage in innovative political efforts and are not afraid to substantively engage with politicians when given the opportunity. Future research should participate in higher levels of social media listening, where it is possible to examine exactly what the populous is thinking and feeling about specific issues. By triangulating this methodology with more traditional research methods, such as polling and survey analysis, it is possible that a better understanding of how people currently engage, why they perhaps choose not engage, and how they may potentially be persuaded to engage more substantially could be developed. President Obama's 2012 campaign actually conducted a great deal of its own research using similar strategies, collecting and analyzing large scale data to model behaviors, predicting the types of individuals who may be the most persuadable, and then coordinating and targeting their communications based on this information.[60] Researchers have a vast amount of data before them that, if effectively considered, may shed an entirely new light on the efficacy of the political Internet.

CONCLUSION

The political Internet will likely never live up to the romanticized version of what could be and public political engagement and deliberation will likely never take place at the levels in which many scholars would consider transformational. However, as discussed in this volume, YouTube has greatly expanded the amount of political information that the populous has access to, altered politicians' abilities to speak directly to constituencies, enhanced opportunities for advertising and fundraising, and increased potentialities for public deliberation and engagement. If harnessed correctly, YouTube can be useful for reinvigorating an evolving and expanding public sphere, providing a base for more diverse political information and deliberation, and establishing a venue for a more emancipated electorate. However, ultimately, there is no way to correctly speculate on the concrete role that YouTube will play in the future of United States' politics because as Joe Rospars, Founder and CEO of Blue State Digital quite aptly stated, "We're flying by the seat of our pants, and establishing new ways of doing things every day. We're going to try new things, and sometimes it's going to work, and sometimes it's not going to work. That's the cost and that's the risk of experimenting."[61]

NOTES

1. Minic Rivera, "YouTube Launches You Choose '08," *The Blog Herald*, March 1, 2007.

2. Tim O'Reilly, "What Is Web 2.0: Design Patterns and Business Models for the next Generation of Software.," *O'Reilly*, September 30, 2005, http://oreilly.com/web2/archive/what-is-web-20.html.

3. Michael Gurevitch, Stephen Coleman, and Jay Blumler, "Political Communication – Old and New Media Relationships," *The ANNALS of the American Academy of Political and Social Science* 645 (2009): 164–81.

4. Ibid.

5. Judson Berger, "YouTube Creates New Site for Political Viral Video," *Fox News.com*, October 6, 2011, http://www.foxnews.com/politics/2011/10/06/youtube-creates-new-site-for-political-viral-video/#ixzz27JQxL8vu.

6. Lee Raine, *Internet Adoption Becomes Nearly Universal among Some Groups, but Others Lag behind* (Washington, DC: Pew Internet & American Life Project, May 30, 2013), http://www.pewresearch.org/fact-tank/2013/05/30/internet-adoption-becomes-nearly-universal-among-some-groups-but-others-lag-behind/.

7. Ibid.

8. Pamela Rutledge, "How Obama Won the Social Media Battle in the 2012 Presidential Campaign," *The Media Psychology Blog*, January 25, 2013, http://mprcenter.org/blog/2013/01/25/how-obama-won-the-social-media-battle-in-the-2012-presidential-campaign/.

9. Ibid.

10. Albert May, "Campaign 2008: It's on YouTube," *Nieman Reports*, 2008.

11. Raine, *Internet Adoption Becomes Nearly Universal among Some Groups, but Others Lag behind*.

12. Jay Samit, "All Politics Is Social: Social Media Engagement Will Decide Election 2012," *SocialVibe*, June 2011, http://advertising.socialvibe.com/political_solutions.

13. Ibid.

14. Kathryn Zichuhr, *Generations 2010* (Washington, DC: Pew Internet & American Life Project, December 16, 2010), http://pewInternet.org/Reports/2010/Generations-2010.aspx.

15. Ibid.

16. Robin Grant, "How Do We Spend Our Time Online?," *We Are Social*, May 9, 2013, http://wearesocial.net/blog/2013/05/spend-time-online/.

17. Ibid.

18. Zichuhr, *Generations 2010*.

19. Rachel Gibson and Ian McAllister, "Do Online Election Campaigns Win Vote? The 2007 Australian 'YouTube' Election," *Political Communication* 28, no. 2 (2011): 227–44.

20. Ibid.

21. Ibid.

22. Pippa Norris and John Curtice, "Getting the Message out: A Two-Step Model of the Role of the Internet in Campaign Communication Flows during the 2005 British General Election," *Journal of Information Technology & Politics* 4, no. 4 (2008): 3–13.

23. Rutledge, "How Obama Won the Social Media Battle in the 2012 Presidential Campaign."

24. Kim Gooyong, "The Future of YouTube: Critical Reflections of YouTube Users' Discussion over Its Future," *InterActions: UCLA Journal of Education and Information Studies* 5, no. 2 (2009).

25. Bryan Caplan, "Mises' Democracy–dictatorship Equivalence Theorem: A Critique," *The Reivew of Austrian Economics* 21, no. 1 (2008): 45–59.

26. Andrew Chadwick, "Web 2.0: New Challenges for the Study of E-Democracy in an Era of Informational Exuberance," *I/S: A Journal of Law and Policy for the Information Society* 5, no. 1 (2009): 9–41.

27. Robert Putnam, *Bowling Alone: The Collapse and Revival of American Community* (New York, NY: Simon and Schuster, 2000).

28. Michael Froomkin, "Technologies for Democracy," in *Democracy Online: The Prospects for Political Renewal through the Internet* (New York, NY: Routledge, 2004), 3–20.

29. Gurevitch, Coleman, and Blumler, "Political Communication – Old and New Media Relationships."

30. Albert May, "Who Tube? How YouTube's News and Politics Space Is Going Mainstream," *International Journal of Press/Politics* 15, no. 4 (2010): 499–511,

31. Bob Boynton, "Going Viral – the Dynamics of Attention," in *YouTube and the 2008 Election Cycle in the United States* (presented at the Journal of Information Technology and Politics Annual Conference, University of Massachusetts - Amherst, 2009), 1138.

32. David Sohn, "McCain Campaign Says Video Takedowns Stifle Fair Use," *Center for Democracy and Technology*, October 15, 2008, https://cdt.org/blogs/david-sohn/mccain-campaign-says-video-takedowns-stifle-fair-use.

33. Rachael Weiner, "Romney's Al Green Video Pulled from YouTube," *The Washington Post*, July 17, 2012, sec. PostTV, http://www.washingtonpost.com/blogs/the-fix/post/romneys-al-green-video-pulled-from-youtube/2012/07/17/gJQAI04sqW_blog.html.

34. May, "Who Tube? How YouTube's News and Politics Space Is Going Mainstream."

35. Nick Couldry and Ana Langer, "Media Consumption and Public Connection: Toward a Typology of the Dispersed Citizen," *The Communication Review* 8, no. 2 (2005): 237–57.

36. William Dutton and Adrian Shepherd, "Trust in the Internet as an Experience Technology," *Information, Communication and Society* 9, no. 4 (2006): 433–51.

37. James Druckman, Martin Kifer, and Michael Parkin, "The Technological Development of Candidate Websites: How and Why Candidates Use Web Innovations," in

Politicking Online: The Transformation of Election Campaign Communication (New Brunswick, NJ: Rutgers University Press, 2009), 21–47.

38. Micha Sifry, "The Battle to Control Obama's MySpace," *Tech President*, May 1, 2007, http://techpresident.com/blog-entry/battle-control-obamas-myspace.

39. Ibid.

40. Morley Winograd and Michael Hais, *Millennial Makeover: MySpace, YouTube & the Future of American Politics* (New Brunswick, NJ: Rutgers University Press, 2008).

41. Sifry, "The Battle to Control Obama's MySpace."

42. Andrew Chadwick, *Internet Politics* (New York, NY: Oxford University Press, 2006).

43. Zichuhr, *Generations 2010.*

44. Nils Gustafsson, "This Time It's Personal: Social Networks, Viral Politics, and Identity Management," in *Emerging Practices in Cyberculture and Social Networking* (Amsterdam: Rodopi, 2010).

45. Ibid.

46. Visible Measures, "Bush vs. Shoes: Viral Video Wrap-Up," *Visible Measures*, December 19, 2008, http://www.visiblemeasures.com/news-and-events/blog/bid/7698/Bush-vs-Shoes- Surpasses-10-Million-Viral-Video-Views.

47. Sebastián Valenzuela, Namsu Park, and Kerk Kee, "Is There Social Capital in a Social Network Site?: Facebook Use and College Students' Life Satisfaction, Trust, and Participation," *Journal of Computer-Mediated Communication* 14, no. 4 (2009): 875–901.

48. Weiwu Zhang et al., "The Revolution Will Be Networked: The Influence of Social Networking Sites on Political Attitudes and Behavior," *Social Science Computer Review* 28, no. 1 (2010): 75–92.

49. Lloyd Morrisett, "Technologies of Freedom?," in *Democracy and New Media* (Cambridge, MA: MIT Press, 2003), 21–33.

50. Maeve Duggan, *Pew Internet: Politics* (Washington, DC: Pew Internet & American Life Project, November 14, 2012), The Revolution Will be Networked the Influence of Social Networking Sites on Political Attitudes and Behavior.

51. Inga Kiderra, "Facebook Boosts Voter Turnout," *UC San Diego*, September 12, 2012, http://ucsdnews.ucsd.edu/pressreleases/facebook_fuels_the_friend_vote.

52. Raine, *Internet Adoption Becomes Nearly Universal among Some Groups, but Others Lag behind.*

53. Aaron Smith and Maeve Duggan, *Online Political Videos and Campaign 2012* (Washington, DC: Pew Internet & American Life Project, November 2, 2012), http://www.pewInternet.org/~/media//Files/Reports/2012/PIP_State_of_the_2012_race_online_video_final.pdf.

54. YouTube, *YouTube Statistics*, 2013, http://www.youtube.com/t/press_statistics.

55. Samit, "All Politics Is Social: Social Media Engagement Will Decide Election 2012."

56. Allison Jones, "Social Media a Powerful Election Tool but No Match for Door Knocking: Experts," *The Canadian Press*, September 18, 2011, http://www.theglobeandmail.com/news/politics/social-media-a-powerful-election-tool-but-no-match-for-door-knocking-experts/article594783/.

57. J Short and K O'Brien, "MP3.com and the Future of the Music Industry: MP3.com Case A: Pre-IPO Background" (London Business School, n.d.).

58. New Politics Institute, "The Technology and Media Transformation of Our Time Compared to Broadcast TV," *New Politics Institute*, 2008, http://ndn-newpol.civicactions.net/about/context/transformation.

59. The Pew Research Center, *Internet Now Major Source of Campaign News* (Washington, DC: Pew Research Center for the People and the Press, October 31, 2008), http://www.people-press.org/2008/10/31/Internet-now-major-source-of-campaign-news/.

60. Rutledge, "How Obama Won the Social Media Battle in the 2012 Presidential Campaign."

61. Joe Rospars, "Our MySpace Experiment," *My.BarackObama.com Community Blogs*, May 2, 2007, http://my.barackobama.com/page/community/post_group/ObamaHQ/CvS1.

Bibliography

Ackerman, Bruce, and James Fishkin. *Deliberation Day* (New Haven, CT: Yale University Press, 2004).

Alexander, Bryan. "Web 2.0 and Emergent Multiliteracies," *Theory into Practice* 47, no. 2 (2008): 150–60.

Allison, Julia. "Internet Memes," *Newsweek*, 2010, http://2010.newsweek.com/top-10/Internet-memes/obama-girl.html.

Ancu, Monica, and Raluca Cozma. "MySpace Politics: Uses and Gratifications of Befriending Candidates," *Journal of Broadcasting and Electronic Media* 53, no. 4 (2009): 567–83.

Anderson, David, and Michael Cornfield. *The Civic Web: Online Politics and Democratic Values.* (Lanham, MD: Rowman & Littlefield, 2002).

Armbruster, Adam. "Local Stations Should Be Socializing; Networking Sites Can Help Viewers Connect to Community, Broadcasters," *TV Week*, April 28, 2008, http://www.tvweek.com/news/2008/04/local_stations_should_be_socia.php.

Armstrong, Jerome, and Markos Zuniga. *Crashing the Gate: Netroots, Grassroots, and the Rise of People-Powered Politics* (White River Junction, VT: Chelsea Green Publishing Company, 2006).

Barber, Benjamin. *Strong Democracy: Participatory Politics for a New Age* (Berkeley, CA: University of California Press, 1984).

Baumgartner, Jody, and Jonathan Morris. "MyFaceTube Politics: Social Networking Web Sites and Political Engagement of Young Adults," *Social Science Computer Review* 28, no. 1 (2010): 24–44.

BBC. "West Wing Week: Producing the White House Video Blog," *BBC*, April 22, 2011, http://www.bbc.co.uk/news/world-us-canada-13166315.

BBC. "YouTube's Website Redesign Puts the Focus on Channels," *BBC*, December 2, 2011, http://www.bbc.co.uk/news/technology-16006524.

Bennett, W. Lance. *News and the Politics of Illusion* (New York, NY: Longman, 1983).

Benoit, Pamela. *Telling the Success Story: Acclaiming and Disclaiming Discourse* (Albany, NY: State University of New York Press, 1997).

Benoit, William. *Communication in Political Campaigns.* (New York, NY: Peter Lang Publishing, 2006).

Benoit, William, and Glenn Hansen. "Presidential Debate Watching, Issue Knowledge, Character Evaluation, and Vote Choice," *Human Communication Research* 30, no. 1 (2004): 121–44.

Benoit, William, Mitchell McKinney, and R. Lance Holbert. "Beyond Learning and Persona: Extending the Scope of Presidential Debate Effects," *Communication Monographs* 68, no. 3 (2001): 259–73.

Benoit, William, Mitchell McKinney, and Michael Stephenson. "Effects of Watching Primary Debates in the 2000 U.S. Presidential Campaign," *Journal of Communication* 52, no. 2 (2002): 316–31.

Benson, Thomas. "Rhetoric, Civility, and Community: Political Debate on Computer Bulletin Boards," *Communication Quarterly* 44, no. 3 (1996): 359–78.

Berger, Judson. "YouTube Creates New Site for Political Viral Video," *Fox News.com*, October 6, 2011, http://www.foxnews.com/politics/2011/10/06/youtube-creates-new-site-for-political-viral-video/#ixzz27JQxL8vu.

Bimber, Bruce. "The Internet and Political Transformation: Populism, Community, and Accelerated Pluralism," *Policy* 31, no. 1 (1998): 133–60.

Bimber, Bruce, and Richard Davis. *Campaigning Online: The Internet in U.S. Elections* (New York, NY: Oxford University Press, 2003).

Blimes, Jack. "Questions, Answers, and the Organization of Talk in the 1992 Vice Presidential Debate: Fundamental Considerations," *Research on Language and Social Interaction* 32, no. 3 (1999): 213–42.

Bohn, Kevin. "Romney Campaign Uses Obama's Line against Him in Attack Ad," *CNN*, June 14, 2012, http://politicalticker.blogs.cnn.com/2012/06/14/romney-campaign-uses-obamas-line-against-him-in-attack-ad/?iref=allsearch.

Bonner, Patricia, Robert Carlitz, Rosmary Gunn, Laurie Maak, and Charles Ratliff. "Bringing the Public and the Government Together through Online Dialogues," in *The Deliberative Democracy Handbook: Strategies for Effective Civic Engagement in the 21st Century* (San Francisco, CA: John Wiley & Sons, 2005), 141–53.

Boyd, Danah. "Can Social Network Sites Enable Political Action?," in *Rebooting America* (New York, NY: Personal Democracy, 2008).

Boynton, Bob. "Going Viral—the Dynamics of Attention," in *YouTube and the 2008 Election Cycle in the United States* (presented at the Journal of Information Technology and Politics Annual Conference, University of Massachusetts - Amherst, 2009), 1138.

Brenner, Joanna, and Aaron Smith. *72% of Online Adults Are Social Networking Site Users* (Washington, DC: Pew Research Center's Internet & American Life Project, August 5, 2013), http://www.pewInternet

Breslau, Karen. "Steve Grove: How to Run for President, YouTube Style," *Newsweek Magazine*, December 22, 2007, http://www.thedailybeast.com/newsweek/2007/12/22/steve-grove-how-to-run-for-president-youtube-style.html.

Burgess, Jean, and Joshua Green. *YouTube: Online Video and Participatory Culture* (Cambridge, MA: Polity Press, 2009).

Cain-Jackson, Bryan. "President Obama Has Changed Social Media Forever," *Technorati*, August 21, 2012, http://technorati.com/social-media/article/president-obama-has-changed-social-media/.

Cammaerts, Bart. "Critiques on the Participatory Potentials of Web 2.0.," *Communication, Culture, and Critique* 1, no. 4 (2008): 358–77.

Campbell, Angus, Philip Converse, Warren Miller, and Donald Stokes. *The American Voter* (Chicago, IL: University of Chicago Press, 1960).

Cannon, Carl. "Generation 'We' - the Awakened Giant," *National Journal Group* 39, no. 10 (2007): 20.

Caplan, Bryan. "Mises' Democracy–dictatorship Equivalence Theorem: A Critique," *The Reivew of Austrian Economics* 21, no. 1 (2008): 45–59.

Carlin, Diana. "Presidential Debates as Focal Points for Campaign Arguments," *Political Communication* 9, no. 4 (1992): 251–65.

Carlin, Diana. "Watching the Debates: A Guide for Viewers," in *Televised Election Debates: International Perspectives* (New York, NY: St. Martin's Press, 2000), 157–77.

Carmody, Tim. "Mitt Romney's Damning '47 Percent' Video and the New Politics of Privacy," *The Verge*, March 14, 2013, http://www.theverge.com/2013/3/14/4103184/romney-prouty-47-percent-video-new-politics-of-privacy.

Castells, Manuel. *The Internet Galaxy: Reflections on the Internet, Business and Society* (Oxford, UK: Oxford University Press, 2001).

Center for Information and Research on Civic Learning and Engagement. *Short Term Impacts, Long Term Opportunities: The Political and Civic Engagement of Young Adults in America*, Unpublished report (Washington, DC: Circle, 2002).

Chadwick, Andrew. *Internet Politics* (New York, NY: Oxford University Press, 2006).

Chadwick, Andrew. "Web 2.0: New Challenges for the Study of E-Democracy in an Era of Informational Exuberance," *I/S: A Journal of Law and Policy for the Information Society* 5, no. 1 (2009): 9–41.

Chaffee, Steven. "Presidential Debates: Are They Helpful to Voters?," *Communication Monographs* 45, no. 4 (1978): 330–46.

Chaffee, Steven, and Jack Dennis. "Presidential Debates: An Empirical Assessment," in *The Past and Future of Presidential Debates* (Washington, DC: American Enterprise Institute, 1979), 75–106.

Chaudhary, Arun. "West Wing Week," *The White House Blog*, April 2, 2010, www.whitehouse.gov/blog/2010/04/02/west-wing-week.

Christensen, Jen. "Obama Outspends Romney on Online Ads," *CNN*, June 2, 2012, http://www.cnn.com/2012/06/03/politics/online-campaign-spending/index.html?hpt=hp_bn5.

Christensen, Rob. "Etheridge Slip Puts Foe on Map," *News & Observer*, June 16, 2010, http://www.newsobserver.com/2010/06/16/535042/etheridge-slip-puts-foe-on-map.html.

Cillizza, Chris, and Aaron Blake. "Mitt Romney's $10,000 Mistake," *The Washington Post*, December 12, 2011, http://www.washingtonpost.com/blogs/the-fix/post/mitt-romneys-10000-mistake/2011/12/11/gIQA9aEQpO_blog.html.

Cisco. *Cisco Visual Networking Index: Global Mobile Data Traffic Forecast Update, 2013-2018*, White Paper, February 5, 2014, http://www.cisco.com/c/en/us/solutions/collateral/service-provider/visual-networking-index-vni/white_paper_c11-520862.html.

Clarke, Paul. *Deep Citizenship* (London: Pluto Press, 1996).

Clayworth, John. "Obama Responds to 'Crush,'" *Des Moines Register*, June 19, 2007, http://web.archive.org/web/20080211114524/http://blogs.dmregister.com/?p=6506.

Cloud, John. "The YouTube Gurus," *Time Magazine*, December 25, 2006.

Coleman, Stephen. "Connecting Parliament to the Public via the Internet: Two Case Studies of Online Consultations," *Information, Communication and Society* 7 (2004): 1–22.

Coleman, Stephen, and John Gotze. *Bowling Together: Online Public Engagement in Policy Deliberation*. (London, UK: Hansard Society, 2001).

Coleman, Stephen, David Morrison, and Michael Syenneyig. "New Media and Political Efficacy," *International Journal of Communication* 2 (n.d.): 771–91.

Commission on Presidential Debates. *Debate Transcript: October 13, 2004* (Commission on Presidential Debates, 2004), http://www.debates.org/pages/trans2004d.html.

Conover, Pamela, and Stanley Feldman. "How People Organize the Political World: A Schematic Model," *American Journal of Political Science* 28, no. 1 (1984): 95–126.

Cooper, Mary. "Low Voter Turnout: Is America's Democracy in Trouble?," *Congressional Quarterly* 10 (2000): 833–56.

Copeland, Henry, and Megan Mitzel. "The Huge Opportunity for Online Political Ads," *New Politics Institute*, n.d., http://ndn-newpol.civicactions.net/sites/ndn-newpol.civicactions.net/files/Advertise_Online.pdf.

Corn, David. "Secret Video: Romney Tells Millionaire Donors What He REALLY Thinks of Obama Voters," *MotherJones*, September 17, 2012, http://www.motherjones.com/politics/2012/09/secret-video-romney-private-fundraiser.

Cornfield, Michael, and Kate Kaye. "Online Political Advertising," in *Politicking Online: The Transformation of Election Campaign Communication* (Mahwah, NJ: Rutgers University Press, 2009), 163–76.

Corrado, Anthony, and Charles Firestone, *Elections in Cyberspace: Toward a New Era in American Politics* (Washington, DC: The Aspen Institute, 1996).

Couldry, Nick, and Ana Langer. "Media Consumption and Public Connection: Toward a Typology of the Dispersed Citizen," *The Communication Review* 8, no. 2 (2005): 237–57.

Crupi, Anthony. "CNN's YouTube GOP Debate Draws Record 4.49 Million Viewers," *Mediaweek*, November 29, 2007.

Dahlberg, Lincoln. "The Internet and Democratic Discourse: Exploring the Prospects of Online Deliberative Forums Extending the Public Sphere," *Information Communication and Society* 4, no. 1 (2001): 615–33.

Dahlgren, Peter. "Introduction," in *Communication and Citizenship: Journalism and the Public Sphere* (London: Routledge, 1991), 1–24.

Dahlgren, Peter. "The Internet, Public Spheres, and Political Communication: Dispersion and Deliberation," *Political Communication* 22 (2005): 147–62.

Dahlgren, Peter. "The Public Sphere and the Net: Structure, Space, and Communication," in *Mediated Politics: Communication in the Future of Democracy* (Cambridge, UK: Cambridge University Press, 2001), 33–55.

Dalton, Russell. *The Good Citizen: How a Younger Generation Is Reshaping American Politics* (New York, NY: CQ Press, 2009).

Davisson, Amber. "I'm In!": Hillary Clinton's 2008 Democratic Primary Campaign on YouTube," *Journal of Visual Literacy* 28, no. 1 (2009): 70–91.

Davis, Richard. *The Web of Politics* (New York, NY: Oxford University Press, 1999).

Deggans, Eric. "YouTube Users to Feed CNN Presidential Debate Questions," *St. Petersburg Times*, June 15, 2007.

Deligiaouri, Anastasia, and Panagiotis Symeonidis. "'YouTube Debate': A New Era of Internetized Television Politics?," *International Journal of E-Politics* 1, no. 2 (n.d.).

Delli Carpini, Michael. "Mediating Democratic Engagement: The Impact of Communications on Citizens' Involvement in Polical and Civic Life," in *Handbook of Political Communication Research* (Mahwah, NJ: Lawrence Erlbaum Associates, 2004), 395–434.

Delli Carpini, Michael, Fay Cook, and Lawrence Jacobs. "Public Deliberation, Discursive Participation, and Citizen Engagement: A Review of the Empirical Literature," *Annual Review of Political Science* 7 (2004): 315–44.

Delli Carpini, Michael, and Scott Keeter. *What Americans Know about Politics and Why It Matters* (New Haven, CT: Yale University Press, 1996).

Dilanian, Ken. "YouTube Makes Leap into Politics: Debate Will Include Q&A from Internet," *USA Today*, July 23, 2007.

Dooley, Jennifer, Sandra Jones, and Don Iverson. "Web 2.0 Adoption and User Characteristics," *Web Journal of Mass Communication Research* 42 (June 2012), http://wjmcr.org/vol42.

Dorsch, Meagan. "Tweeting the Election: Facebook, Twitter and Other Social Media Sites Could Be a Powerful Force in the 2012 Election," *Technology*, April 2012.

Dovey, Jon, and Helen Kennedy. *Game Cultures: Computer Games as New Media* (New York, NY: McGraw Hill, 2006).

Druckman, James, Martin Kifer, and Michael Parkin. "The Technological Development of Candidate Websites: How and Why Candidates Use Web Innovations," in *Politicking Online: The Transformation of Election Campaign Communication* (New Brunswick, NJ: Rutgers University Press, 2009), 21–47.

Duggan, Maeve. *Pew Internet: Politics* (Washington, DC: Pew Internet & American Life Project, November 14, 2012), The Revolution Will be Networked the Influence of Social Networking Sites on Political Attitudes and Behavior.

Dunphy, Jennifer. "How Video Marketing Powers SEO," *Econsultancy.com*, April 12, 2012, https://econsultancy.com/blog/9583-how-video-marketing-powers-seo.

Dutton, William, and Adrian Shepherd. "Trust in the Internet as an Experience Technology," *Information, Communication and Society* 9, no. 4 (2006): 433–51.

Edelman, Murray. *From Art to Politics* (Chicago, IL: University of Chicago Press, 1995).

Eliasoph, Nina. "'Close to Home': The Work of Avoiding Politics," *Theory and Society* 26, no. 5 (1997): 605–47.

Eveland, William, and Myiah Hively. "Political Discussion Frequency, Network Size, and 'Heterogeneity' of Discussion as Predictors of Political Knowledge and Participation," *Journal of Communication* 59, no. 2 (2009): 205–24.

Farrell, David, and Paul Webb. "Political Parties as Campaign Organizations," in *Parties without Parisians: Political Change in Advanced Industrial Democracies*, ed. Russell Dalton and Martin Wattenberg (London: Oxford University Press, 2000), 102–28

Feldman, Lauren, and Dannagal Young. "Late-Night Comedy as a Gateway to Traditional News: An Analysis of Time Trends in News Attention Amongh Late-Night Comedy Viewers during the 2004 Presidential Primaries," *Political Communication* 25 (n.d.): 401–22.

Ferber, Paul, Franz Foltz, and Rudy Pugliese. "Cyberdemocracy and Online Politics: A New Model of Interactivity," *Bulletin of Science, Technology, & Society* 27, no. 5 (2007): 391–400.

Ferenstein, Gregory. "No Online Questions for the next Debate: Tired of Pot and Snowmen?," *TechCrunch*, October 12, 2012, http://techcrunch.com/2012/10/12/no-online-questions-at-next-debate-tired-of-pot-and-snowmen/.

Ferguson, Douglas, and Elizabeth Perse. "The World Wide Web as a Functional Alternative to Television," *Journal of Broadcasting & Electronic Media* 44 (2000): 155–74.

Fernando, Angelo. "The Revolution Will Be Mashed up (and Uploaded to YouTube): Campaign Strategists in the U.S. Are Realizing the Power of Video Ads as Political Weapons," *Communication World* 26, no. 1 (January 2009).

Fineman, Howard. "Many a Hurdle for Hillary," *Newsweek Magazine*, February 5, 2007.

Fisher, Bonnie, Michael Margolis, and David Resnick. "Breaking Ground on the Virtual Frontier: Surveying Civic Life on the Internet," *American Sociologist* 27 (1996): 11–25.

Fishkin, James. *Democracy and Deliberation: New Directions for Democratic Reform* (New Haven, CT: Yale University Press, 1991).

Fitzpatrick, Laura. "Brief History YouTube," *Time Magazine*, May 31, 2010, http://content.time.com/time/magazine/article/0,9171,1990787,00.html.

Folliard, Jim. *2012 Presidential Candidates Use Online YouTube Videos in Campaign* (Fairfax Video Studio, November 20, 2012), http://www.fairfaxvideostudio.com/news/2012-presidential-candidates-use-online-youtube-videos-in-campaign-20121120.cfm.

Fornas, Johan. *Culture Theory and Late Modernity* (London: Sage, 1995).

Fowler, Erika, and Travis Ridout. "Local Television and Newspaper Coverage of Political Advertising," *Political Communication* 26 (2009): 119–36.

Fox News. "Democratic Backers Question GOP Candidates in YouTube Debate," *Fox News.com*, November 29, 2007, http://www.foxnews.com/story/2007/11/29/democratic-backers-question-gop-candidates-in-youtube-debate/.

Fraser, Nancy. "Rethinking the Public Sphere: A Contribution to the Critique of Actually Existing Democracy," in *Habermas and the Public Sphere* (Cambridge, MA: The MIT Press, 1992), 109–42.

Froomkin, Michael. "Technologies for Democracy," in *Democracy Online: The Prospects for Political Renewal through the Internet* (New York, NY: Routledge, 2004), 3–20.

Gamson, William. "Promoting Political Engagement," in *Mediated Politics: Communication in the Future of Democracy* (Cambridge, UK: Cambridge University Press, 2001), 56–74.

Gamson, William. *Talking Politics* (Cambridge, UK: Cambridge University Press, 1992).

Garcia-Castanon, Marcela, Alison Rank, and Matt Barreto. "Plugged in or Tuned out? Youth, Race, and Internet Usage in the 2008 Election," *Journal of Political Marketing* 10 (2011): 115–38.

Gastil, John. "Identifying Obstacles to Small Group Democracy," *Small Group Research* 24 (1993): 5–27.

Gastil, John, and William Keith. "A Nation That (sometimes) Likes to Talk: A Brief History of Public Deliberation in the United States," in *The Deliberative Democracy Handbook: Strategies for Effective Civic Engagement in the 21st Century* (San Francisco, CA: John Wiley & Sons, 2005).

Gibson, Rachel, and Ian McAllister. "Do Online Election Campaigns Win Vote? The 2007 Australian 'YouTube' Election," *Political Communication* 28, no. 2 (2011): 227–44.

Gilmore, Dan. *We the Media: Grassroots Journalism by the People, for the People* (Sebastopol, CA: O'Reilly Media, Inc., n.d.).

Goldstein, Patrick. "Network Fear: The Net as Copilot," *Los Angeles Times*, March 27, 2007, http://articles.latimes.com/2007/mar/27/entertainment/et-goldstein27.

Gonzalez-Bailon, Sandra, Andreas Kaltenbrunner, and Rafael Banchs. "The Structure of Political Discussion Networks: A Model for the Analysis of Online Deliberation," *Journal of Information Technology* 25 (2010): 230–43.

Google. "Hit the Road with President Obama in the First-Ever Presidential Hangout Road Trip," *Official Blog*, January 23, 2014, http://googleblog.blogspot.com/2014/01/hit-road-with-president-obama-in-first.html.

Gooyong, Kim. "The Future of YouTube: Critical Reflections of YouTube Users' Discussion over Its Future," *InterActions: UCLA Journal of Education and Information Studies* 5, no. 2 (2009).

Graber, Doris. *Mass Media and American Politics*, 8th ed. (Washington, DC: CQ Press, 2009).

Graf, Joseph, and Carol Darr. *Political Influentials Online in the 2004 Presidential Election* (Institute for Politics, Democracy, and the Internet, February 5, 2005), http://www.ipdi.org/UploadedFiles/influentials_in_2004.pdf.

Grant, Robin. "How Do We Spend Our Time Online?," *We Are Social*, May 9, 2013, http://wearesocial.net/blog/2013/05/spend-time-online/.

Greenfield, Heather. "YouTube Boom May Mean New Jobs on Campaigns," *E.politics*, January 30, 2007, http://www.epolitics.com/2007/01/30/tech-daily-youtube-boom-may-mean-new-jobs-on-campaigns/.

Grove, Steve. "Hanging Out in the Public Square," *Huffington Post*, February 21, 2013, http://www.huffingtonpost.com/steve-grove/obama-google-plus-hang-out_b_2672215.html.

Gueorguieva, Vassia. "Voters, MySpace and YouTube: The Impact of Alternative Communication Channels," in *Politicking Online: The Transformation of Election Campaign Communication* (New Brunswick, NJ: Rutgers University Press, 2009), 233–48.

Gurevitch, Michael, Stephen Coleman, and Jay Blumler. "Political Communication – Old and New Media Relationships," *The ANNALS of the American Academy of Political and Social Science* 645 (2009): 164–81.

Gustafsson, Nils. "This Time It's Personal: Social Networks, Viral Politics, and Identity Management," in *Emerging Practices in Cyberculture and Social Networking* (Amsterdam: Rodopi, 2010).

Haas, Tanni. "The Public Sphere as a Sphere of Publics: Rethinking Habermas's Theory of the Public Sphere," *Journal of Communication* 54, no. 1 (2004): 178–84.

Habermas, Jurgen. *Legitimation Crisis* (Boston, MA: Beacon Press, 1975).

Habermas, Jurgen. *The Structural Transformation of the Public Sphere* (Cambridge, MA: The MIT Press, 1989).

Halpern, Daniel, and Jennifer Gibbs. "Social Media as a Catalyst for Online Deliberation? Exploring the Affordances of Facebook and YouTube for Political Expression," *Computers in Human Behavior* 29, no. 3 (2013): 1159–68.

Hampton, Keith, Lauren Goulet, Lee Raine, and Kristen Purcell. *Social Networking Sites and Our Lives* (Pew Internet & American Life Project, June 16, 2011), http://pewInternet .org/Reports/2011/Technology-and-social-networks.aspx.

Hanson, Gary, Paul Haridakis, Audrey Cunningham, Rekha Sharma, and J.D. Ponder. "The 2008 Presidential Campaign: Political Cynicism in the Age of Facebook, MySpace, and YouTube," *Mass Communication & Society* 13, no. 5 (2010): 584–607.

Hart, Roderick. "Citizen Discourse and Political Participation: A Survey," in *Mediated Politics: Communication in the Future of Democracy* (Cambridge, UK: Cambridge University Press, 2001), 407–32.

Healy, Patrick, and Jeff Zeleny. "Novel Debate Format, but the Same Old Candidates," *The New York Times*, July 24, 2007, http://www.nytimes.com/2007/07/24/us/politics/24debate.html.

Helft, Miguel, and Matt Richtel. "Venture Firm Shares a YouTube Jackpot," *The New York Times*, October 10, 2006.

Hermes, Joke. "Hidden Debates: Rethinking the Relationship between Popular Culture and the Public Sphere," *Javnost- The Public* 13, no. 4 (2006): 27–44.

Hendricks, John, and Lynda Lee Kaid. *Communicator-in-Chief: How Barack Obama Used New Media Technology to Win the White House* (Lanham, MD: Lexington Books, 2010).

Herrnson, Paul, Atiya Stokes-Brown, and Matthew Hindman. "Campaign Politics and the Digital Divide: Constituency Characteristics, Strategic Considerations, and Candidate Internet Use in the State Legislative Elections," *Political Research Quarterly* 60, no. 1 (2007): 31–42.

Hertzberg, Hendrik. "Obama Wins," *The New Yorker*, November 17, 2008.

Hill, Kevin, and John Hughes. *Cyberpolitics: Citizen Activism in the Age of the Internet* (Lanham, MD: Rowman & Littlefield, 1998).

Hindman, Matthew. *The Myth of Digital Democracy* (Princeton, NJ: Princeton University Press, 2009).

Hollihan, Thomas. *Uncivil Wars: Political Campaigns in a Media Age* (Boston, MA: Bedford/St. Martins, 2009).

Holubowicz, Gerald, and Jean Guillo. *Moneyocracy: The Rise of the United Corporations of America*, Documentary (Insomnia World Sales, 2012), www.moneyocracy-project.com.

Husson, William, Teresa Harrison, Timothy Stephen, and B.J. Fehr. "An Interpersonal Communication Perspective on Images of Political Candidates," *Human Communication Research* 14, no. 3 (2006): 397–241.

Institute for Politics, Democracy, & the Internet and The Campaign Finance Institute. *Small Donors and Online Giving* (Washington, DC: The George Washington University, 2006).

Jagoda, Karen, Rich Berke, Michelle Lambert, and Mike Logan. *Social Networks Supercharge Politics: Turning Action into Votes in 2010* (Washington, DC: E-Voter Institute, 2010).

Janssen, Davy, and Raphael Kies. "Online Forums and Deliberative Democracy," *Acta Politica* 40 (2005): 317–35.

John, Arit. "The White House Tries to Lure Young People to Obamacare with Cuteness," *The Atlantic Wire*, September 27, 2013, http://www.theatlanticwire.com/politics/2013/09/white-house-bringing-cuteness-its-obamacare-push/69947/.

Johnson, Anne, and Lynda Lee Kaid. "Image Ads and Issue Ads in U.S. Presidential Advertising: Using Videostyle to Explore Stylistic Differences in Televised Political Ads from 1952–2000," *Journal of Communication* 52, no. 2 (2002): 281–300.

Jones, Allison. "Social Media a Powerful Election Tool but No Match for Door Knocking: Experts," *The Canadian Press*, September 18, 2011,

Journalism Project Staff. *YouTube Video Creation - A Shared Process* (Washington, DC: Pew Research Center, July 16, 2012), http://www.journalism.org/2012/07/16/youtube-video-creationa-shared-process/.

Jowett, Garth, and Victoria O'Donnell. *Propaganda and Persuasion* (Los Angeles, CA: Sage, 2012).

Kaid, Lynda Lee, and Mike Chanslor. "Changing Candidate Images: The Effects of Political Advertising," in *Candidate Images in Presidential Elections* (Westport, CT: Praeger, 1995), 83–97.

Kaid, Lynda Lee, Mitchell McKinney, and John Tedesco. *Civic Dialogue in the 1996 Presidential Campaign: Candidate, Media, and Public Voices* (Cresskill, NJ: Hampton, 2000).

Kaid, Lynda Lee, and Monica Postelnicu. "Political Advertising in the 2004 Election: Comparison of Traditional Television and Internet Messages," *American Behavioral Scientist* 49 (2005): 265–78.

Kamarck, Elaine. "Assessing Howard Dean's Fifty State Strategy and the 2006 Midterm Elections," *Forum* 4, no. 3 (2006).

Kanalley, Craig. "Google+ Hangout Puts President Face-to-Face with Americans," *NBC News*, January 30, 2013, www.nbcnews.com/technology/google-hangout-puts-president-face-face-americans-24105.

Karl, Jonathan. "Newt Gingrich Announces 2012 Presidential Campaign via Twitter," *ABC News*, May 11, 2011, http://abcnews.go.com/Politics/newt-gingrich-announces-2012-presidential-campaign-twitter/story?id=13578139.

Karpf, David. "Macaca Moments reconsidered...Electoral Panopticon or Netroots Mobilization?," *Journal of Information Technology & Politics* 7 (2010): 143–62.

Katz, Elihu, and Paul Lazersfeld. *Personal Influence* (Glencoe, IL: Free Press, 1955).

Kavanaugh, Andrea. "Community Networks and Civic Engagement: A Social Network Approach," *The Good Society* 11, no. 3 (2002): 17–24.

Kaye, Barbara, and Thomas Johnson. "Online and in the Know: Uses and Gratifications of the Web for Political Information," *Journal of Broadcasting and Electronic Media* 46, no. 1 (2002): 54–71.

Kellner, Douglas. "Intellectuals, the New Public Spheres, and Techno-Politics," in *The Politics of Cyberspace: A Political Science Reader* (New York, NY: Routledge, 1998).

Kelly, Brian. "How Presidential Candidates Can Use Online Video to Run an Effective Campaign," *Huffington Post Tech*, September 19, 2012, http://www.huffingtonpost.com/briankelly/how-presidential-candidat_b_1892222.html.

Kendall, Kathleen, and Scott Paine. "Political Images and Voting Decisions," in *Candidate Images in Presidential Elections* (Westport, CT: Praeger, 1995).

Kendall, Kathleen, and June Yum. "Persuading the Blue Collar Voter: Issues, Images and Homophily," in *Communication Yearbook 8* (Beverly Hills, CA: Sage, 1984), 702–22.

Kenski, Kate, and Natalie Stroud. "Connections between Internet Use and Political Efficacy, Knowledge, and Participation," *Journal of Broadcasting and Electronic Media* 50, no. 2 (2006): 173–92.

Kiderra, Inga. "Facebook Boosts Voter Turnout," *UC San Diego*, September 12, 2012, http://ucsdnews.ucsd.edu/pressreleases/facebook_fuels_the_friend_vote.

Kirk, Rita, and Dan Schill."A Digital Agora: Citizen Participation in the 2008 Presidential Debates," *American Behavioral Scientist* 55, no. 3 (2011): 325–47.

Klotz, Robert. "The Sidetracked 2008 YouTube Senate Campaign," *Journal of Information Technology & Politics* 7 (2008): 110–23.

Kohut, Andrew. *Internet's Broader Role in Campaign 2008: Social Networking and Online Videos Take off* (Washington, DC: Pew Research Center for The People & The Press, January 11, 2008), http://www.people-press.org/2008/01/11/Internets-broader-role-in-campaign-2008/.

Kohut, Andrew. *More than a Quarter of Voters Read Political Blogs* (Washington, DC: Pew Research Center for The People & The Press, October 23, 2008), http://www.people-press.org/2008/10/23/section-1-the-Internet-and-campaign-2008/.

Kraus, Sidney. *Televised Presidential Debates and Public Policy*, 2nd ed. (Mahwah, NJ: Lawrence Erlbaum Associates, 2000).

Kriesi, Hanspeter, Daniel Bochsler, Jorg Matthes, Sandra Lavenex, Marc Buhlmann, and Frank Esser. *Democracy in the Age of Globalization and Mediatization: Challenges to Democracy in the 21st Century* (London, UK: Palgrave Macmillian, 2013).

Kurtz, Howard. "Webs of Political Intrigue: Candidates, Media Looking for Internet Constituents," *The Washington Post*, November 13, 1995, sec. B1.

LaFleur, Jennifer. "White House Gives Agencies Transparency To-Do List," *Pro Publica Inc.*, December 8, 2009, www.propublica.org/article/white-house-gives-agencies-transparency-to-do-list-1208.

Lange, Patricia. "Commenting on Comments: Investigating Responses to Antagonism on YouTube" (presented at the Society of Applied Anthropology Conference, Tampa, FL, 2007).

Lange, Patricia. "Publically Private and Privately Public: Social Networking on YouTube," *Journal of Computer-Mediated Communication* 13, no. 1 (2007): 361–80.

Lau, Rick, Lee Sigelman, and Ivy Brown Rovner. "The Effects of Negative Political Campaigns: A Meta-Analytic Reassessment," *Journal of Politics* 69 (2007): 1176–1209.

Lawler, Ryan. "Political Ads Find Their Way onto YouTube," *Gigaom*, November 1, 2010, http://gigaom.com/2010/11/01/political-ads-find-their-way-onto-youtube/.

Lemert, James. "Do Televised Presidential Debates Help Inform Voters?," *Journal of Broadcasting and Electronic Media* 37, no. 1 (1993): 83–94.

Leung, Louis. "User-Generated Content on the Internet: An Examination of Gratifications, Civic Engagement and Psychological Empowerment," *New Media & Society* 11, no. 8 (2009): 1327–47.

Lever, Rob. "2012 US Election Campaign a Digital Battleground," *Google News*, October 13, 2012, http://www.google.com/hostednews/afp/article/ALeqM5h-83y9eiaiOfOfwRUEOHlkqqpgPg.

Levine, John, and Eileen Russo. "Impact of Anticipated Interaction on Information Acquisition," *Social Cognition* 13, no. 3 (n.d.): 293–317.

Levine, Peter, and Mark Lopez. *Youth Voter Turnout Has Declined, by Any Measure* (University of Maryland's School of Public Affairs: The Center for Information & Research on Civic Learning & Engagement, September 2002), http://civicyouth.org/research/products/Measuring_Youth_Voter_Turnout.pdf.

Levy, Joshua. *The CNN/YouTube Debate: Make It Truly Open* (techpresident, June 14, 2007), http://techpresident.com/blog-entry/cnnyoutube-debate-make-it-truly-open.

Lipsman, Andrew. *Worldwide Internet Audience Has Grown 10 Percent in Last Year, according to Comscore Networks London* (London, UK: Comscore, March 6, 2007), http://www.comscore.com/Insights/Press_Releases/2007/03/Worldwide_Internet_Growth.

Lothlan, Dan, and Becky Brittain. "Obama Hosts Google 'Hangout,'" January 30, 2012, www.cnn.com/2012/01/30/politics/obama-google.

Lupia, Arthur, and Tasha Philpot. "Views from inside the Net: How Websites Affect Young Adult's Political Interest," *The Journal of Politics* 67, no. 4 (2005): 1122–42.

Malcom, Andrew. "Diverse Web Coalition Asks McCain, Obama to Alter Debates," *Los Angeles Times*, September 25, 2008, sec. Nation, http://latimesblogs.latimes.com/washington/2008/09/debates-mccain.html.

Martinez, Jennifer. "Google to Launch YouTube Politics," *Politico*, October 6, 2011, http://www.politico.com/news/stories/1011/65296.html.

May, Albert. "Campaign 2008: It's on YouTube," *Nieman Reports*, 2008.

May, Albert. "Who Tube? How YouTube's News and Politics Space Is Going Mainstream," *International Journal of Press/Politics* 15, no. 4 (2010): 499–511.

McCarthy, Caroline. "MySpace Gets Official Presidential Debate Deal," *CNET*, August 5, 2008, http://www.cnet.com/news/myspace-gets-official-presidential-debate-deal/.

McCarthy, Caroline. "MySpace, MTV Team up for One-on-One Presidential Dialogues," *CNET*, August 22, 2007, http://news.cnet.com/8301-13577_3-9764866-36.html.

McCarthy, Caroline. "YouTube, CNN Aim to 'Revolutionize' Presidential Debate Process," *CNet News Blog*, June 14, 2007, http://news.cnet.com/8301-10784_3-9729506-7.html.

McCarthy, Tom. "Obama Answers Citizens' Questions in Google 'Hangout Road Trip,'" *The Guardian*, January 31, 2014, sec. World News.

McChesney, Robert. *Rich Media, Poor Democracy: Communication Politics in Dubious Times* (Chicago, IL: University of Illinois Press, 2000).

McDonald, Michael, and Samuel Popkin. "The Myth of the Vanishing Voter," *American Political Science Review* 95, no. 4 (2001): 936–74.

McKay, Amy, and David Paletz. "The Presidency and the Media," in *Handbook of Political Communication Research* (Mahwah, NJ: Lawrence Erlbaum Associates, 2004), 315–35.

McKinney, Mitchell, and Mary Banwart."Rocking the Youth Vote through Debate: Examining the Effects of a Citizen versus Journalist Controlled Debate on Civic Engagement," *Journalism Studies* 6 (2005): 153–63.

McKinney, Mitchell, and Diana Carlin. "Political Campaign Debates," in *Handbook of Political Communication Research* (Mahwah, NJ: Lawrence Erlbaum Associates, 2004), 203–34.

McKinney, Mitchell, Linda Kaid, and Dianne Bystrom. "The Role of Communication in Civic Engagement," in *Communicating Politics: Engaging the Public in Democratic Life (frontiers in Political Communication)* (New York, NY: Peter Lang Publishing, 2005), 3–26.

McLeod, Jack, and Lee Becker. "The Uses and Gratifications Approach," in *Handbook of Political Communication* (Beverly Hills, CA: S, 1981).

Mermin, Johnathan. *Debating War and Peace: Media Coverage of the U.S. Intervention in the Post-Vietnam Era* (Princeton, NJ: Princeton University Press, 1999).

Michel, Amanda, and Ed Pilkington. "Obama Passes YouTube Milestone as Online Videos Remake Campaigning," *The Guardian*, July 24, 2012, http://www.theguardian.com/world/2012/jul/24/obama-youtube-milestone-online-videos.

Miller, Arthur, and Michael MacKuen. "Informing the Electorate: A National Study," in *The Great Debates: Carter vs. Ford, 1976* (Bloomington, IN: Indiana University Press, 1979).

Miller, Claire. "How Obama's Internet Campaign Changed Politics," *The New York Times*, November 7, 2008, sec. Technology, http://bits.blogs.nytimes.com/2008/11/07/how-obamas-Internet-campaign-changed-politics/?_r=0.

Montgomery, Kathryn. "Youth and Digital Democracy: Intersections of Practice, Policy, and the Marketplace," in *Civic Life Online: Learning How Digital Media Can Engage Youth* (Cambridge, MA: The MIT Press, 2008), 25–50.

Moore, Kathleen. *71% of Online Adults Now Use Video-Sharing Sites* (Pew Internet & American Life Project, July 26, 2011),

Morrisett, Lloyd. "Technologies of Freedom?," in *Democracy and New Media* (Cambridge, MA: MIT Press, 2003), 21–33.

Moy, Patricia. "Linking Dimensions of Internet Use and Civic Engagement," *Mass Communication Quarterly* 82, no. 3 (2005): 571–86.

Murray Buechner, Maryanne. "50 Best Websites 2007: YouTube's You Choose '08," *Time Magazine*, July 8, 2007.

Muse, Jack. "The Consensus on Last Night's Debate Format," *Huffington Post*, July 27, 2007, http://www.huffingtonpost.com/jack-muse/the-consensus-on-last-nig_b_57608.html.

Neuman, Russell, Marion Just, and Ann Crigler. *Common Knowledge: News and the Construction of Political Meaning* (Chicago, IL: University of Chicago Press, 1992).

New Politics Institute. "The Technology and Media Transformation of Our Time Compared to Broadcast TV," *New Politics Institute*, 2008, http://ndn-newpol.civicactions.net/about/context/transformation.

Nimmo, Dan, and James Combs. *Mediated Political Realities* (New York, NY: Longman, 1990).

Nisbet, Matthew, and Dietram Scheufele. "Political Talk as a Catalyst for Online Citizenship," *Journalism and Mass Communication Quarterly* 81 (2004): 877–96.

Noelle-Neumann, Elisabeth. *The Spiral of Silence: Public Opinion-Our Social Skin*, 2nd ed. (Chicago, IL: University of Chicago Press, 1993).

Norris, Pippa. *The Digital Divide: Civic Engagement, Information Poverty, and the Internet Worldwide* (New York, NY: Cambridge University Press, 2001).

Norris, Pippa, and John Curtice. "Getting the Message out: A Two-Step Model of the Role of the Internet in Campaign Communication Flows during the 2005 British General Election," *Journal of Information Technology & Politics* 4, no. 4 (2008): 3–13.

Noveck, Beth. *Wiki Government: How Technology Can Make Government Better, Democracy Stronger, and Citizens More Powerful.* (Washington, DC: Brookings Institution Press, 2009).

O'Cass, Aron. "Political Advertising Believability and Information Source Value During Elections," *Journal of Advertising* XXXXI, no. 1 (2002): 63–74.

O'Reilly, Tim. "What Is Web 2.0: Design Patterns and Business Models for the next Generation of Software.," *O'Reilly*, September 30, 2005, http://oreilly.com/web2/archive/what-is-web-20.html.

Owen, Diana, and Richard Davis. "Presidential Communication in the Internet Era," *Presidential Studies Quarterly* 38, no. 4 (n.d.): 658–73.

Panagopoulos, Costas. "Technology and the Modern Political Campaign: The Digital Pulse of the 2008 Campaigns," in *Politicking Online: The Transformation of Election Campaign Communication* (Piscataway, NJ: Rutgers University Press, 2009), 1–18.

Panagopoulos, Costas, and Daniel Bergan. "Clicking for Cash: Campaigns, Donors, and the Emergence of Online Fund-Raising," in *Politicking Online: The Transformation of Election Campaign Communication* (Piscataway, NJ: Rutgers University Press, 2009), 127–40.

Papacharissi, Zizi. "Democracy On-line: Civility, Politeness, and the Democratic Potential of On-line Political Discussion Groups," *New Media & Society* 6, no. 2 (2004): 259–84.

Parham, Jason. "iPresident: How Social Media Shaped the Narrative of Barack Obama," *Complex Tech*, January 21, 2013, www.complex.com/tech/2013/01/ipresident-social-media-and-the-narrative-of-barack-obama.

Park, Hun Myoung, and James Perry. "Do Campaign Websites Really Matter in Electoral Civic Engagement? Empirical Evidence from the 2004 and 2006 Post-Election Internet Tracking Survey," in *Politicking Online: The Transformation of Election Campaign Communication* (Piscataway, NJ: Rutgers University Press, 2009).

Parker, Ashley. "His Job Is to Make Public Obama's Candid Side," *The New York Times*, November 11, 2010, sec. U.S., www.nytimes.com/2010/11/12/us/12video.html?_r =0.

Parker, Suzi. "Mitt Romney's 'binders Full of Women,'" *The Washington Post*, October 17, 2012, http://www.washingtonpost.com/blogs/she-the-people/wp/2012/10/17/mitt-romneys-binders-full-of-women/.

Patterson, Thomas. *The Vanishing Voter: Public Involvement in an Age of Uncertainty* (New York, NY: Knopf, 2002).

PBS NewsHour. *Pew Study: More Viewers Choose YouTube for Breaking News* (PBS, July 16, 2012), http://www.pbs.org/newshour/bb/media/july-dec12/pewyoutube_07-16.html.

Peers, Martin. "Buddy, Can You Spare Some Time?," *The Wall Street Journal*, January 26, 2004, http://online.wsj.com/article/0,,SB107508223269211274,00.html.

Perrin, Nicole. "US Digital Ad Spending: Online, Mobile, Social," *Emarketer.com*, April 2011, http://www.emarketer.com/Reports/All/Emarketer_2000794.aspx.

Perse, Elizabeth, and John Courtright. "Normative Images of Communication Media: Mass and Interpersonal Channels in the New Media Environment," *Human Communication Research* 19, no. 4 (1993): 485–503.

Peters, James. "With Video, Obama Looks to Expand Campaign's Reach through Social Media," *The New York Times*, May 14, 2012, http://www.nytimes.com/2012/03/15/us/politics/with-youtube-video-obama-looks-to-expand-social-media-reach.html?_r=0.

Pfau, Michael. "A Comparative Assessment of Intra-Party Political Debate Formats," *Political Communication Review* 8 (1984): 1–23.

Pfau, Michael. "The Changing Nature of Presidential Debate Influence in the Age of Mass Media Communication" (presented at the 9th Annual Conference on Presidential Rhetoric, TX A&M University, 2003).

Pinkleton, Bruce, and Erica Austin. "Media and Participation: Breaking the Spiral of Disffection," in *Engaging the Public: How Government and the Media Can Reinvigorate American Democracy* (Lanham, MD: Rowman & Littlefield, 1998).

Popkin, Samuel. *The Reasoning Voter: Communication and Persuasion in Presidential Campaigns* (Chicago, IL: University of Chicago Press, 1994).

Preston, Jennifer. "New Politics Channel on YouTube," *The New York Times*, October 6, 2011, sec. The Caucus, http://thecaucus.blogs.nytimes.com/2011/10/06/youtube-launches-new-politics-channel/.

Price, Vincent, Joseph Cappella, and Lilach Nir. "Does Disagreement Contribute to More Deliberative Opinion?," *Political Communication* 19, no. 1 (2002): 95–112.

Purcell, Kristen. *The State of Online Video: 69% of Internet Users Watch or Download Video Online; 14% Have Posted Videos* (Washington, DC: Pew Internet & American Life Project, June 3, 2010), http://uploadi.www.ris.org/editor/1276126693PIP-The-State-of-Online-Video.pdf.

Putnam, Robert. *Bowling Alone: The Collapse and Revival of American Community* (New York, NY: Simon and Schuster, 2000).

Quantcast. *YouTube.com Traffic and Demographic Statstistics*, May 10, 2013, https://www.quantcast.com/youtube.com#!demo&anchor=panel-GENDER.

Raby, Mark. "CNN Youtube Debate a Hit among Young Viewers," *TG Daily*, July 25, 2007, http://www.tgdaily.com/content/view/33075/113/.

Rackaway, Chapman. "Trickle-Down Technology," *Social Science Computer Review* 25, no. 4 (2007): 466–83.

Rahn, Wendy, and John Transue. "Social Trust and Value Change: The Decline of Social Capital in American Youth, 1976–1995," *Political Psychology* 19, no. 3 (1998): 545–65.

Rainie, Lee. *Internet Adoption Becomes Nearly Universal among Some Groups, but Others Lag behind* (Washington, DC: Pew Internet & American Life Project, May 30, 2013), http://www.pewresearch.org/fact-tank/2013/05/30/internet-adoption-becomes-nearly-universal-among-some-groups-but-others-lag-behind/.

Rainie, Lee, Aaron Smith, Kay Schlozman, Henry Brady, and Sidney Verba. *Social Media and Political Engagement* (Pew Internet and American Life Project, October 19, 2012).

Reeves, Emily. *Leveraging Online Video*, Digital Whitepaper (Stoneward, October 2012), http://www.stoneward.com/wp-content/uploads/2012/10/October-Digital-White-paper.pdf.

Rehg, William. "The Argumentation Theorist in Deliberative Democracy," *Controversia: An International Journal of Debate and Democratic Renewal* 1 (2002): 18–42.

Reuters, "Will.i.am's 'Yes We Can Song' Video Awarded Emmy for New Approaches in Daytime Entertainment," *Reuters*, July 16, 2008, http://www.reuters.com/article/2008/06/16/idUS145884+16-Jun-2008+MW20080616.

Rheingold, Howard. *The Virtual Community* (Reading, MA: addison-Wesley, 1993).

Ricke, LaChrystal. "A New Opportunity for Democratic Engagement: The CNN-YouTube Presidential Candidate Debates," *Journal of Information Technology & Politics* 7, no. 2–3 (2010): 202–15.

Ricke, LaChrystal. "Debates via Social Media," in *Encyclopedia of Social Media and Politics* (Thousand Oaks, CA: Sage, 2014).

Ricke, LaChrystal. "YouTube," in *Encyclopedia of Social Media and Politics* (Thousand Oaks, CA: Sage, 2014), 1411–31.

Ricke, LaChrystal. "YouTube and the 2012 Presidential Election: An Examination of How Obama and Romney's Official YouTube Channels Were Used in Campaign Communication.," in *Presidential Campaigning and Social Media: An Analysis of the 2012 Election.* (New York, NY: Oxford University Press, 2014), 246–58.

Ridout, Travis, Erika Fowler, and John Branstetter. "Political Advertising in the 21st Century: The Rise of the YouTube Ad" (presented at the American Political Science Association, Washington, DC, 2010).

Rideout, Vanda, and Vincent Mosco. "Communication Policy in the United States," in *Democratizing Communication: Comparative Perspectives on Information and Power* (Cresskill, NJ: Hampton Press, 1997).

Rivera, Minic. "YouTube Launches You Choose '08," *The Blog Herald*, March 1, 2007.

Roberts, Churchill. "From Primary to the Presidency: A Panel Study of Images and Issues in the 1976 Election," *Western Journal of Speech Communication* 45, no. 1 (1981): 60–70.

Roper Center for Public Opinion Research. "A Vast Empirical Record Refutes the Idea of Civic Decline," *Public Perspective* 7, no. 4 (1996).

Rospars, Joe. "Our MySpace Experiment," *My.BarackObama.com Community Blogs*, May 2, 2007, http://my.barackobama.com/page/community/post_group/ObamaHQ/CvS1.

Rubin, Alan. "Ritualized and Instrumental Television Viewing," *Journal of Communication* 34, no. 3 (n.d.): 66–77.

Rutenberg, Jim, and Adam Nagourney. "Melding Obama's Web to a YouTube Presidency," *The New York Times*, January 26, 2009,

Rutledge, Pamela. "How Obama Won the Social Media Battle in the 2012 Presidential Campaign," *The Media Psychology Blog*, January 25, 2013, http://mprcenter.org/blog/2013/01/25/how-obama-won-the-social-media-battle-in-the-2012-presidential-campaign/.

Saenz, Arlette. "Mother of Sandy Hook Victim Delivers White House Weekly Address," *ABC News*, April 13, 2013, http://abcnews.go.com/blogs/politics/2013/04/mother-of-sandy-hook-victim-delivers-white-house-weekly-address/.

Samit, Jay. "All Politics Is Social: Social Media Engagement Will Decide Election 2012," *SocialVibe*, June 2011, http://advertising.socialvibe.com/political_solutions.

Sarno, David. "Obama, the First Social Media President," *The LA Times*, November 18, 2008, sec. Technology, latimesblogs.latimes.com/technology/2008/11/obama-the-first.html.

Schatz, Amy. "In Clips on YouTube, Politicians Reveal Their Unscripted Side: Rival Posts 'Gotcha' Videos in Tight Montana Race," *The Wall Street Journal*, October 9, 2006.

Scheufele, Dietram. "Agenda-Setting, Priming, and Framing Revisited: Another Look at Cognitive Effects of Political Communication," *Mass Communication and Society* 3, no. 2–3 (2000): 297–316.

Schudson, Michael. "Why Conversation Is Not the Soul of Democracy," *Critical Studies in Mass Communication* 14 (1997): 297–309.

Schwab, Nikki. "In Obama-McCain Race, YouTube Became a Serious Battleground for Presidential Politics," *U.S. News and World Report*, November 7, 2008, http://www.usnews.com/news/campaign-2008/articles/2008/11/07/in-obama-mccain-race-youtube-became-a-serious-battleground-for-presidential-politics?page=2.

Schroeder, Alan. *Presidential Debates: Forty Years of High-Risk Television* (New York, NY: Columbia University Press, 2000).

Sears, David, and Steven Chaffee. "Uses and Effects of the 1976 Debates: An Overview of Empirical Studies," in *The Great Debates, 1976: Ford vs. Carter* (Bloomington, IN: Indiana University Press, 1979).

Seelye, Katharine. U.S. Politics to Draw All Eyes to YouTube; Debate May Start a New Phase in Web Campaigning." *The National Herald Tribune*, June 14, 2007.

Shah, Dhavan, Nojin Kwak, and R. Lance Holbert. "'Connecting' and 'Disconnecting' with Civic Life: Patterns of Internet Use and the Production of Social Capital," *Political Communication* 18 (2001): 141–62.

Shea, Daniel, Joanne Green, and Christopher Smith, *Living Democracy* (New York, NY: Prentice Hall, 2011).

Short, J., and K O'Brien. "MP3.com and the Future of the Music Industry: MP3.com Case A: Pre-IPO Background" (London Business School, n.d.).

Sifry, Micha. "The Battle to Control Obama's MySpace," *Tech President*, May 1, 2007, http://techpresident.com/blog-entry/battle-control-obamas-myspace.

Simonson, Peter. "Dreams of Democratic Togetherness: Communication Hope from Cooley to Katz," *Critical Studies in Media Communication* 13 (1996): 324–42.

Sirianni, Carmen, and Lewis Friedland. *Civic Innovation in America: Community Empowerment, Public Policy, and the Movement for Civic Renewal* (Berkeley, CA: University of California Press, 2001).

Slater, Don. "Political Discourse and the Politics of Need: Discourse on the Good Life in Cyberspace," in *Mediated Politics: Communication in the Future of Democracy* (Cambridge, UK: Cambridge University Press, 2001), 117–40.

Smith, Aaron. *22% of Online Americans Used Social Networking or Twitter for Politics in 2010 Campaign* (Washington, DC: Pew Internet & American Life Project, January 27, 2011), http://www.pewInternet.org/~/media//Files/Reports/2011/PIP-Social-Media-and-2010-Election.pdf.

Smith, Aaron. *Civic Engagement in the Digital Age* (Washington, DC: Pew Internet & American Life Project, April 25, 2013), http://pewInternet .org/~/media/Files/Reports/2013/PIP_CivicEngagementintheDigitalAge.pdf.

Smith, Aaron. *The Internet and Campaign 2010* (Washington, DC: Pew Internet & American Life Project, May 17, 2011), http://www.pewInternet.org/~/media//Files/Reports/2011/Internet%20and%20Campaign%202010.pdf.

Smith, Aaron, and Maeve Duggan. *Online Political Videos and Campaign 2012* (Washington, DC: Pew Internet & American Life Project, November 2, 2012), http://www.pewInternet.org/~/media//Files/Reports/2012/PIP_State_of_the_2012_race_online_video_final.pdf.

Smith, Aaron, and Lee Rainie. *The Internet and the 2008 Election* (Pew Internet & American Life Project, June 15, 2008), http://www.pewInternet.org/Reports/2008/The-Internet-and-the-2008-Election.aspx.

Smith, Aaron, Kay Schlozman, Sidney Verba, and Henry Brady. *The Internet and Civic Engagement* (Pew Internet & American Life Project, September 1, 2009), http://www.pewInternet .org/Reports/2009/15--The-Internet -and-Civic-Engagement.aspx.

Sneed, Tierney. "Smoking Herman Cain Campaign Ad: Brilliant or Bizarre?," *U.S. News and World Report*, October 26, 2011, http://www.usnews.com/opinion/articles/2011/10/26/smoking-herman-cain-campaign-ad-brilliant-or-bizarre.

Sniderman, Paul, James Glaser, and Robert Griffin. "Information and Electoral Choice," in *Information and the Democratic Process* (Urbana, IL: University of Illinois Press, 1990).

Sohn, David. "McCain Campaign Says Video Takedowns Stifle Fair Use," *Center for Democracy and Technology*, October 15, 2008, https://cdt.org/blogs/david-sohn/mccain-campaign-says-video-takedowns-stifle-fair-use.

Spigel, Lynn. "My TV Studies . . . now Playing on a YouTube Site near You," *Television & New Media* 10, no. 1 (2009): 149–53.

Stein, Sam. "Obama Campaign Releases Full 17-Minute, First-Term Documentary," *Huffington Post*, March 15, 2012, http://www.huffingtonpost.com/2012/03/15/obama-campaign-documentary-release_n_1350070.html.

Stevenson, Nick. *Cultural Citizenship: Cosmopolitan Questions* (Maidenhead, UK: Open University Press, 2003).

Stewart, Christine. "Christine O'Donnell: Witch Ad Was a Mistake," *CNN*, August 16, 2011, http://politicalticker.blogs.cnn.com/2011/08/16/christine-odonnell-witch-ad-was-a-mistake/.

Stewart, David, Paulos Pavlou, and Scott Ward. "Media Influences on Marketing Communications," in *Media Effects: Advances in Theory and Research* (Mahwah, NJ: Erlbaum, 2002), 353–96.

Stirland, Sarah. "McCain and Obama Campaigns Call for Change in Debate Format," *Wired.com*, October 7, 2008, www.wired.com/threatlevel/2008/10/mccain-and-obam/.

Stirland, Sarah. "New Digital Targeting Helps Romney Campaign Reach Voters," *Tech President*, December 22, 2011, retrieved from http://techpresident.com/news/21546/youtube-facebook-romney-digital-ad-targeting.

Stromer-Galley, Jennifer, and Lauren Bryant. "Agenda Control in the 2008 CNN/YouTube Debates," *Communication Quarterly* 59, no. 5 (2011): 529–46.

Stromer-Galley, Jennifer, and Alexis Wichowski. "Political Discussion Online," in *The Handbook of Internet Studies*. (Chichester, UK: John Wiley & Sons, 2010).

Sundar, Shyam, Sriram Kalyanaraman, and Justin Brown. "Explicating Web Site Interactivity: Impression Formation Effects in Political Campaign Sites," *Communication Research* 30, no. 1 (30-59): 2003.

Sunstein, Cass. *Republic.com* (Princeton, NJ: Princeton University Press, 2001).

Swarts, Phillip. "Obama Videographer: Official Record or Taxpayer-Financed Politics?," *Washington Guardian*, August 8, 2012, http://www.washingtonguardian.com/obamas-video-secrets.

Tedesco, John. "Changing the Channel: Use of the Internet for Communicating about Politics," in *Handbook of Political Communication Research* (Mahwah, NJ: Lawrence Erlbaum Associates, 2004), 507–32.

Tedesco, John, Jerry Miller, and Julia Spiker. "Presidential Campaigning on the Information Superhighway: An Exploration of Content and Form," in *The Electronic Election: Perspectives on the 1996 Campaign Communication* (Mahwah, NJ: Lawrence Erlbaum Associates, 1999), 51–63.

The New York Times. "Changing the Terms of the Debate," *The New York Times*, August 17, 2007.

The Pew Research Center. *How the Presidential Candidates Use the Web and Social Media* (Pew Project for Excellence in Journalism, August 12, 2012), http://www.journalism.org/analysis_report/how_presidential_candidates_use_web_and_social_media.

The Pew Research Center, *Internet Now Major Source of Campaign News* (Washington, DC: Pew Research Center for the People and the Press, October 31, 2008), http://www.people-press.org/2008/10/31/Internet-now-major-source-of-campaign-news/.

The Pew Research Center. *Obama Speech on Race Arguably Biggest Event of Campaign* (Pew Research Center for the People and the Press, March 27, 2008), http://pewresearch.org/pubs/777/obama-wright-news-interest.

The Telegraph. "President Barack Obama's Weekly Address Posted on White House YouTube Channel," *The Telegraph*, January 25, 2009, World edition,

The White House. "Transparency and Open Government," n.d., http://www.whitehouse.gov/the_press_office/TransparencyandOpenGovernment.

Thomas, David. "The Technophilic Body: On Technicity in William Gibson's Cyborg Culture," in *The Cyberculture Reader* (London, UK: Routledge, 2000).

Tian, Yan. "Political Use and Perceived Effects of the Internet: A Case Study of the 2004 Election," *Communication Research Reports* 23, no. 2 (2006): 129–37.

Toff, Benjamin. "Debate Ratings Lag," *The New York Times*, July 27, 2007, http://www.nytimes.com/2007/07/27/arts/27arts-YOUTUBEDEBAT_BRF.html?_r=0.

Towner, Terri, and David Dulio. "An Experiment of Campaign Effects during the YouTube Election," *New Media and Society* 13, no. 4 (2011): 626–44.

Trende, Sean. "Is Etheridge in Trouble?," *Real Clear Politics*, June 15, 2010, http://www.freerepublic.com/focus/news/2534891/posts?page=57.

Trippi, Joe. *The Revolution Will Not Be Televised: Democracy, the Internet, and the Overthrow of Everything* (Harper Collins, 2008).

Uricchio, William. "Cultural Citizenship in the Age of P2P Networks," in *Europoean Culture and the Media* (Bristol, UK: Intellect Books, 2004), 139–63.

Uslaner, Eric. "Social Capital and Net," *Communications of the ACM* 43, no. 12 (2000): 60–64.

Valentino, Nicholas, Vincent Hutchings, and Dimitri Williams. "The Impact of Political Advertising on Knowledge, Internet Information Seeking, and Candidate Preference," *Journal of Communication* 54 (2004): 337–54.

Valenzuela, Sebastián, Namsu Park, and Kerk Kee. "Is There Social Capital in a Social Network Site?: Facebook Use and College Students' Life Satisfaction, Trust, and Participation," *Journal of Computer-Mediated Communication* 14, no. 4 (2009): 875–901.

Vaidyanathan, Rajini. "Barack Obama's Shadow - the Man Who Films the President," *BBC News*, April 23, 2011, http://www.bbc.co.uk/news/world-us-canada-13148700.

Vaidyanathan, Rajini. "Top Hits of the YouTube Election," *BBC News*, October 30, 2008, http://news.bbc.co.uk/2/hi/americas/us_elections_2008/7699509.stm.

Vamburkar, Meenal. "Obama Faces Toughest Grilling about Drones, Not from the Media, but in a Google+ Hangout," February 15, 2013.

Van Eemeren, Frans. "Democracy and Argumentation," *Controversia: An International Journal of Debate and Democratic Renewal* 1 (2002): 69–84.

Vargas, Jose. "Obama Raised Half a Billion Online," *The Washington Post*, November 20, 2008, sec. The Clickocracy, http://voices.washingtonpost.com/44/2008/11/20/obama_raised_half_a_billion_on.html.

Vargas, Jose. "YOUTUBE, TAKE TWO Few GOP Candidates Commit to Debate," *The Washington Post*, July 27, 2007, http://www.washingtonpost.com/wp-dyn/content/article/2007/07/27/AR2007072700283.html.

Vargas, Jose. "YouTube Users Will Quiz Candidates," *The Washington Post*, July 19, 2007.

Verba, Sidney, Kay Schlozman, and Henry Brady. *Voice and Equality: Civic Voluntarism in American Politics* (Cambridge, MA: Harvard University Press, 1995).

Visible Measures. "Bush vs. Shoes: Viral Video Wrap-Up," *Visible Measures*, December 19, 2008, http://www.visiblemeasures.com/news-and-events/blog/bid/7698/Bush-vs-Shoes- Surpasses-10-Million-Viral-Video-Views.

Wallsten, Kevin. "Yes We Can: How Online Viewership, Blog Discussion, Campaign Statements, and Mainstream Media Coverage Produce a Viral Video Phenomenon," *Journal of Information Technology & Politics* 7 (2010): 163–81.

Ward, Jon. "Mitt Romney's First Direct-To-Camera Ad Comes At Make-Or-Break Moment In Campaign," *Huffington Post*, September 26, 2012, http://www.huffingtonpost.com/2012/09/26/mitt-romney-ad_n_1915665.html.

Warschauer, Mark, and Douglas Grimes. "Audience, Authorship and Artifact: The Emergent Semiotics of Web 2.0," *Annual Review of Applied Linguistics* 27 (2007): 1–23.

Waxman, Olivia. "YouTube Videos Mentioning Obama and Romney Reach 2 Billion Views," *Time Magazine*, August 29, 2012, http://techland.time.com/2012/08/29/youtube-videos-mentioning-obama-and-romney-reach-2-billion-views/.

Weiner, Rachael. "Romney's Al Green Video Pulled from YouTube," *The Washington Post*, July 17, 2012, sec. PostTV, http://www.washingtonpost.com/blogs/the-fix/post/romneys-al-green-video-pulled-from-youtube/2012/07/17/gJQAI04sqW_blog.html.

Weprin, Alex. "Fox News/Google Debate Most-Watched GOP Primary Debate Yet," *TVNewser*, September 23, 2011, http://www.mediabistro.com/tvnewser/fox-news-google-debate-most-watched-gop-primary-debate-yet_b89147.

Werner, Erica. "Obama Helps Woman with Husband's Resume," *Huffington Post*, February 1, 2012, http://www.huffingtonpost.com/huff-wires/20120201/us-obama-husband-s-resume/.

Wilhelm, Anthony. *Democracy in the Digital Age: Challenges to Political Life in Cyberspace* (New York, NY: Routledge, 2000).

will.i.am, "Why I Recorded Yes We Can," *Huffington Post*, February 3, 2008, http://www.huffingtonpost.com/william/why-i-recorded-yes-we-can_b_84655.html.

Wing, Nick. "Bob Etheridge Attacks Student: North Carolina Congressman Gets Rough with Interviewer," *Huffington Post*, June 14, 2010, http://www.huffingtonpost.com/2010/06/14/bob-etheridge-attacks-stu_n_610978.html.

Winograd, Morley, and Michael Hais, *Millennial Makeover: MySpace, YouTube & the Future of American Politics* (New Brunswick, NJ: Rutgers University Press, 2008).

Witt, Linda, Glenna Matthews, and Karen Paget. *Running as a Woman: Gender and Power in American Politics* (New York, NY: The Free Press, 1995).

Whitney, Lance. "Google+ Now Connects with YouTube, Chrome," *CNET*, November 4, 2011, http://news.cnet.com/8301-1023_3-57318595-93/google-now-connects-with-youtube-chrome/?part=rss&subj=news&tag=2547-1_3-0-20.

Wolford, Josh. "Note to 2012 Presidential Candidates: Your Social Media Presence Is a Big Deal," *WebProNews*, November 1, 2011, http://www.webpronews.com/note-to-2012-presidential-candidates-your-social-media-presence-is-a-big-deal-2011-11.

Wyatt, Robert, Elihu Katz, and Joohoan Kim. "Bridging the Spheres: Political and Personal Conversation in Public and Private Spaces," *Journal of Communication* 50, no. 1 (2000): 71–92.

Yankelovich, Daniel. *The Magic of Dialogue: Transforming Conflict into Cooperation* (New York, NY: Simon & Schuster, 1999).

YouTube. "CNN, YouTube Team up to Host First-Ever Voter-Generated Presidential Debates.," June 14, 2007, http://www.youtube.com/press_room?morgue=yes.

YouTube. "Fox News/Google Debate: Digging into Your Questions," *YouTube Official Blog*, September 19, 2011, http://youtube-global.blogspot.com/2011/09/fox-newsgoogle-debate-digging-into-your.html.

YouTube. "The 2010 Election on YouTube: By the Numbers," *YouTube: Official Blog*, November 1, 2010, http://youtube-global.blogspot.com/2010/11/2010-election-on-youtube-by-numbers_01.html.

YouTube. *You Choose '08 Spotlight*, April 11, 2007, http://youtube-global.blogspot.com/2007/04/you-choose-spotlight-mitt-romney.html.

YouTube. "YouTube Town Hall by the Numbers: It's the Economy, Stupid," *YouTube Official Blog*, August 16, 2011, http://youtube-global.blogspot.com/2011/08/youtube-town-hall-by-numbers-its.html.

YouTube. *YouTube Statistics*, 2013, http://www.youtube.com/t/press_statistics.

YouTube. "Why Use YouTube?," n.d., retrieved from http://www.youtube.com/yt/politics101/

YouTube Trends Team. "Videos Mentioning Obama or Romney Top 2 Billion Views," *YouTube Trends*, August 27, 2012, http://youtube-trends.blogspot.com/2012/08/videos-mentioning-obama-or-romney-top-2.html.

Zhang, Weiwu, Thomas Johnson, Trent Seltzer, and Shannon Bihard. "The Revolution Will Be Networked: The Influence of Social Networking Sites on Political Attitudes and Behavior," *Social Science Computer Review* 28, no. 1 (2010): 75–92.

Zichuhr, Kathryn. *Generations 2010* (Washington, DC: Pew Internet & American Life Project, December 16, 2010), http://pewInternet.org/Reports/2010/Generations-2010.aspx.

Index

About the Author

LaChrystal D. Ricke (Ph.D., University of Kansas) is an assistant professor of Mass Communication at Sam Houston State University. Her primary area of research is the intersection of Web 2.0 technologies, specifically YouTube, and politics, with a focus on increasing democratic engagement and deliberative interactions. Her research has appeared in the *Journal of Information Technology and Politics*, the *Encyclopedia of Social Media and Politics*, and in the book *Politics and Popular Culture*. Her primary teaching interests are mass media theory and criticism.

CPSIA information can be obtained at www.ICGtesting.com
Printed in the USA
BVOW05*1117040814

361412BV00003B/6/P

DATE DUE	RETURNED